UNFOLLOW ME

KATHRYN CARAWAY

This is a work of narrative nonfiction. Dialogue and scenes have been reconstructed to the best of the author's recollection. Names and some identifying characteristics of people, locations, and events have been changed to protect the privacy of those involved.

Unfollow Me™

Copyright © Kathryn Caraway 2025

All rights reserved. The scanning, uploading, and distribution of this book without permission is theft of the author's intellectual property. If you would like to use material from this book, other than for review purposes, please contact media@adink.com. Thank you for supporting the author's rights.

After Dark Ink Publishing Co.

www.adink.com

After Dark Ink Publishing Co. books may be purchased in bulk. For more information, please contact the publisher at info@adink.com.

ISBN: 979-8-9990545-0-0 (paperback)

ISBN: 979-8-9990545-1-7 (ebook)

LCCN: 2025946218

Dedication

In attempted murders of women by an intimate partner, 85% were stalked beforehand. In murders of women by an intimate partner, 76% were stalked before being killed[i].

I am not one of these statistics.
At least for now.

This book is for those who are.

AUTHOR'S NOTE

For every 1,000 incidents of stalking, an estimated 287 incidents are reported to law enforcement, 159 police reports are filed, 12 arrests are made, and 1 is convicted[i].

The other 999 are free to stalk among us.

He is a predator, but you won't know this the first time you meet him. He looks normal; there is nothing remarkable about him to suggest danger ahead. He creates the façade of an honorable man to hide the cruelty that lies beneath the surface, waiting to erupt. Like a volcano, his pyroclastic flow will incinerate every element of your life, forcing you into a dark world of doubt, disbelief and distrust. What is left in his wake of destruction are distant memories of a life you once had and the person you once were.

He is a predator of the worst kind: a stalker.

My name is not Kathryn Caraway. The stalker knows my real name, but you don't because I finally got away from him. I don't want him to find me. Ever. Again.

Living life as the target of a stalker is like being a rabbit caught in a trap. Waiting. Always waiting.

Kathryn Caraway

The name I hide behind is an imaginary badge of bravery I use to share what it's like to be stalked in the hopes that people will come to understand stalking. Today's vernacular minimizes, normalizes, and even romanticizes stalking, rather than criminalizing it.

My kids are my world. For their sake—and that of my family—I have chosen to keep their part minimal in this story, included only when it is essential.

~

Stalking, by its legal definition, is a pattern of behavior that would cause a reasonable person to feel fear. A more nuanced definition, however, is hard to nail down because each state has slightly different guidelines as to what constitutes stalking. It is a difficult crime to prove to law enforcement because, no matter where you reside, a singular act alone does not constitute stalking.

According to a study, one in three women and one in six men in the United States have experienced stalking victimization at some point during their lifetime, in which they felt fearful or believed that they would be harmed or killed[ii].

This is my story, as told by Kathryn Caraway. One day, it might be your story, too.

PART ONE
THE MONSTER REVEALS HIMSELF

CHAPTER ONE

Café Calais was a French bistro in the heart of my sleepy town. It was a place that gave me a warm sense of comfort at the very thought of it. From the moment I stepped inside, the savory scent of fresh, buttered bread and finely chopped garlic swaddled me. There, nestled at my favorite table, I would enjoy the well-choreographed cadence of the meal while spending quality time with friends or delving into business with colleagues.

However, tonight there would be no casual conversation, no effortless sense of calm. Instead, as I sipped my glass of Merlot, I sat facing Todd. His eyes were wild with rage, his face beet red, and the volume of his voice was increasing. My eyes darted around as he slammed his fist on the table.

"Are you listening to me?!"

"Yes." I nodded. "Just, please, keep your voice down."

As he continued to rant, I drained my glass of wine and signaled to Brandi—my favorite server, who sometimes worked behind the bar—that I wanted another. Todd's eyebrows knitted as beads of sweat formed on his upper lip. He was coming unglued.

As Brandi placed another glass of wine in front of me, Todd continued. "I would have thought you'd try harder to salvage things between us when

I ended it. I guess I was wrong. You're too selfish to think about anyone but yourself. It's pathetic."

"Todd, like your email said—"

"I don't want to hear it. You are self-absorbed, self-righteous, and so fucking spoiled. You have some major issues to work on, but you wouldn't do the work, would you? Instead, you're sleeping with a married man!"

People were looking at us, whispering as Todd continued to berate me and speed through all the reasons I was wrong, how ungrateful I was, and how he was sure I'd soon run off and sleep with yet another guy. Even though the things he was saying about me were completely false—bizarre even—I couldn't defend myself. One word from me would escalate this into a nasty scene. It was clear that my silence was agitating him. He was getting out of control saying anything he could to elicit a reaction. The only time he paused was when Brandi returned to the table with our entrees. She looked at me with concern and I thanked her, forcing a smile despite feeling mortified.

The rest of the dinner was the same. Todd continued his tirade while I dug into my filet au poivre, topped with crabmeat. I couldn't even enjoy the delicious dish I loved because I couldn't stop focusing on my racing heart and wondering how I was going to get out of this situation. I knew if I left, it would only heighten his anger. Cause a big scene. So, I clenched my fork and knife and remained quiet. On the outside, I was calm and collected. Inside, I was dizzy from the disorienting Jekyll and Hyde behavior.

After what seemed like hours, Todd snatched the bill. I had planned to pay for dinner but made no effort after being humiliated by him. While we waited for Brandi to run his credit card, I considered a covert bathroom trip to find another way home. But it was Todd, and I was becoming numb to the chaos. I just wanted to get the hell out of there. So, I clutched my purse tightly against my body as we walked to his truck. I yanked the door open and climbed into the passenger seat before pulling the door shut. Todd got in and slammed the door so hard the truck rocked.

As the engine rumbled to life, Todd paused his tirade for a moment. I stared out the window, trying to remain calm long enough to get to my house, run inside, and lock the door.

Just a few minutes longer.

We rolled up to the stop sign at the end of Main Street. Instead of making a right toward my house, Todd turned left. My face felt hot, and my stomach clenched.

"Where are we going?" I asked, trying not to sound panicked.

"I'm not finished with you yet," he replied, with no inflection.

The hairs on the back of my neck prickled as though tiny insects were nibbling. "Take me home. I—"

"Are you kidding me? I'm not taking you home."

My breath hitched in my throat; I couldn't breathe. With my dinner threatening to come up, my throat was closing. I insisted he pull over and let me out. I needed to remain calm to avoid triggering him further, so I was careful not to raise my voice over his. I sat, clenching my fists, digging my nails into my palms. My intuition was screaming, begging me to get out of the truck. I chewed the inside of my cheeks as trees sped by in big, booming bursts.

I thought about the white cross—the one that sat on the side of the road, close to where I grew up. It marked the spot where a young woman had jumped out of her kidnapper's vehicle and died. I remembered when the news broke and how I wondered what those last moments must have been like for her. How desperate would someone have to be to jump out of a moving vehicle?

Now I knew.

Terrified, my eyes fixed on the door handle. My hands trembled as I imagined flinging it open and rolling onto the pavement. Time was running out, but I couldn't make myself pull the handle. We were off the main road, winding through the city streets toward his house—a place I did not want to go for fear of never making it out alive. Before this moment, I hadn't considered the possibility that Todd was a violent man. But now...?

Todd's anger reached a fever pitch. He was yelling, oscillating between spewing personal disparaging remarks at me and acting as though I were every female who had ever wronged him. He was hitting the steering wheel, droplets of spit flying from his mouth as he cursed. I'd never seen anyone this angry.

After what felt like an eternity, we arrived at his driveway. The porch light illuminated the inside of the truck as he cut the engine and looked over at me. An eerie calm settled over him as he drew a breath and said, "The world would be a better place if you just weren't in it."

With those words, my adrenaline spiked so explosively that I became dizzy with fear. I leaped out of the vehicle and ran toward the road, wobbling in my brand-new shoes that were cutting into the backs of my heels. I was too far to run home. I didn't know where to go. I stopped at the end of the driveway, fumbling for my phone. My stomach dropped when I noticed he was standing just a few yards to my right, shouting. I wanted to run onto the road away from his house, but fast-moving traffic caused me to hesitate. In the chaos of my mind, it didn't occur to me to flag someone down. I turned back and bolted toward his truck, hoping he'd see how scared I was and back down.

"Get inside the goddamn house, Kathryn!"

I dug through my purse desperately searching for my phone. I shifted from foot to foot as he approached. The blisters on my heels tore my flesh, now raw and exposed.

"Get in the house *now!*"

"*No!*"

I imagined his neighbors watching TV, bolting to their windows as they heard the yells. I looked desperately across the street at the jogging trail next to the protected green space.

Please, God, I prayed. *Let someone look over.*

I knew if I stayed outside, I would have a fighting chance. If I entered his house, I worried I might not make it out; I had never seen anyone this unhinged before. Frantically, I fumbled with my phone, my hands trembling. I began to dial 911.

Todd grabbed my hair and yanked wildly. "You're not leaving!"

I screamed. He snatched the phone.

With my long hair tangled in his knuckles, he pulled me toward his house. My scalp was on fire, as my arms flailed, desperate to grab hold of anything I could. My nails clawed into his arms. I lost my balance, my bleeding heels dragging through the gravel as I tried to get my feet back under me.

Nothing was in reach.

I found solid ground and regained my footing. I had one hand wrapped around his arm, and with the other, I pulled back my fist and brought it down on his head as hard as I could.

We both stumbled and I fell to the ground. In a chaotic blur, Todd let go of my hair.

"You bitch!"

He threw my phone as I scrambled to get up. He brought his palm to his head where my punch had landed. Unwilling to back down, I got to my feet and threw my fist as hard as I could a second time, striking him in the face. Shocked, he bent over with his head in his hands.

Todd slowly lifted his gaze, his eyes ablaze with rage. A trickle of blood ran from his nose where my fist had connected. I realized the gravity of what I had done. Starting toward me again, his movements were deliberate and threatening. Panic surged through my veins. I turned and ran. My feet slipped on the loose gravel, grinding tiny stones into the raw skin of my heels.

By fighting back, I feared I'd only provoked him further.

CHAPTER TWO

One year before that harrowing day, I had no idea I was about to enter the darkest period of my life. I was agonizing over the recent disintegration of my two-year marriage, thinking life couldn't possibly get any worse. Jason moved out in July, and by October, I was still a mess.

I stood in front of the fridge, looking at the expired milk, realizing I couldn't put off a trip to the grocery store any longer. I managed to grab a few items from the shelves when I ran into Monica. She was an acquaintance—mostly a friend on social media—who had been through her own divorce recently.

"What you need to do is pull yourself together. Let's get together for a glass of wine. Misery loves company." She tilted her head and smiled sweetly.

"I don't know." My brows furrowed, but I knew inside I needed to get out of the house. I decided meeting Monica for drinks would be the perfect step back into the social world. We agreed to meet on Thursday at Oskar's, my favorite local hot spot.

I took my time getting ready. Leaning closer to the mirror, I parted my lips as I swiped mascara onto my lashes. I opened my eyes wide to make sure I'd coated each lash. The black eyeliner and mascara made my golden brown eyes pop. One section at a time, I curled my dark hair before giving it one last fluff with my fingers.

Hair and makeup done, I slipped into a pair of ankle-length pants. I chose a white satin button-up blouse and a chunky pearl necklace to complement my black pants. Then came the decision about shoes.

Shoes were my guilty pleasure. I had an impressive collection of sixty-two pairs. To an outsider, these shoes might seem purely functional. To me, they embodied my journey through life. My array of conservative heels showed how far I'd advanced in my career, while the spicier heels reminded me of amusing times spent with friends or suffering through botched dates. On this night, I slipped on a pair of black, strappy kitten heels. I stood in front of the mirror and smiled.

I deserve to have a good time.

Especially since Jason blamed his infidelity on the weight I'd gained during our brief marriage. It had been gradual—the weight gain almost imperceptible. We married two weeks after my fortieth birthday, and age had taken a toll. It wasn't a first marriage for either of us, so what did he expect?

I thought about another time I stood in front of this same mirror, when Jason had promised to put effort into our marriage. It was a chance to reconnect and get back on track after what he called a "mistake." I had chosen the perfect dress for our evening out, eager for his approval. Instead, his face contorted into a grimace when he saw me.

"What's wrong with the dress?" My heart sank.

"You're brave for wearing that. I thought you were trying to lose weight?"

Tears pricked the corners of my eyes. A deep sense of shame and doubt replaced my excitement. The awkward silence that night at dinner. The guilt I felt for every bite I took or calorie I consumed. The damage was done. My self-esteem plummeted to an all-time low. I realized that what I wanted in a partner—what I thought I had in Jason—was completely off the mark.

Now, the combination of a well-chosen outfit, freshly done hair, and makeup boosted my self-esteem, and on this night, I savored the boost. I hadn't been out for a fun night like this in ages. I couldn't wait to sit down at the bar and relax. I took one last look in the mirror, grabbed my purse, and headed out the door.

Heading down Main Street, I drove past the protected green spaces and the magnificent oak trees draped in swaying Spanish moss. I felt a sweet, soaring love for the place I called home. I pulled into the familiar parking lot of Oskar's, known for its extensive wine collection and the best steaks in town. My heels clickety-clacked on the pavement as I made my way over, fluffing my hair once more. The air conditioner above the heavy oak door roared, blasting me with cool air. Living in the Deep South, it's not noticeable when fall arrives because the temperature doesn't change.

The savory aroma of sizzling steaks wafted toward me as I stepped inside. Friendly chatter and glasses clinking complemented the soft jazz music filling the air. It took a moment for my eyes to adjust to the dimly lit interior, rich hardwood floors, and crushed blue velvet chairs. I scanned the room until I saw Monica sitting at the bar.

"Kathryn!" she called out.

"Hi, Monica." I greeted her with a friendly hug.

The bartender, Chuck, waved. "Good to see you again, Kathryn. It's been a while."

I sat on a stool and took a deep breath, ready for a drink. Admittedly, I was a wine snob with champagne tastes on a beer budget. But on this October night, I splurged on my favorite wine, which I hadn't had in ages.

Chuck placed the glass in front of me. I took a long, slow sip, letting it linger on my tongue. It was an oaked red wine, with flavor so full that it tasted like I was drinking it directly out of the barrel. It had been too long since I let myself have a break like this, and it was easy to let my shoulders drop a little.

"So," Monica began, eyes keen. "How's the nonprofit?"

Over the years, I'd raised so much money for a local children's nonprofit that they invited me to be a board member to help determine how the funding would be spent. I had worked so hard to promote the nonprofit that it seemed like everyone in the community associated me with it.

"The last meeting, we spent hours brainstorming funding for summer programs. I'm still waiting to see if our grant gets funded. It's exhausting, but seeing the impact we're having makes it worth it."

"Funding for what, exactly?"

"It's this big push to expand our literacy initiatives." I heard the excitement in my voice and didn't bother to hide it. "We're reaching more kids than ever before."

Monica and I fell into a fun, flowing conversation. We sat with our arms resting on the bar, facing each other. We talked about work, life, and our love-hate relationship with cooking.

"I know, it's silly, but I miss cooking. It's hard to justify putting the time into it when you're making a meal for one," I said.

"It's funny how we hate cooking when we *need* to do it, but it can be so nostalgic when we don't *have* to."

"Exactly!" I took another sip of the oaky red, savoring its flavor.

"I—" she paused, looking over my shoulder.

I watched as Monica reached out, touching the shoulder of a man walking by.

"Todd, hi. How are you?"

"Hey there, Monica. I'm doin' well. How's it goin'?" Todd stretched out his arms and embraced her.

"I'm great." Monica reached over and placed a hand on my shoulder. "This is my friend, Kathryn."

Meeting a man was the last thing on my mind, considering the smoldering wreckage my life had become. Yet here I was, pasting on a polite smile, meeting a man.

"Nice to meet you," I said.

Todd's hands were warm, his handshake firm. He had striking blue eyes that reflected a softness. Standing around five-and-a-half feet tall, he had neatly combed blonde hair. He wasn't tall, but he wasn't short. He wasn't lean, but he wasn't large either. Somewhere in between, much like me.

"Pleasure to meet ya, ma'am." His words were a melody of Southern hospitality that transported me to a place of front-porch conversations and sweet tea shared among family.

As we chatted, I learned Todd works for the police department, providing IT support. I listened intently as he spoke, looking into his eyes. It was like looking into the ocean. They held a calm intensity that once you notice, you can't look away from.

"Wow, that must be an interesting job."

"I don't work full time for them. They call me when they need me. And even when they don't, I hang around the station. I also do freelance work on the side. I don't have an office or nothin'. I run my business out of my house." His distinctive drawl lingered in the air, creating a comfortable rhythm of conversation.

Monica and I listened as he talked about some of the cases he worked on. It was clear that he took great pride in using his skills to support law enforcement and help bring criminals to justice. I was genuinely impressed.

"I've even been called as an expert witness for data collection." He swirled the wine in his glass and took a sip. "Computers, cell phones . . . if you delete it, I can usually retrieve it."

My head swam as the wine took hold. Even though he wasn't the type of guy I was usually attracted to, Todd was not only charming, but seemingly trustworthy given his work with the police department. As he flirted with me, I found myself volleying back, playfully throwing a hand on his shoulder as he made jokes.

I felt . . . something when we made eye contact, but I couldn't quite put my finger on it. While Monica rambled on about her ex, my thoughts drifted to when I first met Jason. I had stopped off for coffee one morning —a rare treat. I didn't notice him at first, but when I went to grab napkins, Jason introduced himself. BAM! There it was—that electric jolt that romance flicks have us all searching for.

I believed Jason would set a strong example for the boys—he was reliable and had a solid career. He brought laughter that filled the empty spaces, and hands ready to share the load. Life was good. No, life was wonderful.

Until I gained weight.

Until he cheated.

But that something I sensed with Todd? It wasn't like that at all. What sparked with Todd was more like a soft ember, mysterious and lingering. I couldn't be certain that it wasn't just drunken politeness.

I was taught that being a lady meant always being polite. I can still recall finishing etiquette school and feeling like I'd achieved something significant, even though I was just eight years old.

Putting others' needs before my own was something I picked up early on, almost naturally. As I grew older, this ingrained politeness served me well in many ways. Teachers praised my quiet, cooperative demeanor. Friends confided in me, trusting my discretion and gentle advice. I was the consummate good girl, the one adults pointed to as an example. I'll leave my faith out of this, but at the end of every day, I wanted to be a good person. The one that everyone could call a friend.

Little did I know that this deeply rooted politeness would ensnare me in a stalker's web.

CHAPTER
THREE

The pulse of the bar faded in and out, while my mind was caught in a loop, weighing the urge to flee against the pressure to stay. Monica and Todd exchanged banter while I mulled it over. It was, after all, getting late.

Todd leaned forward, his eyes wide with curiosity. "What do you do for work?" Genuine interest colored his voice.

"I do fundraisers on the side for various charities and causes. But my main job is with a company based in Chicago. We have a facility about thirty minutes from here, and that's where my office is located."

"Really? That's impressive. What kind of work is that?"

"I manage their operations across the state. On that note, I should head home. Tomorrow's a workday." I smiled, a silent applaud to my exit strategy.

I signaled to Chuck for the bill, but Todd wouldn't hear of it. He insisted it was his treat. I fumbled for words to refuse, but Monica's hand gently settled on my arm, her eyes sparkling with a knowing look. Feeling a pleasant warmth from Todd's unexpected generosity, I rose from the barstool.

Todd offered to walk me to my car. His hands were tucked into his pockets, a soft smile playing on his lips. At my car, he held the door open—a small gesture that spoke volumes and rattled the quiet, guarded spaces inside me.

"Would you like to go on a date?"

I smiled. "I'm sorry, but I'm not quite ready to date yet. I'm going through a divorce."

"Man, I understand." He shook his head. "I'm going through a breakup myself. Maybe we can keep each other company?"

"Sure," I said politely. It seemed harmless to exchange phone numbers.

The divorce from Jason wasn't my first rodeo. I moved here fourteen years ago with Mark, my husband, and our two kids. Mark's job had transferred him, but I didn't adjust well living in a new state. Growing up as a small-town girl in the Deep South, I was connected to the familiar rhythms of my community. I graduated from the same high school where my parents had once walked the halls as students. The doctor who brought me into this world was the same kind, reassuring presence who had delivered my children. Now, that place was a long drive—too far to make a round trip in one day. Visiting required an overnight stay, making those drives rare.

Leaving behind those roots was tough. Mark and I called it quits shortly after the move—seven years of marriage, gone. Instead of moving back home, I stayed to share custody of our kids. Being a single mom hadn't been part of the plan, but then, plans tend to change when you least expect it.

Dylan was three and Caleb was five when Mark and I divorced. We agreed on everything except child support. Even though I desperately needed it, I never sought it to keep the peace—a pattern of conflict avoidance I didn't realize I had until years later.

In the beginning, it was a bit of a bumpy ride. Mark and I decided to sell the house, and we got places of our own just three miles apart. It worked out well, since the boys could hop on the bus after school and end up at either of our doorsteps. Buying that house was a big deal for me—it was the first piece of real estate I bought entirely on my own.

After years of marriage, re-entering the dating world was a challenge—dating sites and, after the first iPhone came out, apps. It wasn't like that when I met Mark in the late 1990s. I was working at a store when he walked in . . . a typical boy-meets-girl story. After we split, dating became all about swiping and messaging, trying to connect through a tiny screen. I couldn't bring myself to use a dating app, which probably explains why I didn't remarry for eleven years after Mark and I divorced.

Now, going through a divorce from Jason, I still couldn't see myself using a dating app. But I knew I wasn't ready to start something new, either. And Todd? I wasn't sure yet what to make of him.

After that night at Oskar's, I made more of an effort to be social. And when I did, I kept running into Todd. Whether out with friends or running errands, he seemed to appear everywhere. It felt strange—then again, maybe he'd been there all along, and I hadn't noticed him before.

One Saturday morning, I stopped by the coffee shop to indulge in a seasonal favorite, another mundane attempt to add flavor to my flavorless life. Thanksgiving was around the corner, so I decided to do some Christmas shopping early.

While standing in line, letting the scent of roasted beans invigorate me, I noticed Todd come in. There was a simple ease in the way he smiled and waved, as if we were already old friends.

The line inched forward when Todd joined me.

"Hi, Kathryn."

He stood close—closer than I expected. The air between us was thick with his cologne, an intoxicating blend of spicy cedarwood and crisp citrus that wrapped around me like an embrace, making the space feel intimate.

"Yeah." I turned, trying to match his casual tone. "Hi, Todd."

"What are the odds?" He laughed as if we were sharing a private joke. "We keep running into each other."

"Small town." I gave a half-shrug.

"How about you let me stand in line for you? Maybe you can snag a table, and we can catch up—if you're not in a hurry."

I hesitated, my grandmother's voice echoing in my mind, *"Cat got yer tongue?"*

Todd gestured to the tables. "Go ahead, grab one before the crowd gets any worse. Let me guess—cappuccino?"

"I was actually going for a pumpkin spice latte," I said over my shoulder. I picked a cozy table and settled into it. When I looked back at the line, I saw the elderly lady who had been in front of me was now placing her order. She began to fret, rifling through her purse and apologizing profusely.

The barista's face grew impatient, her eyes narrowing at the woman's increasing embarrassment. I saw Todd leaning in and tap his card, a thoughtful smile on his face. I relaxed into my seat, my heart warming at the interaction.

Todd's demeanor shifted the moment the woman left. Judging from the barista's reaction, his kindness had been replaced with something cold and biting. The barista looked down, her defiance replaced by a flicker of shame. This was a different side of him. I felt my heart skip a beat—a jolt of something I couldn't quite place—again.

As quickly as his demeanor changed, it shifted back. Todd made his way over with our coffees, his smile easy and untroubled.

"A pumpkin spice latte for the lady, as ordered."

I was speechless—a jumble of impressions and doubts. The cup was warm in my hands, but my thoughts were jumbled into a strange, tangled brew all their own.

Every time I ran into Todd over the next few months, he would ask with genuine interest how I was, how things were going, and how I was processing the divorce. It surprised me—his persistence, his concern. Each encounter left me in knots, touched by what seemed like real care, yet wary of what it might mean. I'd been struggling to figure out where I stood, how to respond. Beneath the surface, I felt the tension of his expectations.

Each time he asked me out, I declined. But Todd's persistence was endearing, which only made it tougher to keep saying no. I didn't feel that chemistry, and even if I did, I wasn't sure I could trust it anymore.

CHAPTER
FOUR

By January, the divorce from Jason had taken a nasty turn. It never failed to surprise me just how far we'd drifted and how ugly things had become. This was a man I'd been deeply, madly in love with. I'd trusted him to take on a paternal role in my boys' lives. Now, dividing the community property was a struggle we couldn't seem to overcome.

I was determined to make the new year great and put everything behind me. But then I received yet another email from Jason—this one demanding that I return the laptop he purchased for me during our brief marriage. I closed my eyes and rubbed my temples, willing away an impending headache. I didn't have to return it, but I didn't want to fan the flames over something so trivial, either.

I knew I'd need to remove my data first. My mind instantly went to Todd. Since he was so tech-savvy, I knew he'd be able to help me remove my data from the hard drive.

He answered on the first ring. "Hey there, Kathryn."

I smiled. His excitement was palpable through the phone. I explained my situation with the laptop and before I could even ask the question, he offered to do it for me.

"It'd be my pleasure. I could come over now if you'd like . . ."

Right now? I quickly glanced in the mirror and realized I needed a few minutes to freshen up. "Uh . . . well, maybe thirty minutes? If it's not too much trouble."

I suggested paying him for his time, but he refused.

"I hardly ever get a chance to enjoy a home-cooked meal. That'd be payment enough." His drawl filled the phone and settled warmly in my chest.

"Sure. I can do that, but I'll need a bit more time. How about this evening at six?"

"That works for me."

After we hung up, I remembered the night I met Todd. I had been talking to Monica about how much I missed cooking for the kids. I wondered if he had overheard our conversation. It was cold outside, so I decided to make soup—an unimpressive meal that didn't scream romance.

Todd arrived with his shirt tucked into his jeans, emphasizing the bulbous shape of his belly, and his hair neatly combed. I was sure he hoped dinner would turn into something more, but I made sure the setup was anything but intimate.

He smiled when I opened the front door. "Ya know your Christmas decorations are still up?"

"I know." I laughed. Even though it was two weeks into the new year, there were still wreaths on my upstairs windows, and I'd need to get on the roof to take them down. "How 'bout you get up there and help me?"

I wasn't being serious, but within ten minutes, Todd was on the roof taking down the wreaths. Once back inside, he sat down with a glass of wine, his left hand resting atop his belly. As we drank, he shared more details about his recent breakup with his girlfriend, and I shared more about my divorce.

After about an hour, I served dinner. Steam danced off the bowl of homemade chicken tortilla soup in front of him. He took a slurp from his spoon, closed his eyes, and declared, "This is the best soup I've ever had."

We lingered at the table after dinner as he worked on my laptop. It was small at first, but I admit I felt a spark of connection ignite between us—a tentative ember, fragile yet promising, hinting at the possibility of something more.

As Todd stood to leave, he hesitated for a moment before turning to me with a smile. "I had a great time tonight," he said softly. "Maybe we could do this again sometime?"

I felt my heart skip a beat at his words, a swirl of emotions inside me. "I'd like that."

Without realizing it, I was slowly dropping my guard.

Cash was tight, but I was ready to reconnect with friends. For years before Jason, I enjoyed happy hour after work with an eclectic group at Café Calais. It was the high point of my week, but it had been two years since I last participated. At the center of the group was Lauren. We were tight—more than friends. Lauren and I were like sisters. Sure, she could be loud and opinionated, but that's what made her special—that and her heart of pure gold.

I grabbed my phone and texted Lauren.

ME
Wine Down Wednesday?

LAUREN
Yes! U coming?

ME
I'll be there next week

LAUREN
About time. Miss u

On the first Wednesday of February, I pulled on jeans and a sweater before slipping into a pair of ankle boots. I felt genuine joy when I walked into the bar, waving to the girls. It wasn't long before I started to feel like myself again, a feeling I'd been craving.

As we chatted, I noticed a familiar face walk in—Todd. We spoke briefly, but he was clearly outnumbered. Happy Hour Girl Code dictated that no men were allowed, so I cut short the small talk with Todd.

"Okay, I get it," he said with a small laugh. "But can I call you tomorrow?"

"Sure," I replied.

He left the bar without ordering anything, and the girls and I continued our evening of boisterous laughter and fun. Still, in the back of my mind, I couldn't believe how odd it was that I kept seeing Todd in the most unexpected places.

When he called the following day, he asked again if I'd like to go out on a date. I explained that I still wasn't interested in dating but was flattered by his persistence over the past four months.

"I hate to admit it," he said with a hint of sadness that piqued my interest, "but Valentine's Day is hard for me."

"I'm not really a Valentine's Day gal," I responded, jokingly. "It seems like a way for greeting card companies to make money."

He laughed. "I know, but when you're alone, Valentine's Day feels cruel, you know? What if we just had a casual dinner?"

I could hear the pain in his voice. As much as I wasn't ready to date, I didn't want Todd to be sad and lonely.

When Valentine's Day arrived, I made no effort to dress up, fearing it might send the wrong message. Instead, I swept my hair into a low ponytail and wore jeans with a chunky sweater and flats—easy-breezy.

I was excited for dinner because I had something important to discuss with Todd. The Chicago-based company I worked for had announced it was closing its offices in my sweet Southern state. The cost of doing business along the Gulf of Mexico had increased significantly since it opened. As the senior employee, I was responsible for managing the closure and the layoffs of hundreds of employees—an awful task.

I could stay on and temporarily move to a work-from-home position, with the expectation that I'd relocate to Chicago. It was uncommon for companies to allow employees to work remotely at that time, and I could tell my boss wasn't thrilled about the idea. He begrudgingly allowed it after I promised to relocate once Dylan graduated from high school. He had just started his junior year, giving me a year and a half to find a new job. I knew I'd never move to Chicago—I loved my small town.

Since the company was publicly traded, and I had access to confidential financial information, network security was critical. I was tasked with finding a local contractor to set up the necessary infrastructure. Of course, Todd came to mind. If the police department could trust him with sensitive data, I figured I could, too.

Over dinner, I asked if he would be interested in helping and explained the nuances of my job. He was elated at the idea and seemed happy to have a new client.

"I'm so glad you'll help," I said, taking a bite of my pasta and hoping flecks of parsley wouldn't lodge themselves in my teeth. "Oh, by the way, I looked up your company and saw that your business license has expired. Looks like you need to file your annual report."

A flicker of emotion crossed Todd's face—anger. His eyes narrowed, and his lips pursed into a thin line. "So what? Are you investigating me now?" A vein in his neck visibly pulsed.

"No." I was taken aback. "A publicly traded company wouldn't allow anyone access to their network without verifying their business entity." The sudden tension caught me off guard.

"Oh, that makes sense." His face settled back into his usual, relaxed smile.

I stared into my plate of Italian sausage tortellini. Maybe Todd was concerned about protecting his work at the police department and for his other clients. I was sure that the explanation was that simple.

CHAPTER FIVE

Four years after my divorce from Mark, he remarried. The kids now had a stepmother, and she didn't bother hiding the fact that she wasn't my biggest fan. It was tough, especially when I was struggling. I hustled to cobble together an income, working multiple jobs while juggling the kids' school and activities. But it wasn't enough. I fell behind on my bills, especially my mortgage, and the bank began foreclosure proceedings. I put my beloved house up for sale to stop the foreclosure, taking on extra jobs until I could catch up on the mortgage. It wasn't easy, but then again, I've never been one to shy away from hard work.

I'd saved my beloved house.

Now I'd have to save it again.

Jason, who loved the outdoors, bought a large center console fishing boat right after our wedding. My house was just forty miles from the Gulf of Mexico. Tributaries flowed through my small Southern town to the gulf, making boating and jet skiing popular pastimes in my community.

The boat was huge, and the monthly dry storage fees were pricey. Jason proposed building a garage onto my house instead. I'd lived in my home for eleven years without one, but it seemed like a good idea.

The garage, designed to fit the boat, was almost a thousand square feet.

The contractor mentioned that adding a room above wouldn't significantly increase the costs, so we decided to go for it. My parents often stayed at a hotel when they visited, and Jason's parents lived several hours away. It would be a nice space for visitors, so we added a bathroom with a walk-in shower.

When Jason moved out and took the boat with him, the garage was mostly finished. It was attached to the house, with a door leading into the kitchen. But the upstairs construction had stalled. I was finishing it as best I could with the limited money I had.

With all the costs on top of the divorce, no walls had been built except around the bathroom and a small closet. The laminate floors had been laid, but there were no baseboards. The windows were installed, but the sills hadn't been added. The space could be accessed either through the back of the garage or via an outside entrance.

Once Todd corrected the issue with his business license, my company approved him. On the day of the installation, he arrived at my house with the tools and equipment he needed. I took him through the garage and up the unfinished stairs.

"Your garage is huge. How many cars can you fit in here?"

I scoffed. The garage had been a financial weight, dragging me down.

As Todd looked around, he remarked, "I'm so jealous that you have all this space up here, and it's separate from your house. I work out of a bedroom at my place. This is great." He tapped on the walls, searching for the best spot to install the router. "What if I rented some of it for my freelance work? I'm pretty handy and could help finish some of this myself. I used to help my dad flip houses."

I tilted my head, surprised by his suggestion. I wasn't sure how to respond, but I wasn't immediately put off by the idea. The space was larger than I needed for my home office. The construction and divorce had left me financially compromised, so the thought of rental income and extra help was appealing. Todd continued his pitch, reasoning that since he did IT work, Internet speed was critical. He would pay for it, meaning one less bill for me. I agreed.

I handed Todd my spare garage door opener to access the workspace since I didn't know where the keys to the external entrance were. In exchange, he handed me a check for the first month's rent.

I handed it back.

"Could you write 'rent' on the memo line for me, please? Just to keep my records in order."

He took it and did as I asked, but I swear I saw a sneer pass over his face.

Todd was quick to move his office in. We positioned our desks on opposite sides of the room. I arranged things so that he wouldn't be visible if I needed to join a video call. Although the company's firewall secured my work computer, it didn't secure Todd's. He relied solely on Wi-Fi to connect his devices.

I had always thrived in the social office environment and had never worked from home before. Sharing my office space with Todd eased the sting of solitude. Sometimes, I would go days without seeing anyone but Todd. He'd ask if I needed anything from the store and bring groceries, so I didn't have to leave the house. He would never accept my offers to reimburse him, even when I'd discreetly leave money in his desk drawer.

We talked constantly, and the more I got to know Todd, the more comfortable I became. Our banter ranged from the weather to the challenges of being single. Not having a plus-one for events, for example, so I understood exactly what he meant when he mentioned needing a plus-one for a charity event.

"Please come?" he begged. "You know I need a plus-one."

Since I often attended my own fundraisers alone, I knew how much it would mean to him if I went. So, I agreed. Later that week, we made our way to the event sponsored by the police department. As he drove, he explained that his ex might be there.

"If she's there, we should avoid her. She's been stalking me and will try to talk to me, but I want to make sure I don't engage her. Just stick close to me and ignore her, okay?"

I nodded. If Jason were there, I'd want to avoid him, too.

When we arrived, I stayed close to Todd. I smiled graciously and offered firm handshakes to his friends and colleagues. Soon, he pointed out his ex-girlfriend, who curiously made no eye contact with either of us. In fact, she seemed to do her best to stay on the opposite side of the room. She carried herself awkwardly, as if she were uncomfortable.

After she made her way across the room, she sat with her foot nervously tapping the floor. In truth, she looked . . . *scared*. It wasn't long after Todd pointed her out that she left, as though she didn't want to be there.

This seemed like nothing more than a bad breakup, and I dismissed it. I'd been through plenty myself. We enjoyed the swirling cocktails and raising money for the police department's foundation. After the event, Todd and I decided to stop by Oskar's for a nightcap.

"It's been tough. I just haven't found the right woman yet."

I listened as tidbits about his life flowed—his relationships and the women who had taken advantage of him. There was the manipulative mother of his two children, the ex-girlfriend who cheated on him, and now, the crazy ex-girlfriend who was stalking him.

"I haven't seen my kids in over seven years." His voice cracked, and his eyes were trained on the ground. My heart ached for him, and I was angry at the thought of any mother keeping a good man's children from him. After all, I'd only stayed in this state so my boys could have their father in their lives.

"I'm sorry," I offered. "That must be awful."

His eyes lifted to his glass, looking vulnerable. Even in the dim lighting, I could see tears beginning to pool in the corners of his eyes.

I saw him not just as someone I had met by chance but as a complex, intricate soul with layers waiting to be unraveled. I found myself wanting to reach out—to touch him, to comfort him. In that instant, I realized I felt a connection that transcended the lack of physical attraction. I was beginning to care about him in ways I never expected.

CHAPTER SIX

Later that week, as we worked in the office, Todd said he had a camera system he wouldn't be using. "You should let me install it for ya," he said casually. "Especially since I have my equipment here. I'd be happy to do it—maybe for another home-cooked meal?"

Todd was quick to point out the right-of-way running the length of my backyard. Anyone could drive up to the back of my property without my knowing it. I'd owned the house for fourteen years without issue. However, Todd worked for the police. I reminded myself that while I spent my workday crunching numbers, he was dealing with criminals. Of course, his mind would go there.

I couldn't hear the doorbell while in the office. Cameras would at least let me know if someone was at my front door, so I agreed.

"Great." He smiled. "I'll feel better knowing you've got 'em."

The next day, Todd installed the cameras while I worked. He never asked where I wanted them placed—he just did it. I didn't mind since I wasn't paying for them. He installed one at my front door, one at the side door angled over the driveway and into the garage, another in the backyard showing the patio and back door, and one on the side of the house, looking at my bedroom window. I could access the footage on a TV or through an app on my phone. The system even had a DVR with full playback capability.

"All done. I just need your phone to get the app configured," he said, putting his drill on his desk. "Hey, did you know your car has an app? You can unlock doors, check oil levels—things like that."

I looked at him, puzzled. *Why would someone check oil on an app rather than look at the dash?* But I figured Todd was really into technology. It was his job.

"You don't know how many stolen vehicles get reported that we can't find because people don't set up the app."

I hesitated, then thought, *Why not? It can't hurt.* "Okay." I handed him my unlocked phone. Within minutes, he had both apps downloaded, the logins created, and he walked me through how to use them.

"If Caleb or Dylan ever borrow your car, you can click here for their location. That way, you'll know they're where they say they're going to be."

I thanked him, even though I knew I'd probably never use the car app. Caleb and Dylan had their own vehicles. I assumed Todd had become somewhat paranoid—possibly because of the work he did with the police department. Out of respect, I didn't pry into his job, but I was curious about what he was exposed to that made him so safety-conscious.

That evening, Todd stayed for dinner. I made roast chicken with garlicky potatoes and a side of fresh, crisp green beans. After eating and sharing a few glasses of wine, we headed outside and pulled up chairs around a fire pit beside the towering pine trees. The calendar had just turned to April, so it was still in the high fifties outside. Together, we sat in the pulsing glow of the fire, talking about life beneath a sky strewn with twinkling stars over wine. A bit tipsy, I felt warm in the sweatshirt I was wearing. When I lifted it over my head, my T-shirt came up with it. I pulled the sweatshirt back down and laughed at the mishap. Todd stood and took my shoulders. Our eyes met. That's when he kissed me—and I let him. Something about it felt right.

After our first kiss, Todd and I began openly flirting more. Although I tried to set a slow pace, he was far ahead of me. He texted and called constantly, spending as much time as he could at my house. We watched shows on Netflix or cooked dinner together. I wasn't ready to be intimate with him, but it was nice having someone to relax with after work.

It became normal for Todd to be at the house. I'd always been firm about my rule—no men staying over when Caleb and Dylan were around. So, Todd wasn't spending the night. Caleb was at college, just a thirty-minute drive away. Dylan was always out until his ten o'clock curfew, involved in after-school activities, a part-time job, and hanging out with friends rather than with me.

I noticed Todd never invited me to his place, and I couldn't help but wonder if it was because he was embarrassed. He told me he owned his house, but later asked to spend the night at mine because his landlord was fumigating his. I never pushed the issue; it didn't matter to me whether he owned or rented.

One Saturday morning, I was eager to reconnect with Nathan. We'd met years ago when I had my first local job working the front desk at the gym. He was a commanding yet comforting figure who embodied wisdom. His full head of white hair was matched only by a neatly trimmed white beard.

There was an unmistakable paternal aura about Nathan, filling the void left by the physical distance between my parents and me. He'd become like my local dad. He had seen me face challenges as a single mother, including the struggle to save my house from foreclosure.

For over ten years, we'd met for breakfast on Saturday mornings—a tradition I'd given up because Nathan didn't like Jason, and it was mutual. To avoid conflict, I stopped going. I missed our time together and was looking forward to reconnecting. Yesterday, I sent him a quick text to see if he wanted to resume our weekly breakfasts.

NATHAN
Glad to have you back, kiddo.

ME
See u at our usual spot at 8:30.

Not long after the text messages, Todd called. He invited me to a home and garden show at the convention center. He was enthusiastic about it, claiming it'd give me ideas to spruce up my place. Looking back, it seemed like he was preparing my house for himself, deepening his delusion about a future life together.

I told him I had plans to meet Nathan for breakfast. He asked to join us, and I didn't see the harm. We walked in together, and my eyes immediately locked onto Nathan. He was sitting at our usual table, where the roles of mentor and protégé blurred into something more familial.

"Hey there," Nathan called out, his voice rich and welcoming.

"Mornin', Nathan." We hugged, and I directed his attention to my guest. "I'd like you to meet Todd."

Throughout breakfast, Todd subtly steered the conversation in ways that left me feeling off-kilter. *Why is he commenting that Nathan must have a hefty retirement to meet me every week? And why does Nathan's age matter?* Todd's questions probed into areas that felt too personal for a first meeting.

I sensed a hint of sarcasm in Nathan's responses. His naturally jovial demeanor was strained, a palpable tension lingering at the edge of conversation. It was awkward, but I felt Todd was trying to make a good impression—he just went about it the wrong way. It didn't surprise me when Nathan later called and asked that I not bring Todd again.

"Why?"

"I don't know, but there's something off about him. He gives me the creeps."

While I deeply respected Nathan, we'd become so close over the years that I wondered whether he would approve of anyone I introduced him to. I was beginning to overcome my lack of attraction to Todd, realizing that maybe love wasn't about that immediate spark I'd found with Jason. Perhaps it was more about a kindling—something to nurture and grow into a strong, bright future.

I was planning to talk to Todd about the personal questions he asked Nathan when he surprised me with concert tickets—second-row seats, along with a backstage pass—to see my favorite band. And not just any tickets—these felt like more than an innocent gift. I once told him that when I was happily married to Jason, one of my best memories was when he surprised me with concert tickets to see this band. It almost seemed like Todd's way of making amends for Jason's mistakes.

Caleb was visiting from college and got in late. In the early morning hours, my phone pinged text alerts. I'd already heard Caleb come in through the garage, and knew he was home safe. Seeing Todd's name on the screen, I ignored the texts.

Then he called. And he called again.

> **TODD**
>
> I'm concerned that Caleb left the garage door open.
>
> Did he leave it open?

I set my phone on the floor so the carpet would absorb the vibration. When I woke the next morning, I had several more missed calls and texts.

> **TODD**
>
> Did you check the garage?
>
> Check with Caleb.
>
> It's not safe to have your door open like that all night.
>
> Call me.

I stopped reading when they escalated from concern to fury when Caleb came downstairs, ready to leave to head back.

"Did Todd call you? He called and texted me like twenty times, but I didn't recognize the number, so I ignored it."

"Yeah," I said casually, hiding how annoyed I felt. "He was concerned because you didn't close the garage when you came in last night."

"Why does he care?" Caleb asked, grabbing a soda from the

refrigerator. It was a good question which I had no answer for. "I think it's weird. It's creepy that he's even monitoring the garage door."

Caleb kissed me on the cheek and rushed out the door. My anger simmered as I sat there, staring at my phone with Todd's messages still on the screen. Before I could second guess myself, I hit the call button. He picked up on the first ring.

"What the hell, Todd?" I demanded, not even giving him a chance to say hello. "Why are you accessing my cameras in the middle of the night?"

"Whoa, whoa, calm down," he said in a patronizing tone. "I was doing a routine check of the cameras for all my clients to make sure the cameras were functioning properly. It's part of my job. Do you know how many times I've seen a store that was robbed whose cameras weren't functioning?"

"In the middle of the night?" I asked, not buying it for a second.

"Best time to do maintenance. Look, in your perfect, utopian bubble, cameras are always reliable, right? Welcome to the real world, where technology isn't always plug and play. That's why they pay me. I was doing you a favor, but I don't have to."

I was speechless. The way Todd spoke to me—like he was wise and I was a naïve child—was unsettling. As much as I hated to admit it, he had a point. I hadn't seen the things he had during his time at the police department. I didn't know what kind of threats were out there.

"Trust me." He paused. When he spoke again, his tone was softer, almost coaxing. "I've got your best interests at heart."

I thanked him and ended the call, feeling a mix of embarrassment and unease. As I sat there, staring at the now blank screen of my phone, something about it didn't sit right with me. Todd's explanation made sense, but how did he get Caleb's number? I was sure there was a simple explanation. Knowing Caleb, it was probably on the Internet.

CHAPTER
SEVEN

Time seemed to blur and before I knew it, two months had passed. Todd had woven himself into every aspect of my life—his presence now as familiar in my home office as the desk lamp, as expected in my kitchen as the coffee maker. He would drop by unannounced, bearing gifts—a book he thought I might enjoy, a scented candle to help me relax. He even warned me about Monica, claiming she had said unfavorable things about me. I didn't hesitate to cut her out of my life. I didn't need friends who talked unkindly about me, so I unfriended her on social media. I was thankful Todd had my back.

But there were moments when something felt off—a nagging sensation I couldn't quite place, like that night Todd called Caleb about the garage. I never asked him about it because I believed him when he said he had my best interests at heart. But there were other things—like the way Todd's gaze would linger a beat too long, or the casual touches that hinted at unspoken expectations to move our relationship into a physical realm even though I made it clear I wasn't ready. I dismissed these feelings, telling myself they were lingering emotional wounds from Jason's betrayal. Without realizing it, I was blocking out what should've been red flags.

One morning, when he walked into the office in a suit, I was surprised. He normally just wore pants and a collared shirt.

"What's the occasion?"

"A case I worked on is going to trial. I have to testify today. Which tie do you like?" He held up a red one with navy blue pin dots against the light blue striped tie he had on.

"The red one."

As he took off his tie and swapped it for the other, he offered more details. "It's a robbery case. I took the camera footage from the convenience store and ran it through facial recognition software against the driver's license database. Once I got his name, I checked his social media accounts and found a picture he'd posted a block away from the scene less than an hour before the robbery. Idiot," he snarled. "See? Cameras are good—they work."

I nodded and returned to my work while Todd prepared for his testimony. As I jostled a stack of papers, Todd rose from his seat across the room and moved closer to me, his hand reaching out to gently brush against mine. "I know we've been spending a lot of time together," he began, his voice soft yet hesitant.

Whatever was coming, I didn't want any part of the conversation. I quickly withdrew my hand. "I'm behind on a deadline. I really need to work. Don't you need to head to court soon?" I tried to keep my tone light.

Todd's smile faltered, but he quickly recovered, taking a step back and holding up his hands in a gesture of surrender. "Of course. Dinner tonight? I'm already dressed."

I forced a smile. "We'll see."

The vibration of my phone against the desk broke the tension.

He glanced over my shoulder, and I knew he saw it was my dad. He slumped and walked away, defeated. Part of me felt bad, but I couldn't let myself go there. Somewhere inside, I knew he wanted to talk about our relationship, and I wasn't ready.

The call was brief—my dad let me know he was coming in on business. He'd be staying at a hotel across town, and I'd only get to meet him for dinner on his last night. I looked forward to seeing him. Even though we weren't close, I was eager to catch up.

Todd offered to join us for dinner, but I wasn't ready for that either—especially with the divorce from Jason still pending and the breakfast with Nathan still fresh in my mind.

"I don't think that's a good idea. I haven't seen my dad in a while, and I'd like it to be just the two of us."

The atmosphere changed as if the temperature dropped. Todd's nostrils flared, and I sensed an oncoming storm. He was angry. He threw his hands up. "You just won't let anyone in, will you, Kathryn?"

I shook my head. Two weeks had passed since our first kiss, so I couldn't blame him for asking. Deep down, I knew he didn't understand my need to wait—not at all.

"You're overreacting because of choices you made in the past. It's not my fault that no one else would put up with you." He continued his tirade about how emotionally damaged I was, and honestly, I couldn't disagree.

Perhaps the lack of attraction isn't about Todd at all; maybe it's me. I spent the next few days drowning in guilt over how I was treating Todd, questioning my actions. Wasn't this what I'd longed for during those years between Mark and Jason—someone who truly saw me for who I am? Over the past six months, Todd had demonstrated a genuine desire to be with me, and yet I was sabotaging it all.

My dad and I met at a restaurant across town, near the hotel where he was staying. When I walked inside, he was sitting at a table, looking at the menu with his reading glasses propped on the end of his nose. We chatted as we ate our way through wood-fired steaks. He was passionate about guns, and our visits usually included a trip to the shooting range. But not this time—he had an early morning departure.

"Have you done any shooting lately?" Dad asked with a grin. He'd given me a handgun for my eighteenth birthday, and he'd taught me everything—shooting, cleaning, taking it apart, and putting it back together. I'd never part with it.

"Not lately. It's a shame we can't hit the range while you're in town. I bet the boys would love to go."

"When was the last time we took them? Two or three years ago?"

"I think it's been close to three years."

Dad knew I'd taken the boys out to the range frequently. Having a firearm in the house was normal for me—something I grew up with. My dad always emphasized respect for guns, a trait I passed on to my boys.

Before we left, he kissed my forehead, just like he used to when I was a little girl. I checked my phone after I got in the car and saw texts from Todd that had come in throughout dinner. He knew I was visiting my father, so it annoyed me that he'd sent so many messages.

> TODD
>
> How is it going?
>
> How is dinner?
>
> How is your dad?
>
> Want to grab a drink after? I'd love to hear about it.
>
> What time are you getting back?
>
> You're out late.
>
> I'm getting worried.

I continued scrolling through them. The messages were simultaneously sweet and irritating. It was nice to know he cared, but the volume was overkill. I messaged him that I'd just finished dinner and was heading home. Soon after, he called, but I let it go to voicemail. I wanted the soft hum of the engine to envelop me as I reflected on my time with my father.

As I was leaving the parking lot, waiting to turn left, a familiar truck passed in front of me. I recognized it immediately—Todd. I was shocked to see him, since this wasn't a part of town that either of us usually visited. It couldn't have been a coincidence that he was in the same area. I was already annoyed by the texts, and this didn't make sense. So, instead of turning left to go home, I turned right and followed him.

He parked at a store, and as he got out of his truck, I pulled alongside and rolled down my window. "Odd running into you like this," I said, raising my eyebrows.

"Are you following me?" he snapped, suspicion lacing his voice, his posture tense with accusation.

Surprised, I responded defensively. "No, I had dinner with my dad over there." I gestured toward the restaurant. "You passed right in front of me when I was leaving."

"Oh." He looked directly into my eyes, not even blinking. "I started a new exercise routine, and I'm here to pick up a few things. Want to go shopping with me?"

"No, I'm just gonna head back home. I'm exhausted from the day."

"Okay, I'll see you there."

"It's been a long day, and I'm just gonna go to bed. I'll see you in the office tomorrow." I kept my tone gentle but firm.

"Fine, if that's what you want." His words were clipped, his jaw clenched. "But don't come crying to me later when you're feeling lonely."

With that, he turned on his heels, leaving me stunned. I sat there for a moment, hands gripping the steering wheel, trying to make sense of it all. Was I wrong to assert my need for solitude? Was he right—that I was damaged, broken in some fundamental way?

Instead of enjoying the warmth of my visit with my dad, I drove home in a fog. I supported his desire to start exercising, but this was the first I'd heard about it. He was so open about his life that I couldn't help but wonder what had suddenly spurred this on.

Something didn't feel right.

CHAPTER
EIGHT

The cool morning air surrounded me as I sat at my kitchen table, sipping my second cup of coffee. I heard the garage door open and knew it was Todd, but I couldn't bring myself to greet him with a smile.

He walked in, a smile on his face. "Mind if I join you?"

"Help yourself to coffee," I said. My tone was clipped.

With a mug in hand, he sat down at the table. "Beautiful day."

"Yes, indeed." I turned to face Todd. "Why did you get so upset about not being able to meet my dad?"

He chuckled. "Well, aren't you being dramatic this morning? It wasn't a big deal. Don't make it one."

The string of text messages flashed through my mind—the way he drove by me on the other side of town weighed heavily. "What were you *really* doing across town? If you wanted workout gear, there are closer stores."

Todd stared at me in disbelief. "You're being delusional. You followed me to the store, remember?" His tone turned ice-cold. "I was already at the electronics store, buying an external hard drive. How was I supposed to know where you were meeting your dad? I wasn't invited. Or did you forget that, too?" He shook his head, his tone firm.

"Oh. I didn't know that." I tucked my hair behind my ear. The only electronics store in our area was, in fact, near the restaurant where I had been.

"Do you need me to tell you every time I go to the store?" He threw his hands up. "You are needy, but this takes it to a whole different level."

"No . . . I just . . . it struck me as weird that you'd be driving by at the exact moment I'm pulling out of the parking lot."

"If you're accusing me of something, then just come out and say it already. Otherwise, I'm done with this conversation."

Maybe Todd was right. The revelation about the electronics store put it into focus for me. I slumped in my chair, feeling small. I sounded ridiculous.

The following Wednesday, I was at happy hour, trying to shake off the unsettling encounter with Todd. As we sipped our martinis, Gwen leaned in, her brow furrowed with concern.

"Hey, Kathryn, I heard something strange the other day. Todd's been telling people you're stalking him. Following him around town?"

My stomach dropped. "What? No, that's not what happened at all." I explained the coincidental run-in after dinner with my dad, how Todd had passed right in front of me. "I was just surprised to see him there. I wasn't stalking him."

Gwen nodded sympathetically. She cut the conversation short, leaving me in the wreckage of my humiliation. The damage was done. I paid for the one drink I didn't even finish and left to confront Todd.

"Why are you spreading lies that I'm stalking you?" I demanded, my voice steady but simmering with anger.

"Kathryn," he replied coolly, "you almost ran me over in the parking lot after your dinner with your dad."

"That's a complete fabrication, and you know it," I shot back. My fury was bubbling over.

"Well, you have your version, and I've got mine." He shrugged, a smug smile playing at his lips.

I was slowly realizing that in our gossip-hungry town, the first story to circulate was the one that stuck. But little did I know, the whispered tales were just the beginning—real public humiliation lurked just around the corner, waiting to strike when I least expected it.

The next day, I received a call from Todd. My frustration with him still simmered beneath the surface. I answered, expecting to hear an apology.

"Listen," he said dismissively, "nobody in this town cares about what you do. You're making a big deal out of nothing and worrying too much about what others think."

"It's not that I care about their opinions," I replied, trying to assert my truth. "But I'm on the board of a nonprofit that serves children. I can't have people thinking I'm some psycho stalker. Especially because it's not true."

He let out a long, exaggerated sigh, as if I were being unreasonable. "If your reputation is really that important to you, I'll go with you to Oskar's tonight for drinks. When everyone sees us together, they won't think you're stalking me. Problem solved, right?"

I wasn't thrilled about the plan, but I agreed. As the time drew near for me to leave, Todd called.

"Hey, I'm nearby. Want me to swing by and pick you up?"

I'd ridden in his truck more times than I could count, so I figured, why not? We pulled up to the restaurant, and suddenly, Todd was all charming and flirty. I didn't know what to make of this change in behavior, but I played along to salvage my pride and reputation.

By this point, I had painfully realized that Todd and I would never transition into a romantic relationship. The thought of asking him to leave the office we shared weighed heavily on my mind, but I was at a loss for how to bring it up. It felt like I'd be betraying our friendship, putting my comfort ahead of his. So, I took the easy way out, hoping that our work arrangement and friendship could withstand the strain of his unrequited feelings. I kept telling myself it would all smooth out eventually. And I was right. We fell back into a comfortable routine.

One day, while we were working in the office, Todd let me know a client was dropping by. He rambled about an attorney who needed him to retrieve text messages for divorce proceedings. Moments later, Todd's phone rang, and he directed his client to enter through the garage and upstairs to the office. The downstairs door creaked open, and a friendly voice called out, "Hello?"

"Come on up!" Todd shouted.

I looked up from my desk to see Adam, a young attorney from a prestigious law firm. His firm was one of the donors to the nonprofit board I served on. "Adam. How are you?" I said, offering a hug.

"Kathryn, this is your house?"

"Yes, Todd and I share an office."

"Among other things." Todd smirked from across the room.

Adam looked around. "Wow, this is a nice space. I'm jealous you get to work from home."

"Hey, Adam," Todd interjected. "Did you bring the phone?"

The two of them talked as Todd worked, and Adam explained he only had an hour to return the phone. I tried not to listen, but—let's face it—it was juicy. I was still in the middle of my messy divorce, and misery loved company.

"Kathryn, where did you put those flash drives that were delivered yesterday?"

I pointed to a box on the floor next to his desk. "They're right there."

Todd loaded a flash drive and handed it to Adam before signing an affidavit attesting to the digital download.

Occasionally, Todd would order computer parts and have them delivered to my house. It seemed he was spending more time in our shared office than at the police department. Even so, he rarely did any work. He'd putter around, installing soft-close toilet seats, tightening loose cabinet handles, and doing odd jobs that weren't on my priority list. I was thankful it distracted him so I could work.

I was curious about how he managed to generate income, but it wasn't my place to ask. He hadn't paid rent since that first check but he more than made up for it with groceries, dinners, and chores. As long as he kept paying the Internet bill, I didn't complain.

Over time, I realized that once Todd was at my house, it was impossible to get him to leave. He would offer to make lunch or pick something up. Before I finished for the day, he was already inquiring about dinner plans. Anytime I mentioned wanting to have a night alone, he'd get his feelings hurt. It was as if he took it personally whenever I wanted to spend time by myself, which usually resulted in my caving and spending evenings with him, too.

When an opportunity came up to make plans with my friend, Carleigh, I didn't hesitate. We'd shared countless adventures and swapped recipes, and I'd even stood by Carleigh's side as a bridesmaid at her wedding. With her husband away on business, she dreaded spending the evening alone. We settled on experimenting in the kitchen on a new dish she'd found online. I gathered my keys to set out to the grocery store to gather the ingredients when Todd stopped me.

"Where are you going?" Todd's voice cut through the air, sharp and demanding.

I paused at the door, feeling a knot of annoyance tighten in my chest. "Just heading out to grab a few groceries. Do you need anything?" I tried to keep my tone light. After all, he'd done the same plenty of times, so offering seemed only fair.

"What're you getting?"

Frustration simmered beneath my skin. "My friend, Carleigh, is coming over for dinner tonight," I explained, already grasping my keys in anticipation of escape.

His demeanor shifted instantly, curiosity sparking in his eyes. "Carleigh Lopez, right?"

I nodded, feeling the weight of his interest.

"I saw y'all are friends on social media. She works for one of the law firms that contracts their IT work to me. I'd love to have her over for dinner tonight."

He said it so casually, as if he had a key to my house and a permanent seat at my table. A wave of unease clenched my stomach.

"Her husband is out of town, so we're just having a girls' night," I called back over my shoulder, my feet moving swiftly toward the door, eager to escape the tension building in the room.

"I have a lot of work to do tonight anyway."

"That's fine. Stay in the office as long as you need," I said, hoping he'd take the hint. But deep down, I knew he wouldn't.

I rushed through my shopping, my mind swirling with thoughts of Todd's intrusion. As I drove back home, I couldn't help but wonder if this was what my life had become—constantly navigating around Todd's expectations, even in my own space. The thought made my grip tighten on the steering wheel, a physical manifestation of my frustration.

Back at home, I busied myself unpacking groceries and prepping for Carleigh's arrival. The mundane tasks provided a welcome distraction, helping me push away my misgivings about Todd.

The doorbell rang, and I welcomed Carleigh with a warm hug. We chatted and laughed as we cooked, the aroma of garlic sautéing in olive oil filling the air. Dinner stretched into the night, conversations flowing as freely as the wine, until the table was a cozy mess of empty plates and satisfied smiles.

Then Todd appeared. "Smells good," he said, walking through the door.

Carleigh's eyes flicked from him to me, a silent question lingering in the air. I shrugged, a gesture that said more than words could.

"Don't mind me. Just here to snag a plate, if there's anything left?" Todd asked, eyes scanning the remnants of our feast.

"Sure, help yourself," I replied, trying to keep the mood light.

And just like that, the lively chatter faded into an awkward hush.

"I'll leave you ladies to your evening," he said, retreating with his plate.

Carleigh looked at me. "What was that about? I thought y'all weren't seeing each other anymore."

I gave another nonchalant shrug. "It's . . . complicated."

And indeed, those words carried a truth heavier than the night that wrapped around us.

CHAPTER NINE

When the boys were young, I had a tight-knit group of friends, but as the decade wore on, many moved away. We stayed connected through a group chat and had planned an out-of-state gathering, renting a cozy house so we could maximize our time together. I needed to be with friends who had no motive other than to support me.

I was packing the day before the trip when Todd asked if he could come along. Nobody else was bringing their spouse or significant other, and to be honest, Todd wasn't either of those to me.

"I'm sorry. It's just us girls. It wouldn't be right to have you there."

He balled his fists, and I sensed his anger brewing.

"Well, at least let me take you to the airport," he said, surprisingly even-toned. He left shortly after, and I didn't hear from him for the rest of the day.

The next morning, he arrived to drive me to the airport. He handed me an envelope when he dropped me off.

"Open it once the plane is in the air." He smiled sweetly and told me to have a good time.

As the plane gained altitude, I stared at the envelope I had placed in the seatback pocket in front of me. Curious, I opened it once we were above the clouds. It was a sweet sentiment, letting me know he would miss me.

When I arrived at my destination, I found other envelopes he had secretly tucked into my suitcase, labeled for each day I would be gone; the last one marked for the plane trip home. The thought of Todd rifling through my suitcase made me uneasy. But it was Todd. He meant well, but he didn't know how to respect boundaries.

The trip was perfect. My friends and I overindulged in food during the day and alcohol at night. We laughed a lot, allowing for a real, solid escape, especially from the nagging doubts I had about Todd.

Even so, every morning when I woke up, I anxiously read that day's card. Each one was sweeter and more flattering than the last:

> I enjoy the meals you cook & our dinner conversations.
>
> I like when you wear your hair down and curl it.
>
> You're sexy when you wear dresses above the knee and show off your legs.
>
> You are beautiful, especially when you wear the color red.

This made me want to wear my hair down and curled every day. I wanted to buy every red dress above the knee I could find. Despite the back-and-forth with Todd, I still struggled with self-esteem. His messages made me feel special, as if he truly saw me. I started doubting my doubts about him, if that was even a thing. Maybe I was being too hard on myself. Maybe I wasn't letting myself open up enough, and I was inadvertently fueling his volatility. Maybe the problem was me.

When I returned, I couldn't help myself. I wanted him to know how much I appreciated his kind words, his gestures, his genuine desire to make me happy. I let that be my guide, letting go of all my doubts and insecurities. Nearly two months after our first kiss, I became intimate with him. He'd been patient while I wavered, unsure if I was ready, so I knew this made him happy.

I nestled my head against Todd's chest, feeling the steady rise and fall of his breathing beneath my cheek.

"I really missed you while you were gone. We have this software at the office that does age progression—you know, like for missing persons cases."

I nodded, wondering where this was going. It sent a ripple of unease through me. By now, I was used to awkward moments—something I had come to expect from my time with Todd.

"Let me tell you," Todd exaggerated. "You're gonna be hot when you hit fifty."

Was this his idea of a compliment? I wondered.

As intimacy grew between us, I hoped my romantic feelings toward him would, too. Over the weeks, we fell into a comfortable routine where he spent most of his time at my place, which now included nights since Dylan was mostly staying at his dad's. Mark and his wife had a young son, and with Caleb away at college, Dylan preferred to stay with his younger brother. Even though Todd had a place of his own, it was like I woke up one day and realized we were practically living together. I began withdrawing, urging him to go home.

The more I pulled back, the more he pushed forward.

Todd had a never-ending list of self-appointed chores—an excuse to be at my house all hours of the day and night. He busied himself with finishing the stairs leading up to the office, installing baseboards, and adding windowsills. Sure, the house needed these things, but it didn't bother me as much as it seemed to bother Todd. At first, I accepted his help because money was tight, and I knew he wanted to take care of things for me. Over time, I began to feel increasingly unsettled.

Especially when I walked into the house one day after working above the garage and heard Todd. I turned the corner and found him in the guest bathroom, removing wallpaper.

"What are you doing?" I asked, my eyes wide.

"You said you didn't like it, so I'm taking it off."

I scratched my head. "When did I tell you that?" I tried to recall any mention of disliking the Western toile wallpaper—I actually liked it.

"Just the other day. You don't remember?" His response was quick. "You're getting forgetful."

No, I didn't remember. But since he was already halfway through peeling it off, what could I say? Annoyed, I rolled up my sleeves and joined him.

I was relieved when my phone rang. I smiled when I saw it was Lauren, so I went to the front porch to answer.

"Hey there!"

"Hey, girl. I think my phone's acting up. I haven't had any calls or texts from you in a while." She laughed.

"Yeah. Sorry . . . I've been busy. Todd decided to remove wallpaper, and the bathroom's a disaster." Even though Lauren had never met Todd, I'd told her about him.

"Oh, isn't he handy? If that's the case, do you think he'd help me install a new toilet?" Like me, Lauren was single, and we often commiserated about the responsibilities of homeownership.

"I'll ask him and let you know."

After we hung up, I spoke to Todd. He said his schedule was light in the morning and that he didn't mind helping Lauren. His willingness to help a friend of mine—someone he hadn't even met—was heartwarming. To alleviate Lauren's comical concern about her phone, I even followed up with a text letting her know Todd would be by in the morning.

When he returned from helping Lauren, Todd came up to the office where I was working.

"I'm going to paint the bathroom today. What color do you want?"

I already felt suffocated by his constant presence and wasn't in the mood to discuss paint colors, so I snapped at him. "I'll paint it when I'm ready."

"What's gotten into you today?"

"Todd, it's just that . . . all this work is great, and I appreciate it. But I don't want you to feel like I'm using you for home improvements." The words tumbled out before I had a chance to think.

He looked hurt, and my heart sank.

"I'm doing this for *us*." His eyes widened, and his hand went to his chest. "I love you, Kathryn."

When someone says that, you want your belly to flutter. You want the feeling of forever to stretch out before you, a seemingly endless expanse of time spent intertwined. But when Todd dropped the L-bomb, the words hit me like a pile of bricks. I knew I wasn't in love with him. I stared blankly, unable to speak. I watched his face shift from happy to excited to confused, and finally, to disappointed.

"I'm sorry, Todd. That's just not where I am."

"What do you mean?" His cheeks flushed.

"If I'm being honest, all of this has become . . . smothering."

There. I said it.

He rolled his eyes, incredulous. "That has nothing to do with me. That's *your* problem. Things are great. You're just scared to let someone love you. It's really sad, actually."

Honestly, I agreed with him. But it didn't change the fact that I wasn't in love with him. After that, Todd pulled back and stopped coming over every morning. It felt like a relief, confirming that I'd been feeling suffocated.

Although my job was going well, I knew the company would want me to decide soon whether to relocate to Chicago. I wasn't confident they'd allow me to continue working from home in a state they no longer did business in.

I thought about those early years, after my divorce from Mark. I'd struggled to work my way up from the front desk at the gym. After the house was out of foreclosure, I applied for higher-paying positions but was routinely passed over because I didn't have a degree. I was exhausted from juggling low-paying jobs and couldn't let not having a degree stop me. I enrolled in college and studied when the kids went to bed or to Mark's house. Finally, I had gotten a bachelor's degree and a year later, a job offer from a Chicago-based company. I started as a shift manager and was later promoted to operations manager. The company had seen potential in me and even paid for me to get my MBA. Once I had that, they promoted me to the highest position in the state—Director of Operations.

But I had to face reality. The company pulled out of the state entirely, leaving me as the lone remote employee. They changed my title to Director of Special Projects, but I feared the list of projects would eventually run out.

With Dylan starting his senior year of high school, I knew my job could be in jeopardy. I reverted to what I knew best. Instead of working nights and weekends on fundraisers, I decided to try consulting to rebuild my savings. I set up an LLC and connected with a few contacts, spreading the word. It wasn't long before I landed my first client on a monthly retainer. Over the next few months, I settled into a steady rhythm—my nights filled with consulting work and my days dedicated to my job, leaving less room for Todd.

CHAPTER TEN

It seemed like we had finally reached an understanding since Todd confessed his love, and I hadn't returned the sentiment. Todd would let himself in through the garage and up to the office as if nothing had happened. It wasn't an everyday occurrence like it had been, and I was grateful for that. We'd even gone to a shooting range for target practice. He didn't try to hold my hand; we just stood in separate shooting lanes next to each other, focused on our own targets.

Today, I had the office to myself, which was great because I had a ton of work on my plate. I was immersed in my tasks when a notification sounded from my phone. It was a breaking news alert, announcing the presumed accidental death of a local, well-known, and well-liked woman—someone who worked at a church less than a mile from my house. She'd been found at her house, which was a little over ten miles away, near Todd's. Although I had only met her once, I felt sad for her family.

A few hours later, Todd stopped by. He casually asked if I had seen the news alert and whether I knew the woman.

"No, not really," I said, staring at my computer screen, trying to convey that I needed to work.

"I did. I installed the security camera system at her house. She was a real bitch." His tone was harsh as he dropped into the chair behind his desk.

It felt like he was baiting me into a conversation about it. His comment struck me as odd. Todd always claimed everyone was a good friend. Other than his exes and criminals, this was the first time I'd heard him speak negatively about anyone.

"My boss is on me to get this report out. I really need to stay focused."

"You know, you're not going to find another guy out there who will love you like I do. I'm the best thing that will ever happen to you."

I pretended to stay focused on my work and didn't respond. My stomach twisted into anxious knots. Deep down, a small part of me feared he might be right. I'd never been lucky in love, and my forty-third birthday was quickly approaching. Despite my doubts, a tiny part of me hoped that if Todd would just slow down, we could find a real connection.

Todd left shortly after. Over the next week, I saw very little of him. I figured he was busy with work at the police department. Then he stopped by with lunch. We were eating at our respective desks when our phones simultaneously sounded with another breaking news alert. I glanced down, saw it had something to do with the woman's death, but I didn't read the article. Todd, however, stared at his phone, reading for several minutes. I figured he'd give me an update, but instead, he abruptly said he had to go and left.

The next evening, he asked if I wanted to meet for dinner. I wasn't interested in going out, so I declined. Less than an hour later, he showed up at my house with a bag of takeout.

"You need to put some meat on your bones, Kathryn." He held up the bag and then waltzed into my kitchen. The irony struck me—Jason had shamed me for my weight.

Todd and I sat down at the table as he pulled containers from the bag. I didn't bother getting dishes or cutlery, as I would have if I'd been grateful for a delivered meal. Instead, we ate right from the containers.

"Did you hear that the coroner's office announced their findings on that woman?" The disdain dripped from his words. "Apparently, she didn't die accidentally. She was murdered." He said it like we were talking about the weather.

"Yeah, that's awful." Our county had four murders the previous year, so this was big news in our small town.

"When I saw the coroner's announcement, I left here and went to her funeral. It was at the church just up the road from here."

I thought maybe he'd gone to the police station to offer help with any IT aspects of the case. Now I wondered why her cause of death would prompt him to go to her funeral, since he didn't speak fondly of the woman. But I didn't bother to ask.

"She was shot in the head. Then whoever did it set fire to the house."

"How terrible," I responded, mindlessly scraping my plastic fork against the side of the container. In my mind, there was no sense in talking badly about the newly departed.

"I mean, shot in the head. I wonder if she knew it was coming." Todd shook his head. "Would you want to see death coming?"

The question caught my attention. I thought it was rhetorical, but then I looked at Todd. His piercing stare seemed to demand a response. "I don't know . . . I guess . . . I'd rather not."

Little did I know, my innocent words would become a dark invitation, summoning something sinister. It was like signing a contract with the devil himself, sealing my fate in ways I couldn't possibly imagine.

As the investigation into the woman's murder gained more media attention, Todd's presence at my home dwindled. Instead of using the time to really see what was going on, I kept reminding myself that he was different than the other men I'd had in my life. And maybe "different" was exactly what I needed, even if I couldn't see it.

One morning, I was unloading the dishwasher. Through the window above the sink, I noticed Todd's truck pulling into the driveway. I dried my hands on a dish towel and turned around when he walked in, with a brightly wrapped package tucked under his arm. His eyes met mine, a smile playing at the corners of his mouth.

"Happy birthday, beautiful." He held out a present.

I was caught off guard. I hadn't planned on celebrating my birthday, so Todd's thoughtfulness touched me.

"Thank you." I took the gift. "You didn't have to get me anything."

"Of course I did." He pulled me into a hug. "You deserve to be spoiled on your special day."

I pulled out a mountain of tissue paper to reveal two Amazon Alexa devices. Although I was familiar with them, I didn't have one, much less two.

"You can put one in the house and one in the office. We can link them together and use them as an intercom system." Todd was more excited about the gift than I was.

"Thanks." I hesitated. I wasn't thrilled about introducing this technology into my home.

"I know you're not into technology, but you're going to love these. I activated them already, so they're plug-and-play."

He set one up in the office, then plugged the other into the kitchen.

"Look, just say 'Alexa, play Country,' and she'll play music. And to use it as an intercom, you just say 'Alexa, drop in on the kitchen!'"

I nodded, feigning appreciation for the gift.

Still, when Todd tried to steer things toward romance, I pulled away. I slowed down on responding to his texts. Sometimes he'd send two or three messages before I responded. This tactic finally wore him down. He emailed saying he couldn't continue seeing me. It was short and to the point—things weren't working out, and he would relocate his office back to his house. I felt a wave of relief and responded, wishing him the best.

With every shred of romance gone, I believed it was only fair to let him take the move slowly. He would occasionally come by, saying he needed something from the office, but I did my best not to encourage him to hang around.

One time, I texted to let him know that a large, heavy package had been delivered.

> **TODD**
>
> It's a server for the police department. I'll need to come over to configure it before I can install it. Do u mind if I stop by tomorrow?

> **ME**
>
> Sure.

> **TODD**
>
> They're running out of storage for all the dashcam and body cam footage we're required to maintain.

His message caught me off guard. He rarely talked about his work at the police department. I wasn't sure what to say, so I didn't respond. Then my phone chirped again.

> **TODD**
>
> I have court in the morning to testify on some texts I downloaded from an offender's phone. I should be over in the afternoon.

The next day, while I was on a conference call, Todd came by and spent an hour working on the new server. Initially, I was concerned it might be awkward, but there was a natural, comfortable silence between us as he worked. He quietly exited, waving goodbye as he left. It seemed we had settled into an easy, unspoken friendship.

CHAPTER ELEVEN

Nine months had passed since I first met Todd. The heavy, humid summer air of the Deep South made it hard to breathe. I wiped the sweat from my brow as I poured a cold glass of sweet tea and sat on my front porch swing. I hadn't been outside for even fifteen minutes when Todd pulled into the driveway.

"Whatcha doin' out here?"

"Just mopped the floors, so don't go inside. You workin' today?" It was Saturday—not a normal workday for Todd unless there was a network outage.

"Nah, I was just out runnin' errands and thought I'd stop by." It wasn't unusual for him to just drop by on a whim. I'd become numb to those kinds of excuses.

"I better get back inside." I stood up from the swing, and he reached for my hand.

"What's your rush?"

"My mom is coming into town. She'll be here in a bit." I faked a look at my watch.

His face lit up. My heart dropped.

"I can't wait to meet her!" he exclaimed.

Here we go again, I thought. With my situation with Todd so tenuous, it seemed like a bad idea to have them meet. "Oh, come on, Todd."

"I tell you what. I'll plan a group dinner with friends. Please? It'll be casual and fun. It'll give you two something to do."

I should've said no. But the memory of what happened the night of my dad's visit was still fresh. A group dinner didn't sound bad. Mom was planning to stay with me for a couple of days, so after some thought, I saw no harm in it. With my permission, he invited the friends we had in common and planned the details.

Mom and I arrived at the restaurant late, so we could skip the small talk. To my relief, there were two seats opposite Todd instead of next to him. The dinner was casual and uneventful—Todd mostly conversed with friends, interjecting now and again to engage Mom in conversation. Once dinner wrapped up, Mom limited her comments to how enjoyable the food was and how wonderful the conversation had been.

The next morning, I had planned brunch with Nathan, Mom, and me. My parents knew Nathan well and always wanted to see him when they were in town. The restaurant was a favorite of Nathan's, but not so much mine. I loved the waterside location, but the food wasn't anything I was excited about. In fact, I hadn't been there for quite some time and had certainly never been there with Todd. We were seated at a table outside with a perfect view of the water, enjoying conversation over mimosas, eggs Benedict, waffles, and a delicious assortment of pastries topped with fresh fruit.

Mom saw him first—her gaze trained on him like a mother protecting her young, which caught my attention. I turned to see. My stomach flipped. There, huffing and puffing, was Todd in workout clothes, jogging on the lake trail directly across from the restaurant. His face was red, and his hair was drenched with sweat—a far different look than when Mom saw him the night prior.

Todd had told me he was participating in triathlons, but I didn't recall ever seeing him exercise. I thought about the time Todd drove past my car on his way to buy swim goggles for a supposed new fitness regimen the night I had dinner with my dad. It now seemed like he only exercised when my parents came to visit.

I could see Mom glaring at him disapprovingly. I had seen this look on her face before and was more familiar with it than I cared to be.

"Is that Todd?"

"It is," I replied, trying to sound casual. "I guess he decided to go for a jog on the lakefront." *Why am I making excuses for him?* I wondered.

We tried to get on with our meal, but Todd soon looked over and waved, hustled across the street, and stopped at our table. He wiped at the sweat that dripped from his brow and said, "So funny seeing you here! I was just out for a run."

"I see that," I said, my eyebrow raised.

"How was y'all's night after dinner?" He edged closer to the one empty seat at the table. His distinct Southern drawl, which I once found charming, was now irritating.

"It was fine," Mom said, with a curt nod.

"Good." He placed his hand on the chair back and stared at Mom. "I'm sorry we didn't get a chance to talk much last night."

"That's all right," Mom said, flatly. And I could tell from her mannerisms, she meant it.

"Well, we're going to get back to our brunch. I'll talk to you soon," I said, hoping he would get the hint.

He stood silent for a beat, then replied, "Sounds good." He waved, then jogged back across the street onto the trail, but not before looking back over his shoulder at us.

"There's something not right about that guy," Mom said, looking directly at Nathan, who nodded in agreement.

I admit, I took her opinion with a grain of salt. Mom had been an emergency room nurse before taking a job at a psychiatric facility. Her proximity to the insane made her an expert, in her mind.

As we drove back to my house, Mom expressed her concerns about Todd. I glanced over at her—she was wringing her hands. "He seemed fixated on you at brunch. He was staring at you with soulless eyes."

I gripped the wheel more tightly, my knuckles white.

"I'm telling you; it's a look I've seen before, from a patient I treated at the psychiatric facility. It gives me the chills."

For my entire life, she'd asserted her opinion, analyzing my relationships. I was therefore numb to the psychiatric analysis on Todd that she offered to substantiate her comment. I hate to admit it, but I tuned her out. It turns out, I should have listened. This time, Mom was right.

Soon after my mom's visit, streams of water rushed down the walls in my bedroom. So did the tears. I watched the water pool on the floor from what turned out to be a burst pipe upstairs. When I entered my bathroom, water was pouring from the ceiling in there, too. My bedroom, my sanctuary—destroyed. The problem with humidity in the Deep South was that wherever there had been water, there would be black mold. I had to act fast.

Todd and I had been texting, so I let him know what was going on and asked if I could borrow his wet/dry vacuum. It was barely twenty minutes before he was in my house, cutting up soggy carpet and setting up fans to dry out the walls. He did all he could to help mitigate the damage, and I was grateful.

As I started repairs, I hit my insurance policy limit quickly. The financial burden was sizable. I had a considerable installment past due to the contractor for the roof installed over the office. Negotiations between Jason and me had been stalled for months now, leaving me drained emotionally and financially.

Todd's presence and his willingness to help were a reminder that while I might be lonely, I wasn't alone. Todd took the lead on getting the water leak repaired, which was a wonderful gesture. However, nothing with Todd was simple. Now that he had come in for what seemed like an innocent favor, he started to overstay his welcome. Again.

The daily routine of Todd coming by the house for coffee in the morning had resumed. And he had a great excuse. He made what repairs he could and coordinated contractors for the ones he couldn't. I was starting every day on the wrong foot, frustrated and willing him to leave.

After nearly two months, the repairs were complete. I could have my house back. No more shared coffee pots or morning nods of acknowledgment. I was relieved that Todd's reason to be at my house had fizzled.

However, several days had passed since the bathroom was finished, and Todd was still showing up for coffee every morning. It was September now and I'd been riding this emotional roller coaster with him for nearly a year.

Back in February, when Todd had installed the security cameras, he'd installed a large TV that displayed all four cameras on a split screen. I was working in the office when a movement alert popped up on the TV. I watched as Todd's truck pulled in, already wincing about the small talk I'd have to make with him to keep the peace.

Todd chatted away about the football season when he stopped mid-sentence. I looked up and saw him glancing at his phone. He said that he'd just received a text and was needed in court. "Do you mind if I borrow your shower?" It was an odd question, considering his house was less than six miles away.

Sensing my hesitation, Todd responded, "I always carry a set of clothes in my truck in case I get called into court. I need to be there in thirty minutes; otherwise, I would run home."

"Okay. That makes sense."

"Besides," he chuckled, "it'd be nice to take the bathroom for a test drive after all the work I put into it."

The only bathroom affected by the water leak was in my master bedroom. I didn't like the idea of Todd using my personal space, but I felt obligated since he'd been such a help. He was just going to take a quick shower. What could possibly go wrong?

CHAPTER
TWELVE

After I finished work for the day, I stayed in the office to prepare a report for one of my consulting clients. His company handled medical claims for the healthcare industry, and I was hired to measure productivity. I'd been given half a dozen spreadsheets to sort through. I'd already done the legwork but needed to put together a final report showing average processing times based on CPT codes. Mom's nursing background was coming in handy.

Exhausted, I made my way into my bathroom that night for a hot bath at the end of a long day. I stopped in the doorway as my eyes fixed on the counter—a razor and a can of shaving cream sat next to the sink. My hamper lid was open. A breath caught in my throat. There, on top of my laundry, were *his* clothes.

Frustration comes in various shapes and sizes. It comes on suddenly and without warning, like a bucket of ice water dumped over your head. I felt it in my chest, but there was nowhere for it to escape.

I jogged to my utility room, grabbed a grocery bag, and came back to the bathroom. I turned the bag inside out, placed it over my hand, and cringed as I removed his dirty clothes from the hamper. I tossed his razor and shaving cream on top, tied up the bag, then went back upstairs to the office and dropped it on his chair. I pulled my clothes out of the hamper in disgust and put them in the washing machine. I was being petty, and I knew it. I refused to let Todd insert himself back into my life.

The next morning, I sat at my breakfast table, having coffee and watching the morning news, when the door opened.

"Mornin'," he said cheerfully.

I glared as he strode past me, still seething from seeing his dirty laundry. I thought he was going to the coffee pot, but instead, he headed to the refrigerator.

"Good morning," I responded flatly.

He pulled a carton of eggs out and started rustling through the cabinet where I kept the frying pans. My eyebrows shot up, and my mouth fell open in disbelief.

"You want eggs for breakfast?" he asked with his back to me, fumbling for a pan.

My cheeks felt fiery as I blurted uncontrollably, "*Todd, you don't live here!* We are *not* in a relationship. Go to your house if you want to make breakfast."

Todd threw the pan onto the counter and glared at me; his nostrils flared. The blue eyes that once reflected kindness turned into icy daggers. "You don't appreciate anything I do for you."

I didn't respond. It was like a switch had instantly flipped in Todd, and I had no idea how to handle it.

"This is what a relationship is, Kathryn," he said, his voice laced with sarcasm. "But you wouldn't know. You couldn't even make a marriage work in your forties."

I was stunned he threw that in my face. He knew how devastated I was about Jason's infidelity, but I feared Todd might be right. Maybe I didn't know what a real relationship was. After what seemed like an eternity, I broke the silence. "You need to leave." My voice was nearly a whisper now.

His eyes narrowed into a fierce scowl as he fixed his gaze on me. Without a word, he grabbed the carton of eggs from the counter, raised it high, and slammed it down with force, causing a sharp crack to echo through the kitchen. Thick, golden yolks oozed out, cascading over the edge of the counter. They dribbled down the face of the cabinet and pooled into a sticky mess on the floor.

My eyes widened, pupils dilating in disbelief. The door shook violently as he flung it open. It slammed shut behind him with a resounding bang. I sat in stunned silence, watching the translucent egg white glisten as it slowly stretched from the cracked shell. Gravity took over, and it plummeted to the floor with a soft splat.

After cleaning up the mess and mopping the kitchen floor, I received an email from Todd. He sent it to my personal account, then to my work email and another email address. He demanded items from my house that he wanted back because he was "absolutely done" with me. He claimed I manipulated him into doing the water leak repairs and demanded payment for materials he had purchased. He provided a transaction list from his bank of payments to the hardware store, but no receipts. Of course, I ignored it. He insisted on doing the repairs. Since he hadn't paid rent for the office, I figured we were even.

Just when I thought the worst was behind me, the phone rang with more bad news.

"You're not going to believe this," Lauren said, her voice strained. "Todd's been going around badmouthing you to anyone who will listen."

My stomach clenched. "What's he been saying this time?" I asked hesitantly, not sure I wanted to know.

Lauren sighed. "He's telling people that you used him—that you manipulated him into doing all this work for you and then kicked him to the curb. He's painting you as a conniving, self-centered bitch who takes advantage of people. He says you owe him money and don't pay your bills. What's going on, Kathryn? Are you in some sort of trouble?"

I sat down, my mind reeling. This couldn't be happening again. "I don't understand why he's doing this. I never forced him to do anything," I said helplessly. "I thanked him profusely each time he helped me out. I even tried to pay him, but he refused."

"Well, I know it's not true, and you know that. You have that fundraiser coming up, and him spreading rumors that you don't pay your bills looks bad," Lauren said.

She was right. After we hung up, I sat at my desk, debating what to do about Todd. I opened my email to tell him I'd reimburse him if he would stop spreading rumors about me. But then I saw he'd been sending the same email repeatedly. Within two hours, I had nearly twenty identical messages. In each, he claimed a police escort had been requested to retrieve his office equipment from my house. Given that Todd worked at the police department, I was certain he would show up with an escort. And I didn't want my personal life to become a public spectacle.

I was furious. No way in hell was I going to extend an olive branch now. Instead, I forwarded one of Todd's emails to Adam, who I thought might help mediate a resolution since he already knew of our working arrangement. It was embarrassing, given his company donated to the nonprofit I serve on the board of. But I didn't want to engage with Todd while he was acting this way.

I was relieved when Adam called to say he had spoken to Todd. Arrangements were made for him to come by and pick up his things the next day. At the agreed-upon time, Todd pulled into the driveway and politely knocked on the door instead of letting himself in through the garage. I opened it and said, "Thank you for knocking."

His eyes were red and swollen, as if he'd been crying. "Can we talk?"

I took a breath. I felt I could have handled the shower situation better, especially considering how helpful he'd been with the water leak. I tried to see things from Todd's perspective: he offered to cook me breakfast, and I flipped out on him. I felt bad about how I handled my frustration, but what I really wanted was to shut down the rumor that I didn't pay my bills.

"Sure." I nodded.

Todd came inside and sat down. His shoulders slumped. "I'm sorry," he said, his voice barely above a whisper. I looked into his eyes and saw a flicker of genuine remorse, the kind that seemed to reach deep into his soul.

"For which part? The rumors you've been spreading about me not paying my bills? Or the fact that I'm a . . . how was it put to me? A conniving, self-centered bitch?"

His fingers fidgeted nervously with the hem of his T-shirt. He couldn't even look at me. Finally, he cleared his throat, his voice barely above a whisper. "I never meant to hurt you. I'll move my stuff out of the office, but I need to line up someone to help."

His eyes glistened as he finally met my gaze, and I could see the sincerity etched on his face. I watched him closely, noticing the way he shifted uncomfortably in his seat, the way his back arched as if carrying the weight of his regret. I felt a flicker of empathy stirring within me. Slowly, the anger and resentment waned. What sat before me was a broken man, and I wasn't without fault.

"That's fine," I said. "We'll also need to coordinate when you cancel the Internet service so I can have it reconnected the same day. Over a weekend would be preferable."

My anger completely dissipated. That's why, when a package arrived for him at my house, I decided to deliver it in person.

I knew his address but had never been to his house. As I drove up, I finally understood why. His home was a small duplex that had not been cared for. One window screen lay discarded in the yard, while another barely clung to its frame. The flower beds were overrun with weeds, the lawn needed mowing, and the shrubs desperately needed trimming. A rusty bicycle lay abandoned on its side, blocking the front door. To the right was a carport where Todd's truck was parked, and I spotted a side door leading into the house.

Before I could step out of my car, Todd stormed out with a scowl on his face. His stance was stiff, and an immediate sense of guilt washed over me. "What're you doing here?"

I plastered on a smile, acting unfazed by the sight of his home. "I just wanted to drop off your package." I held it up for him.

His scowl softened slightly. "Thanks." He took it from me.

"You're welcome."

He looked like as if he were about to say more but then abruptly turned and went back inside. As I drove home, guilt settled in my stomach. It was clear he was ashamed of where he lived, which explained why he always preferred being at my house.

Todd always saw the best in me. I wanted to do the same for him. But in doing so, I blinded myself to the disturbing truth lurking beneath Todd's charismatic veneer. Despite how irrational his behavior was, I somehow convinced myself it made sense. In reality, I was unwittingly laying the groundwork for my own undoing.

CHAPTER
THIRTEEN

I'd been waiting a week for Todd to collect his belongings from the office and was beginning to doubt he ever would. He dropped by occasionally for one thing or another but didn't stay long. I had convinced myself the seemingly endless roller coaster ride had finally stopped.

The divorce with Jason was still pending a division of community property, and I was growing increasingly frustrated with the mounting attorney fees. Jason would verbally agree to a settlement but then refuse to sign the agreement my attorney drafted. He didn't hire an attorney, so I was left bearing the brunt of the legal expenses. My personal life left a lot to be desired, but I looked forward to an upcoming meeting.

The nonprofit sent out the accounting report ahead of our monthly board meeting, which gave me something other than work to focus on. We had a lot on the agenda to discuss, including the summer literacy program I helped put together. I was reading through the documents when my phone rang.

It was a local business owner, Ryan. I first crossed paths with him years back at the gym, and ever since, he had been a steadfast supporter of the fundraisers I'd organized—especially the political ones. Ryan's company was in the business of developing neighborhoods, and he needed Nathan's expertise. He barely knew Nathan and was counting on me to arrange a meeting. After a series of texts, I'd confirmed we'd meet at Magnolia Bistro, a local Southern fare restaurant that had recently opened, later that evening.

It wasn't long before I received a call from Todd. My instinct was to send him to voicemail, but I had learned to pacify him. If I didn't answer his calls or texts, he'd show up claiming he needed to get something from the office. So, I answered.

"Hey, there. Would you like to go to dinner with me tonight?" he asked, sounding chipper.

I balanced my phone between my ear and my shoulder as I worked. "I can't tonight." I didn't feel the need to explain to Todd that I had dinner plans. He peppered me with questions about my evening, which I ignored. Eventually, he took the hint and ended the conversation.

It was a Tuesday evening, and the restaurant was practically deserted. We settled into a booth in the bar. I slid into one side, my slacks squeaking against the vinyl, and Ryan slid in next to me with Nathan sitting across from us.

Over steaming meals of local flavors, Ryan filled us in on his plans to develop a new subdivision. In mid-sentence, my eyes focused on a familiar man walking in—Todd. He glared at me as he walked to the bar, his face twisted in anger. He sat at the bar close enough to our table for me to hear him ordering a beer. It was hard not to notice him, constantly glancing over his shoulder in our direction.

"Excuse me for a second," I said to the group. Livid, I walked over to Todd and leaned against the bar. "Funny seeing you here."

"I had no idea you were here," he responded, staring straight ahead. "I called in an order an hour ago. I'm just here to pick it up."

"So why are you at the bar?"

"It's not ready yet. I'm grabbing a drink while I wait."

I said nothing and walked back to the table while Todd sat, sipping his beer and playing with his phone. After a bit, the hostess handed Todd a bag, and off he went. As relieved as I was to see him go, something in my gut told me this wasn't right. The restaurant wasn't that busy, and it wouldn't have taken an hour to prepare the food. There were too many coincidences, too many convenient excuses. No matter where I went, it seemed Todd wasn't far behind.

When our meeting wrapped up, the three of us headed out to the parking lot to say our goodbyes. My mind raced, hoping Ryan hadn't picked up on the tension crackling beneath my composed exterior. I had worked hard to forge a reputation as a pillar of professionalism—one that Todd was too eager to destroy.

As soon as everyone was in their respective cars, I went back into the restaurant. I asked the bartender, "That man who was at the bar earlier—the one who got takeout—had he ordered it before he came in?"

"No," she responded. "He ordered it when he arrived."

My gut instincts had been correct. Todd somehow knew I was at the restaurant. I had caught him in a lie; I was furious. I was beginning to have unsettling misgivings about this kind of sick behavior. Todd's following me felt sinister. I wondered if my mother was right—was I dealing with someone with serious mental health issues? Regardless, I needed this to stop. I thought the only way to make it stop was to confront him. I fumbled through my bag as I got into my car, pulled out my phone, and dialed him. He answered on the third ring.

"I know you didn't call ahead and place an order. Why the hell were you there?"

"I know you're having an affair with Ryan, Kathryn. He's a married man!"

"What are you talking about? We've been discussing his project!" As I spoke, I realized that I didn't need to defend myself. But Jason's cheating was still a fresh wound, and to be accused of sleeping with a married man made me feel sick.

Before I knew it, we were locked in a heated battle. The more despicable insults he hurled at me, the more I called him out on his lunacy. He yelled, cursed, called me names, and accused me of having Ryan in my bed as we spoke. I yelled, cursed, and called him an asshole before hanging up on him.

He called back.

Then he texted.

Then he called again.

And again.

And again, firing off obscene text messages in between since I was ignoring his calls. This went on for hours after I returned home. I yearned to turn my phone off but didn't dare, in case my boys needed anything.

I was setting the coffee pot to start its automatic brew for the next morning when something flitted across my backyard—a shadow. I dismissed it, but then I heard a noise, like a stick breaking beneath something heavy. Because the pond was close to the fence, I assumed it was a possum or a raccoon. It was common to see critters out there, especially at night.

Once in bed, I arranged my pillows beneath my head, anxious to leave the day's events behind. When I plugged in my phone to charge, I was disgusted by the number of missed calls and text messages from Todd. I decided that if I were going to get any sleep, I would have to silence his text notifications.

Lying there in the dark, I thought about blocking Todd. I needed to get away from him, but I knew he wouldn't take it well. The rumors would start back up; only now, he'd tell people I was sleeping with a married man. I decided I would distance myself from him and refuse to engage in his erratic behavior. Eventually, he would give up and move on.

I started to drift off to sleep when there was a knock on my bedroom window. Alarmed, I jumped out of bed and eyed the window uneasily. It was too dark to see who was out there, but I already knew. Through the window, I heard Todd's muffled voice. "You won't answer your phone, so I have no choice. We need to talk."

I said nothing. Anger surged through my veins, and I could feel my heart pounding wildly.

"We need to talk," he repeated more firmly.

I walked back over to my bed and grabbed my phone from the nightstand. He knew I had guns inside the house, so I called out, *"I have my gun. You need to leave!"* I didn't have my gun pulled out—yet—but he didn't need to know that.

"We need to talk," he shouted louder.

"No, you need to leave."

"Please, I'm just so hurt."

"Go away, Todd!"

I pulled the charging cable from my phone and gripped it tightly. I considered calling 911, but I hesitated. It was Todd, and, like I told Nathan, he's harmless. If he meant to do me any harm, he would've just opened the garage and come into the house.

"Kathryn, please." His voice cracked. "I just need to understand why you—"

"No jury will convict a single woman who shoots a man dead outside her bedroom window. Leave!"

I was posturing, saying anything to get him to go away.

And the message seemed to get through to him because he finally left after yelling, "You're a psychotic bitch!"

I watched his shadowy figure retreat. My heart was still pounding, adrenaline coursing through my body. As I settled into bed, I felt drained and shaky. I had a sinking feeling he was just getting started. If anything, tonight just might have been the calm before the inevitable storm.

CHAPTER
FOURTEEN

The clock's bright-red digits screamed the early hour and my failure to get even a moment's sleep. I lay in bed, wide-eyed, choking on memories and regret. I'd thought about calling Monica all night to see if I could learn more about Todd. Everything I knew about him was from him. But something inside me crumbled. What if Todd was right, and she really had said those things? I should have called her when Todd first told me, but he'd been so convincing that she had been talking about me unkindly behind my back. Was I that desperate to have someone on my side—anyone—that I blindly accepted what he said? I'd backed myself into a corner. I was too embarrassed to make the call.

I pulled myself out of bed and dressed. It was Wednesday and I had to log in to work. The coffee mug felt heavy in my hands. I leaned against the counter, the cold surface seeping into my skin. I took a scalding sip, letting it burn the inside of my mouth. I didn't know what to do about Todd or his erratic behavior, but I did know I needed it to stop.

The office was cluttered—papers and drafts in precarious piles—but it was familiar. I sank into the chair and wanted to dive into work to forget the night's events. As hard as I tried, I couldn't help but look across the room at Todd's desk. I just wanted him and his chaos out of my life.

My phone vibrated against the desk. I glanced at the screen, half expecting to see Todd's name. To my surprise, Ryan's name glowed on the display.

"Hey, do you know a guy named Todd?"

"Yes," I said tentatively. "He was the guy at the restaurant last night that I spoke to."

"I figured. I hate to tell you this, but he contacted my wife."

"What?" The thumping in my chest accelerated. I inhaled sharply and held it, willing it not to be true.

"Yeah, he reached out to her on social media and made it seem like something . . . nefarious was going on between us. He sent her a picture of us at the restaurant."

I rubbed my temples in disbelief at what I was hearing. The image of Todd sitting at the bar, sipping his beer and playing with his phone, flooded my mind. He wasn't just playing with his phone—he was taking pictures.

"I'm so sorry. Do you want me to talk to your wife?"

"No, she's fine. I'm more concerned about you. This is an odd situation."

"I'm okay. Todd and I sort of work together, and we dated, but this is unacceptable."

My cheeks flushed with anger. I felt like an idiot. I wondered if this could have been avoided if I had just told Todd I was having a business dinner with Ryan. But I had no obligation to do so. Not only were Todd and I not a couple, but I also knew that would open the door for him to know all my social comings and goings.

But this? This was too far—like an invasion. To go to Ryan's wife and make a false accusation could have dire consequences. And then, it hit me: How did he even know it was Ryan?

The truth is, if it had been anyone else who had done such an egregious thing, I would have blocked them. But it wasn't some random stranger. It was Todd, a man whom I believed cared for me. Maybe I was wrong. Maybe I should have told him I was meeting Ryan for dinner to discuss his business development. Doubts swirled in my head as I tried to figure out how to handle a situation I'd never faced before.

Part of me wanted to storm over to Todd's place, demanding answers for his bizarre antics and making it crystal clear he'd stepped way out of bounds. But the sensible side of me knew better—any confrontation would just fan the flames. Todd was a loose cannon, and I couldn't afford to rile him up any more than he already was. No, I had to handle this with caution before he went public with the picture and rumors that I was sleeping with a married man. And quick!

The click of my heels echoed in the hallway as I strode past the hors d'ouerves and sodas into the conference room on Thursday evening. Inside, a few other board members were already seated around the large wooden table, chatting. I settled into my usual spot, pulling out my notebook and pen. I was keenly aware that nobody greeted me or made an effort to talk to me. I felt like a leper. Out of the corner of my eye, I saw another board member approach.

"Hey, Pastor Nick." I turned and greeted him with a smile. "Ready for tonight's meeting?"

He shook his head. "It's going to be a long one, I'm afraid."

"Yeah, no kidding." I held up the two-page agenda and laughed.

Pastor Nick leaned in close. "A friendly word of advice, Kathryn. Keep your house in order. I'm hearing things from various individuals and what affects you impacts all of us here."

"What've you heard?"

But I already knew. Carleigh had reached out. She worked at a place where Todd provided tech support. We were close enough that she asked if I was "messing with a married man," so it didn't take much to connect the dots.

"That doesn't matter. What does matter is the hard work we do for the community. People don't recognize the effort we put in, but they will take notice if... say... one of us is involved in behavior unbecoming of a board member."

"Thanks, Pastor Nick. That's good advice. I'll take it to heart."

Pastor Nick was someone I respected. Years ago, after Mark remarried, they wanted Caleb and Dylan to spend a week at their house over Christmas to celebrate their new family. I agreed, but I wasn't looking forward to spending the holidays alone. Pastor Nick led a large congregation. Even though I wasn't a member of his church, he had invited me to join the midnight Christmas Eve candlelight service. When I arrived, I hadn't realized how emotional I was. Pastor Nick welcomed me, and I immediately broke down in tears. He prayed with me, and from that moment, our bond grew. The last person I wanted to disappoint was Pastor Nick.

The meeting dragged on well into the night. By the time I stepped out into the darkness, my head was spinning. I drove home on autopilot, barely registering the empty streets. I knew I needed to get Todd out of my life. The spark I once thought was there would never have a chance to ignite. But it frustrated me to think I might have another unstable conversation with him. He had proven himself volatile, and he was more than willing to say anything to anyone to paint himself as a victim. And he knew a lot of people.

Pastor Nick had opened my eyes; it wasn't just my reputation I had to protect, but also that of the board's. The last thing I wanted was to be the cause of disgrace for the important work we were striving to accomplish.

I needed someone I could confide in—someone who could give me solid advice. My regular Saturday morning breakfast with Nathan arrived. Over steaming mugs of coffee, I told him about Todd contacting Ryan's wife and Pastor Nick's comments.

"That's insane. Who does that?" Nathan shook his head. "You need to get away from this guy, Kathryn. I told you the first time I met him he gave me the creeps. It's called a gut instinct, and you should listen to yours."

"I've been trying to let him down easy, so he doesn't explode. And don't forget, he knows a lot of people. He could really damage my reputation if he takes his anger public. I, for one, wouldn't put that past him."

"You're in a tough spot, but your safety has to come first."

I shook my head. "It's not a safety issue. He's a gnat that you can't swat away. Todd's not going to bite."

Little did I know, he'd bite with the savage ferocity of a ravenous lion.

CHAPTER
FIFTEEN

It was time to have a conversation with Todd. I wasn't looking forward to it, but I knew it was necessary. This was one of those adult responsibilities I didn't enjoy. The days of dealing with a bully by going to the principal's office were long gone. It was up to me to put an end to this.

I looked at the phone in my hand, mentally rehearsing what I wanted to say. I dialed Todd's number, and he picked up on the first ring.

"We need to talk. Is this a convenient time for you?" I kept my tone steady. I hoped that my politeness would disarm him.

"I can talk."

"When do you plan on moving your office out?"

"Let me make a few calls and see if I can line up some help. I'll call you back once I know, and maybe we can have a conversation then?"

It sounded reasonable, so, of course, I agreed. The curse of being an empath is that I absorb others' feelings like a sponge. I feel it swell in my chest and I'm usually the first one to shed a tear.

Todd's sorrow was unmistakable, and I'd caused his pain. I had called him to put an end to the chaos and the rumors swirling around, to make him own up to the mess he caused. But instead, I found myself soothing his wounded heart.

Instead of calling back, Todd sent a text suggesting we talk about his moving out and other matters over dinner. I was conflicted. On one side, meeting in a public setting might help keep the conversation calm. On the other side, I suspected he might try to charm his way back into my life. I was prepared for that tactic, and it wouldn't sway me. I agreed to meet him for dinner at Café Calais since it was Sunday and Oskar's was closed. To Adam's point, there was no reason for animosity. I saw dinner as an opportunity to reimburse him for the camera system he had installed, since I hadn't paid for it when he thought there was a possibility of more between us. He wouldn't have equipment at my house anymore, and I didn't want the cameras taken down, leaving gaping holes in the soffit of my roof. It was the right thing to do.

On the day of the dinner, I was getting ready to leave the house when the phone rang. I saw it was Todd and answered, expecting to hear a last-minute cancellation. Instead, he was in the neighborhood and offered to pick me up for dinner. It seemed innocent enough, so I agreed—a decision I would soon regret.

Seated at the table, Todd waited until we ordered before launching into his real purpose for the dinner. He was offended that I had not tried to salvage the relationship. I could see his anger growing, taking shape in the flushed cheeks and fixed stare he directed at me. Now, resorting to shaming me and name-calling, his words were bitter and sharp. I sat, bewildered, trying to reconcile the vile words coming out of his mouth with the man who once spoke so compassionately. I was trying to understand where this anger was coming from. He gained steam in his vitriol with each passing minute.

After what seemed like an eternity, the bill came, along with overwhelming relief that it wouldn't be long before I was back at my house. I had already planned to pay the bill, but after being called 'ungrateful,' among other things, I lurched forward to grab it before he could make a scene about it.

"You are *not* paying this." He snatched the bill from me.

He refused, reminding me that he was none of the things he had described me as. In fact, he was chivalrous, and paying the bill for such ungrateful company, in his mind, proved it. As we left the restaurant, I made sure to walk in front of him and open the door for myself, out of rebellion.

Riding away from the restaurant, I remained silent to avoid triggering him any further. I just wanted to go home. We pulled up to an intersection, and instead of turning right toward my house, Todd turned left. A wave of nausea came over me as I realized he wasn't taking me home. He started speeding. In a flash, we were back at his house, locked in a physical altercation on his lawn. I couldn't understand how the hands that once comforted me were now claws tearing the hair from my scalp.

Less than thirty minutes later, I stood across the street, my eyes fixed on Todd as he stood on his lawn, still holding his face. My heart raced as I considered bolting—running as fast as I could toward home, but my feet were in so much pain, and I had lost my phone.

Breathless and hopeless, I turned my attention to an oncoming jogger and frantically waved. The jogger was getting closer and had finally reached me just as Todd got into his car and drove off.

"Are you okay?" the jogger asked.

Still out of breath and disoriented, I managed to say, "Can I use your phone? Something just happened, and my phone is somewhere in the woods."

"Of course." He took his phone from his sweaty armband and handed it to me.

I called Lauren, the only phone number I could remember. When I told her what had happened and where I was, she shouted, "I'll be right there!"

The second call I made was to my phone. We listened, finally hearing it ring about fifty feet into the woods. The jogger watched as I wobbled into the marshy brush, my new shoes grinding into the raw flesh of my heels. When I retrieved my smashed phone, I told the jogger I would be fine.

Although I was still shaking, I didn't want to burden the stranger with my drama. He reluctantly said, "Goodbye," looking back over his shoulder as he jogged away. Once he was out of sight, I tucked myself between two bushes, trembling.

The screen on my phone was broken, but when Lauren called, I could still answer. Crouched low in the bushes facing Todd's house, I kept her on the line as I started making my way toward a fire station. I darted between trees and bushes, like a scared animal cowering from a predator.

Lauren narrated each turn of her drive. I couldn't stay in one spot for too long, or Todd might find me, so I methodically guided Lauren to my ever-changing location. She was getting close, and the fire station was still another two blocks away, but it felt much further given my bleeding heels. I felt like Todd was watching my every move.

"I promise, I'm going as fast as I can. Just stay with me," she said.

Finally, I stopped walking and slipped between towering pine trees, crouching down and trying to slow my breathing. I remained motionless, scared that any movement would draw attention to me. I worried that if Todd was near, he could hear me breathing. I hadn't seen his truck pass by, so I thought maybe he was searching on foot. I clutched my phone tighter, knowing it was my lifeline to Lauren. When a nearby dog barked, it alerted me to a vehicle approaching. My heart pounded as I strained to see in the growing darkness—was it Todd or Lauren?

Suddenly, I saw headlights low to the ground and instinctively knew it was a sedan. After confirming Lauren's location, I emerged from my hiding spot.

"Can you see me?"

"I'm looking, but I don't see you yet."

"Look to your right, Lauren!" I shouted, desperately waving my arm.

"I see you! Get in quickly!" Lauren pleaded, now scared that her own safety was in jeopardy. Her car jarred to a halt in the middle of the street as she leaned over to open the passenger door.

I sprinted toward her, leaping into the passenger seat. Before I could close the door, Lauren was already speeding away. I let out a sigh of relief.

Tears burned the backs of my eyes, then spilled onto my cheeks as the gravity of the situation flooded over me. I sobbed desperately, uncontrollably, while she quietly consoled me.

Instead of taking me back to my house, Lauren took me to hers. She loaned me a pair of sweatpants and a sweatshirt, along with bandages for my bleeding heels. As my adrenaline subsided, the physical pain set in. My head was pounding from being dragged by my hair, and my knuckles were scraped up. I thought maybe a finger was broken after Todd stomped on my hand, but it wasn't.

I was broken.

CHAPTER
SIXTEEN

Lauren poured me a glass of whiskey and led me outside to a chair next to her pool. I stared into the bright blue water, the surface rippling softly.

"I just can't figure out what I did to make him so angry. I'm sure he didn't plan on hurting me if he got me into his house, right?"

"I think he's a fucking psychopath."

"I know, but I probably could have handled it better."

Lauren looked me in the eyes. "With the divorce and all the other crazy shit you have going on, you don't need this drama in your life."

"I know." I felt utterly defeated. "Let's just go to bed."

I'd crashed at Lauren's countless times before, never needing to ask because she was that kind of friend. And now, she was the kind of friend who would rescue me from the side of the road without hesitation.

As I stood at the sink, rinsing my glass, I heard Lauren's phone chirp sharply, slicing through the silence. She turned her phone to me.

"Do you know this number?"

My shoulders sagged. My heart plummeted. It was Todd's number. He was, after all, an IT guy who had managed to get in touch with Ryan's wife. But that didn't explain how he knew where I was.

"Did you give him your number when he helped you with the toilet?" I asked.

"No."

The shock etched on her face was a mirror reflecting my own. A wave of guilt crashed over me, suffocating and relentless. It felt as though I was becoming toxic, contaminating the lives of those I cared about.

Our heads almost touched as our eyes read the message:

> **UNKNOWN SENDER**
>
> Hi, Lauren. I want to make sure that Kathryn is okay. We had an argument that got heated and she left my house angry. She was very upset. Did she make it to your house all right? Please do me the kindness of letting me know. I still care about her and want to know that she's safe.

"What the actual fuck, Kathryn? He has my number now. I don't want to be dragged into this shit."

Three dots pulsed as Todd typed more, each one a heartbeat I couldn't control. All I could do was shake my head in disbelief. "I'm so sorry," I whispered, my voice cracking with emotion. "I never meant for you to get pulled into this nightmare."

Lauren sighed heavily and set down her phone. "It's not your fault, Kathryn. This guy is unhinged, and I just blocked him. We need to figure out what to do next. Should we go to the police?"

I hesitated, unsure. Part of me feared that involving the authorities would only make Todd more volatile and dangerous. But another part recognized that his behavior was escalating.

"I don't know." I slumped onto a stool at her kitchen counter. "What if going to the cops just makes things worse? You know how manipulative Todd can be. He might spin it to make me look like the crazy one. I hit him. He was bleeding."

Lauren reached out to squeeze my hand. "Hey, we'll get through this together, okay? Let's sleep on it."

As much as I tried, I couldn't sleep. My nerves were on fire, and my mind was reeling. I'd come to learn there were hidden depths within a person that only reveal themselves when they're thrust into the crucible of a moment. For me, I had no inkling of the fierce, untapped power lurking beneath my calm exterior until I was engulfed in a whirlwind of adrenaline. I had never hit anyone before, not even as a kid in school. I never imagined I possessed the raw strength and primal instinct to land a punch, let alone unleash a second one. I had made Todd bleed. I was appalled at my capacity for violence, even in self-defense.

Todd would take it as a personal affront if I were to report him to his colleagues. He'd spin it so that he was the victim of an assault rather than the perpetrator of an attempted kidnapping. I spent hours weighing my options, as women who have experienced domestic violence tend to do.

I made excuses for him.

I was concerned about hurting his reputation at the police department, an income stream I knew he relied on. In hindsight, I was giving Todd courtesies he never afforded me.

The next morning, Lauren drove me home. I had to get to work. Although I was an emotional wreck, I didn't feel like I had a choice. I needed my job, my income. My boss was not happy about my working remotely, and I feared that if I didn't log in and show I was online, he would use it as an excuse to let me go.

When I got home, I went to my bathroom to wash my face. I looked puffy and sad, my eyes still rimmed with remnants of makeup from the night before. I cleaned my face, then changed clothes before grabbing a cup of coffee and heading upstairs to log in. When I sat down at my computer and wiggled the mouse, the normal sign-in screen wasn't popping up. I turned my computer off and back on, hoping that would fix the problem. I clicked everywhere I could, and tapped at the keys, but nothing helped. My entire network was down. Since Todd was still paying for the Internet at my house, I wondered if he had disconnected it.

I glared at my shattered phone screen—a sharp, agonizing reminder of the chaotic, violent night I'd endured. The events felt so unreal, like a twisted dream. If it hadn't been Todd, I would have called it a desperate, nightmarish attempt at kidnapping. My frantic escape, the heart-pounding moments hidden in the bushes . . . it all played out like a scene from a high-stakes thriller rather than my terrifying reality. The phone screen was the sole, undeniable evidence that it had all truly happened.

With trembling hands, I tapped on the screen. Although it was badly damaged when he threw it, the phone was somewhat usable. I called the service provider and was surprised to learn the Internet was still connected. The representative said the issue was not on their end but on mine. I closed my eyes and gritted my teeth. Given his profession, it didn't take much for me to connect the dots and realize who was responsible. I had no idea how to get it working again, so I loaded my computer into the car and returned to Lauren's house to use her Internet.

Todd had gone too far. He was deliberately messing with my ability to work, knowing how much I needed my job. Why should I care about reporting him to the police?

At Lauren's urging, I pushed past my nerves called the sheriff's department since neither Todd nor I lived in city limits. I filled out the form with tears in my eyes and a shaky voice. I'd never filed a police report before. It felt like a huge, scary step. I wasn't sure what to expect. Would Todd be angrier than he was last night? After that experience, I no longer believed he was harmless. I became scared. I second-guessed myself. I downplayed my handwritten statement, making it seem like it was just about his malicious destruction of my phone, my personal property. When I handed my statement over to the deputy, my hand lingered on the edge as if my fingers were unwilling to let go.

"Are you sure you don't want charges filed?"

"No, just the report documenting the incident is all I'm asking."

"Now, I'll get this filed, but you need to sever all communications with Todd, do you understand?"

"I do. Thank you, officer."

If only it were that easy.

When the day ended, I was exhausted in ways I'd never been before. I just wanted my own bed to curl up in, so I headed home. In my mailbox was a statement from my divorce attorney showing the legal fees I was behind on paying—fees for conversations with Jason to negotiate a divorce settlement I filed for thirteen months ago. My head and neck ached, my brain was foggy, and my life was a hot mess. I moved through my evening as if snowed by static. I forced myself to eat something before getting ready for bed.

But there was still one thing I needed to do. Todd had sent text messages earlier that morning. I didn't have the strength to even open them. As much as I didn't want to read his messages, I needed to know if he found out I'd filed a police report. My thumb hovered over the broken screen. My pulse pounded in my ears. The weight of dread settled heavily in my chest, but a nagging voice in the back of my mind urged me on.

The shattered screen of my phone looked like a spiderweb, with jagged cracks radiating out in every direction. I slid my finger across the fractured glass. The messages loaded, flickering and distorted on the compromised display. I started with the most recent one and worked my way back.

TODD

I'm going to call for a police escort. Give me a date and time when I can have someone accompany me to your house.

Quit being a fucking bitch. I just want my things back.

The sad thing is, I really cared about u.

U are so childish.

Give me a date and time when I can come pick up my things.

> This is so immature.
>
> Please give me a date and time when I can come pick up my things.
>
> I realize working from your house is not a good idea. I want to come pick up my equipment from the office.

Tears pricked at my eyes, but I blinked them back furiously. I wanted to throw the phone across the room, scream until my voice gave out, and curl into a ball. I didn't want to give him the satisfaction of knowing he'd gotten to me. I had to be strong, to put on a brave face and pretend he hadn't traumatized me. I stared at my shattered screen and dictated a response, careful not to say anything that could incite him.

ME
> Since I am working from home, I can make whatever is most convenient for you work.

I curled up in bed, eager to put the day behind me. But that was easier said than done. I turned on the television and binge-watched episode after episode to quiet my mind. I don't know what time I finally fell asleep. I was just grateful I had slept at all.

Seventy-two hours after he attempted to force me inside his house, Todd arrived to collect his things. And he didn't come alone.

CHAPTER
SEVENTEEN

My heart slammed against the walls of my chest. I had planned for this to be a cordial "best of luck to you in the future" exchange with Todd, but that was now out of the question. I barricaded myself inside the house, all doors locked. At this point, I didn't care what Todd took from the office. He could have anything he wanted, as long as he never contacted me again.

I sat beneath a partially open bedroom window upstairs that overlooked the driveway. At times, I felt completely ridiculous, crouching down under the windowsill; at others, I wondered how things had gone so terribly wrong. I listened as Todd and Jason commiserated about how glad they were to have saved themselves from me. They spoke about me as if I were a flesh-eating monster, eroding what little self-esteem I had regained since separating from Jason.

With the roar of a truck, I peeked out of the window just in time to see Jason leaving. Todd was still in the driveway next to his truck, staring down at his phone. He sent a text to let me know he had loaded everything and asked if I wanted to walk through the office with him before he left. I declined politely, but as soon as I hit send on the message, in my head I was yelling, *Get the fuck off my property!*

Now that the driveway was clear of ex-whatevers, I closed the garage door. I rushed up to the office and felt relief when I saw the empty space where Todd's desk had been. Still bewildered, I called Lauren. It took me nearly ten minutes to get past her cussing in disbelief before what I was saying sank into her head.

The next morning, I was back in my home office, staring blankly at the computer screen. The cursor blinked, mocking my inability to focus. I had a report due by the end of the week, but my mind kept drifting to Pastor Nick's "friendly advice" about rumors. His words echoed in my head, a reminder of the precarious situation I was in.

I leaned back in my chair, rubbing my temples in a futile attempt to alleviate the tension. The sunlight cast a warm glow on the room, but it did little to lift my spirits.

Focus, Kathryn. One crisis at a time.

I contacted my company's IT group feigning ignorance about what the problem could be to avoid humiliation. Since they weren't able to remotely access my firewall, a new device had to be overnighted to me. I cringed. I knew how much my boss disliked my working remotely, and this could be just what he needed to force me to decide on relocating or getting laid off.

Although the thought of relocating was tempting, I wasn't ready to make such a big decision. Dylan had just started his senior year of high school.

"What do you think happened to the firewall?" I asked in my most innocent voice.

"Who knows? It's an old one from one of the offices we closed."

I felt like I dodged a bullet on that one.

My network was now stable, but I still couldn't find a rhythm at work. I found myself typing tentatively, constantly pausing to check my connection and running through dozens of scenarios in my head. I feared there were other vulnerabilities in my system, and Todd could take it down at any moment.

Worn down from the drone of constant worry, I began to feel like I had overreacted and blown the situation out of proportion by involving the police. Self-doubt crept in. I could almost hear my mother calling me "dramatic."

The weight of a thousand cinder blocks pressed against my chest. Todd's behavior had accelerated so wildly, it was hard to believe it had happened at all. I was an empath, and that meant my default setting was to see the best in others, to manufacture context for even the most egregious of behaviors.

Todd was not physically violent. That was my line in the sand. He never crossed it. He hovered on the other side, toes digging into the dirt, daring me to test him. And I did. I had been the one to hit him. I had been physically violent with him. Maybe I was the one who should be sorry. Maybe he'd inadvertently grabbed my hair when all he meant to do was take the phone so we could talk. The empathy turned me inside out.

I was convinced the red flags I saw in Todd were a prism of my own insecurities. I was certain Todd was suffering as much as I was. Maybe he didn't want to be this way. Maybe he just wanted to be heard. Maybe we were two broken people that just shouldn't be together.

My gut had never done me any favors. My gut told me to stick around after Jason's affair, to forgive him because "everyone makes mistakes." My gut was an idiot.

The phone vibrated—a text from Todd. To pick up the phone would be to acknowledge the control he held over my life, to admit that I was still tethered to the eye of his storm. Yet wasn't there strength in the ability to quell his chaos with a listening ear, as I'd done in the past?

The indecision was poison, seeping through my skin. Guilt and fear warred inside me, tangling into knots that threatened to choke the breath from my body. I squeezed my eyes shut, the darkness a momentary reprieve from the battle raging in my mind.

Flashes of Todd's face, contorted in anger, strobed behind my eyelids. A single tear trickled down my cheek, and I quickly wiped it away. The echo of his voice, once a soothing balm, now sent icy tendrils down my spine. I wanted to be strong, to sever the ties that bound me to his instability. But the desperate desire to fix what was broken—fix Todd—pulled at me with unrelenting force.

My fingers trembled as I traced the jagged crack in the screen, my breath shallow and sharp.

> TODD
>
> Are u ok? I'm worried about u.

I shook my head, trying to dislodge the insidious temptation to respond. I knew better. I had to be stronger than this. Stronger than him. I backed away from the window, my phone still clutched in my hand. Each step felt leaden, as if invisible strings were pulling me back, back to him. I wanted to believe this time would be different—that he would change. He would be that guy who wrote me sweet notecards and bought the elderly lady a cup of coffee out of the kindness of his heart. I'd seen the kindness. I knew it was there.

Tears pricked at my eyes, and I blinked them away furiously. With a shaky breath, I called him before I could change my mind.

"Hello?" Todd's voice crackled through the speaker, both familiar and foreign.

"It's me." My voice was barely above a whisper. "I . . . I wanted to talk."

There was a heavy pause, the weight of the past year settling between us. Todd drew a breath. "Listen, I'm sorry." He paused. "For everything. I know I have issues I need to work on. I started seeing a therapist." His voice wobbled as he spoke. I could tell he was holding back tears.

"Why did you contact Jason?"

"I didn't know how to deal with you since you weren't responding. I found him on social media and contacted him, thinking he might have some insight. Sometimes, I feel like you're a puzzle. I hoped he could help me put the pieces together."

"So, it's my fault?"

"Kathryn, you have so much fight in you. I needed to see that same fight for us. Instead, you just accepted my breakup like I meant nothing to you."

"Todd, there is no excuse for your behavior." I had to keep him on track. Engaging with him would not be productive, so I redirected him. "What did you do to my work computer? I could've lost my job, Todd."

"I ping flooded your network from a spoofed IP address. It overwhelms your system, so it stops functioning. I hoped . . . I mean, I knew . . . I couldn't get you to talk to me after what happened. I thought if your network was down, you'd call me for help."

My head dropped into my hand, thinking, *This man is completely detached from reality.* I couldn't believe the lengths he would go to get my attention. All I managed to say was, "Thanks for telling me."

"There's something I need to tell you about Jason. I know y'all have your differences, but he's actually a really nice guy. Y'all just aren't meant to be together."

"I don't want—"

"Listen." Todd's voice was stronger now. "After we left your house, Jason and I went out for a beer. We talked through a lot of things y'all have been at odds about, and I think I was able to get him to come to an agreement."

I was silent. To my surprise, something welled up from deep within my soul—hope. The anger and fear I felt around Todd and his behavior began to fade. I'd lost so much of myself in the conflict with Jason that I had nothing to gain from the conflict with Todd. If what Todd was saying was true, I could finally get Jason out of my life.

"I know the issues with your divorce are what caused all our problems. But I was able to get him to agree on a solution so you can finally put it behind you."

Perhaps the problems between Todd and me were petty. *Maybe he took things too far and genuinely regretted it. Maybe I, too, was to blame. Could I have been contributing to all this by somehow taking out my pain from the divorce on Todd?*

After a long pause, I said, "It's hard for me to trust you."

"I know, and I'm truly sorry. If you'll let me come by, I can fix everything, and we can get the Internet switched over to your name."

"I'll have to think about it."

"That's fine," he said softly. "I want to reimburse you for your phone. I know it was smashed. I'm so, so sorry about that."

I let the silence linger. But what was really going through my mind was: *Keep your friends close and your enemies closer.*

CHAPTER EIGHTEEN

After speaking with Todd, I felt my body gradually unwind. The oppressive tightness that had gripped my chest eased, allowing me to breathe deeply once more. The tears that had threatened to spill over retreated, leaving my eyes dry but slightly puffy. My heart, which had felt like it was trying to break free from my chest, now settled into a steady, gentle rhythm.

I sat down at my computer and typed up the terms of the agreement Todd said he brokered with Jason. When I clicked "send," I was instantly relieved, knowing it was in the hands of my attorney. I hoped this would be the end of Jason in my life and that I could finally move on.

At my request, Todd came over to fix my network. It turned out I didn't need a new firewall.

"I'm really sorry," he said before going upstairs to fix my network. When he came back down, he told me that he had installed a Google Wi-Fi system at his expense.

Turning his phone toward me, he pointed to an app. "Download this app, and I'll show you how to reset your network if anything goes wrong. I know you don't want to rely on me, and I hope this helps rebuild some trust."

I hesitated but liked the idea of having control over my network. I started the download and placed my phone on the table. Once it was done, Todd picked it up and configured the settings. He walked me through how to use it before we called the Internet service provider and transferred the account to my name. He looked at me with sad, tired eyes and left immediately afterward.

Over the next few days, things seemed okay. It felt like the whole ordeal was behind me. Even my network was now stable. I knew I wanted Todd out of my life, but I wasn't sure how to do it without causing collateral damage.

Nearly a week went by before I received a call from my divorce attorney. "I hate to be the bearer of bad news," she said, "but Jason said he did not agree to these terms."

I felt like I'd been punched in the gut. "What do you mean?"

"There must have been a miscommunication somewhere along the line. Jason claims he never spoke about any of this with your friend, Todd."

I wanted to cry. I'd wanted it to be true so badly that I'd ignored any doubts. I'd been gullible.

"I'll have to charge you for drafting the settlement based on the terms you provided. I also spent about thirty minutes going over it with Jason, so you'll see that as a separate charge on your next bill."

I. Was. Livid.

I snatched my phone from my desk and dictated a message to Todd. Two could play this game. I invited him to meet me for cocktails at Café Calais—the scene of his crime. He seemed genuinely pleased to get the invite but, this time, I was the one with something sinister in store. I threw on jeans and a sweater, then ran my fingers through my hair. I opted for heels to feel powerful. I was irate.

When I arrived at the restaurant, I purposely sat at the corner of the L-shaped bar, forcing Todd to sit facing me.

I didn't immediately see Todd come in; I heard his voice. He was speaking with the owner of the restaurant about contracting to take over their network support. As I sat and listened, I wanted to scream. Todd knew exactly what to say to make himself sound professional and reputable. And, of course, he leveraged his work at the police department to provide credibility.

When he finished his conversation, Todd came over and sat down. "How are you doing?" He pulled out his chair. I didn't wait for him to order a drink or get comfortable before getting straight to the point.

"I'm not doing well. I had a call with my attorney today, and she told me there was no deal with Jason. In fact, there was no conversation with Jason."

He stared at me blankly.

I met his eyes. "Why would you make something like this up? Why would you twist the knife?"

His cheeks turned a shade of pink.

"Well, Todd, if you were trying to prove that I'm an idiot, you've succeeded."

He reached forward and placed his hand on my arm. He stared into my eyes and spoke softly. "I'm sorry that's what you think of me, but you're wrong. We talked. He agreed to every one of the terms I laid out. Jason is lying to his attorney, I guess."

I shook my head in disbelief.

"I'm sorry, but he duped us both into believing he agreed to resolve the differences that have been holding things up." He signaled to Brandi, the bartender, that he wanted a beer. When it was placed in front of him, he narrowed his eyes and took a sip before slamming the bottle on the bar. "I bet this is his way of trying to drive a wedge between us. I can't believe he would stoop so low."

His use of the word "us" disgusted me, but I continued to listen. Todd spoke incredulously about Jason and how angry he was at him for going back on his word, while I sat in silence. He explained how he had worked to come up with terms that were fair, in hopes of wrapping things up—a grand gesture he meant as a peace offering after attempting to kidnap me.

I found myself nodding in agreement as Todd talked with disdain about Jason. He retraced every facet of the conversation he claimed to have had, ordering another round of drinks. Blinded by my anger at Jason, I believed Todd. Everything he said seemed plausible, given my own experience. By the time I was ready to leave, Todd had convinced me not to let Jason's attempt to muddy the waters succeed.

Over the next few days, I wasn't sure what to believe anymore so I didn't respond to Todd's messages. He emailed me an article about how abusers use silence as a tactic to assert power over their victims. I felt a pang of guilt. I'd considered his behavior unacceptable, but now I questioned my own.

I called him and explained I'd been busy and, amid everything, my new phone was giving me trouble. I'd purchased it after my conversation with Todd and hoped the sales associate could transfer my data. Sadly, my old phone was too damaged for that.

"I understand," he said. "Listen, at the very least, I can help you with your new phone."

Within twenty-four hours, Todd had my new phone up and running with everything restored. He even reimbursed me. But I didn't want his money. Instead, I told him we'd call it even for all the work he had done around the house. Still, he insisted. I convinced myself that Todd was actually a good guy who had just made some big mistakes. In reality, what happened should have sent me running.

I never should have looked back.

CHAPTER
NINETEEN

Lazy swirls of steam rose from my cup of coffee as I settled in for work. I'd been burying myself in work over the past two months to distract myself from the reality that was my life. I'd withdrawn—again—socially, just as I did after Jason moved out.

Todd had been on his best behavior. He always texted before he stopped by and would even knock. Gone were the days when he'd breeze in like a gust of air. I'd even forgotten he had my garage door opener, since he wasn't letting himself in anymore. I had settled into a sense of calm, though the scars of that traumatic night in the bushes were never far from my mind. I couldn't imagine ever getting in Todd's truck again.

Scrolling through my email, I saw one from my boss. The subject line read "Chicago." I clicked on it, a knot forming in my stomach. He said I needed to make travel arrangements and plan on being at the office next week. I was certain this was it: my job had come to an end.

I dreaded the trip, already trying to figure out if I had enough consulting work to cover my minimum bills for a month or two while I looked for a new job. When I'd laid off the other workers, they received severance packages—one week of pay for ever year worked. I hoped I would, too.

My boss informed me that the company was eliminating the position they'd temporarily created for me—director of special projects. I gave my best professional smile and thanked him for the opportunity.

"That doesn't mean we're letting you go, Kathryn. You're a valuable employee."

My heart soared. At least one thing in my life was going right.

"That last financial analysis you did? It saved the company a lot of money. You more than paid for your own salary just by making our regular vendors bid for our business. We just got into a rhythm where we order from the same vendors year after year and don't pay attention to when they raise our costs. As a thank you, you'll be getting a bonus that I think you will find expresses the company's appreciation."

I was stunned. I didn't know what to say. My boss was enjoying this moment. "Thank you so much. That's very generous. But if my current position is being eliminated, what will I be doing?"

He explained that I would transition to the corporate finance team to continue my efforts to reduce overhead costs, work on forecasting spending, and handle other miscellaneous financial matters. I would now be reporting directly to the chief financial officer, who was the person I would be meeting with next.

The CFO was a very laid-back guy. I was timid about broaching the subject of whether I'd be allowed to continue working from home. Such a position would surely require me to be in the office. To my surprise, he didn't mind at all and even complimented me on the amount of work I'd done on the recent cost-savings project.

Returning home from my Chicago trip, I needed to do some shopping. Next to the grocery store was a pen of puppies up for adoption, run by a volunteer I knew. I stopped for a chat and was instantly drawn to the sweet, wagging tails and wet noses. I reached in and picked up one of the puppies. I held him above my head and looked into his big, brown eyes before holding him against me. His puppy paws gently tickled my shoulder as he climbed into a spot between my neck and my ear, sighing softly as he settled. This was it—love. He was destined to become mine. I would name him Winston.

The following few weeks were a whirlwind of puppy insanity. There was puppy training on basic manners, housebreaking, and squeezing in as much exercise for him as I possibly could. He was a welcome change in my life.

Winston and I were taking a Sunday stroll down Main Street when I ran into Todd. He was bicycling around, but I noticed he was wearing jeans. A month had passed since I'd met him at Café Calais, and we had talked a few times. Since that awful night at Todd's house, I hadn't heard any rumors, and it seemed that sporadic communication was keeping him stable. While he acknowledged me with a friendly smile, he didn't immediately approach me. It wasn't until he bicycled by me again that he stopped to chat. His arms rested on the bike's handlebars.

I thought the worst was finally behind me, so we chatted as he played with Winston.

"If you go out of town for the holidays, I'd be happy to watch Winston for ya. I don't plan on doin' anything special."

It was mid-November, and the trauma from being trapped in Todd's truck was still fresh. The issues with my divorce from Jason were still making my head spin in all directions. But the spirit of the holidays was in the air, and I'd finally found job security. Not to mention, the generous bonus helped ease the pain in my bank account. I found myself telling Todd about my new position at work and how happy I was that I wouldn't have to relocate.

"That's great! Congratulations." His enthusiasm was evident in the way his face lit up, and I could tell he was sincerely happy for me. He knew what a constant source of unease I had about losing my job.

"Thanks. My new boss doesn't mind that I work from home, so I don't even have to relocate. I can stay close to the boys. The only bad thing is I'll have to be in Chicago for a week at least once a month. That's when we review all the previous month's accounting reports and compare them to the forecast to make sure the company is on track to hit our targets."

As a publicly traded company, the financials were an important part of the process. We were required to do quarterly updates to shareholders, so month-over-month tracking was critical to making sure we had good news to share.

"I'd be happy to puppy-sit while you're in Chicago. Have you heard about doggy daycare? You should look into it. It will help him burn some of that puppy energy and teach him how to socialize with other dogs."

"Thanks, I think I will."

After that day, Winston became the focal point of Todd's attention—something he could latch onto to get me to engage with him more frequently. He would text me to see how Winston was adjusting and offered to pick him up and take him on walks while I worked. He did this a few times without incident.

I enrolled Winston in doggy daycare two days a week—Mondays and Thursdays. On occasion, Todd offered to take him to daycare or pick him up afterward. Sometimes he offered to do both. The truth was, I hadn't been to Todd's house since the day he tried to force me inside. And he knew I wouldn't go back. He'd always pick Winston up at my house and return him. He'd knock on the door, pass the leash, and leave without coming inside. With each passing day, it seemed Todd was respecting my space.

Instead of making a trip back home, I planned time with friends over the holidays so I could spend it with Winston. The boys had always begged me to get a dog when they were younger, so they were ecstatic to spend time with him, too. My plans gave me an excuse if Todd called me. He did.

Todd had been invited to dinner at Café Calais with a detective from the police department and his wife, but he didn't want to go alone. Despite everything that happened, I knew that awful feeling all too well. It seemed harmless enough to attend dinner with a police officer present, and I felt comfortable that it would be far different than our previous dinner, so I agreed.

That night, I pulled on a pink blouse with a high collar and slipped into jeans, determined to send a clear message that I was not in a relationship with Todd. I fastened on the shoes I had worn the night I ran from Todd—I wanted him to notice them. Even though they had torn into my feet, I wanted to convey that his behavior had not been forgotten.

As if on cue, Todd called and said he was in the neighborhood and asked if I wanted him to pick me up. I knew this tactic now and refused to be sucked into it. I wanted to scream, "No way! Are you nuts?" But I managed to temper my reaction and simply said, "No thanks. I'll meet you there."

Less than an hour later, I arrived at Café Calais. I was concerned Todd would make it awkward by introducing me as his girlfriend. During the short drive, I prepared an appropriate, yet kind, response to mitigate any potential awkwardness if that did happen. To my relief, when I entered the restaurant and greeted everyone, Todd acknowledged me with a hug and simply introduced me by name.

When I saw the detective for the first time, he was not what I expected. Despite his commanding presence, broad shoulders, and bald head, he introduced himself as "Peanut." I smiled at the oxymoron—apparently, "Peanut" had been a childhood nickname that stuck into adulthood. Peanut and his wife, Barbara, were older and had a sweet, calming presence.

"I still can't believe they haven't arrested anyone in that woman's murder," Todd said, leaning toward Peanut. "Are there any new suspects?"

Todd's morbid curiosity about the unsolved murder was nothing new. I dismissed it, believing that maybe he was just digging for gossip to satisfy his persistent need to be in the know.

As I drove home past all the houses decorated with twinkling Christmas lights, I reflected on dinner. Todd was as engaging and charismatic as he had ever been. Time and ignorance had dulled the sharp memories of hiding in the bushes with a broken cell phone. Peanut had assured me that Todd was harmless, leading me to realize I was being overly sensitive—if not outright dramatic, as Todd had once suggested. I believed law enforcement was a good judge of character. If Peanut trusted Todd and the police department could depend on him, so could I.

It wasn't long after the new year that Todd called.

"Hey!" His tone was jovial. "I just received a notification on my calendar—it was one year ago today that I helped you take your wreaths down!"

I laughed.

"Need me to get them down for you again?"

"Oh, thanks for the offer. I didn't even put them up this year."

"I get it. Would you like to grab a cocktail with me? I have something for you."

I hesitated.

"Don't worry. It's just something small that made me think of you."

A wave of emotions came over me at this unexpected gesture. The line was silent, waiting for me to respond. I did the polite thing and agreed to meet him. Maintaining contact and allowing him to help me with Winston really stabilized Todd, but I knew I couldn't let my guard down. I set out to find a gift for him that wouldn't muddy the waters.

I came across an inexpensive night-vision monocular that matched the one Todd had described wanting before. I purchased it, threw it haphazardly into a reused gift bag with no tissue paper, and left to meet him for a cocktail at Oskar's.

Somewhere deep down, I knew I shouldn't. Every time I'd talk to Lauren, I conveniently left out that I was talking to Todd again. She wouldn't understand that talking to him kept him calm. And at this point in my life, I needed to keep things calm.

The boundaries seemed firmly in place. It didn't occur to me that it could be a show, a magician's trick to provide a false sense of security. But I was about to find out. The hard way.

CHAPTER **TWENTY**

Todd was at the restaurant when I arrived with my crumpled gift bag. He didn't get up when I approached the bar—a chivalrous move he was accustomed to making—so I took it as a good sign. He was seeing me as a friend. I sipped my wine as we casually chatted about our respective holiday events and the gifts we'd received from others. As we spoke, he casually placed a box on the bar. It was beautifully wrapped, complete with a perfectly tied bow on top.

"I can't accept this."

"It's not big, I promise. Open it." He was smiling, beaming from ear to ear. Whatever it was, he was proud of himself.

I cringed, afraid to see what was in the box. I slowly untied the ribbon and unfolded the paper to reveal a pair of flannel-lined leather gloves.

"For your Chicago trips," Todd explained.

It was brilliant—exactly what I needed. I was surprised at the thoughtfulness behind his gift.

Now feeling a pang of guilt, I set the crumpled gift bag on the bar. "Mine's not wrapped pretty." I pushed it over to him.

He reached in, pulled out the night-vision monocular, and happily exclaimed, "Oh man, this is exactly what I've wanted for so long! Thank you!" In hindsight, I see the irony in this.

I was finally becoming comfortable with the idea that Todd and I could be friends and that his bad behavior was in the past. As cruel as he could be, he was also funny and fun, charming and chatty, and he was nothing if not reliable. He'd remind me, "I love you, and sometimes, you're not easy to love," which is a statement I couldn't necessarily disagree with. He'd poke at old wounds, making me feel lucky to have someone love me despite my shortcomings.

I responded to his messages as a friend would, with one text for every three of his, so I wouldn't send the wrong message. Most of my responses were flat, non-committal, usually a *yes* or *no* to his questions. It seemed to work.

That's why, when my monthly trip to Chicago rolled around, I texted Todd to see if Winston could spend the week with him. Of course, he agreed. I told him I needed to leave for the airport a little early because I had to stop by the high school to pay Dylan's graduation fees. My sweet baby would be graduating in three short months and had already decided to join the military. I was a proud mom!

Chicago awaited, with its towering skyline and lakeshore winds, but my focus was momentarily on the chaos of packing. I'd need to leave in an hour. My phone buzzed from the nightstand. Todd. He'd be here soon to pick up Winston.

A knock on the door sent Winston leaping from the bed to the door, barking and wagging his fluffy tail.

"Hey, Todd." I turned and headed back toward my bedroom to finish packing. My open suitcase lay on the bed, waiting for last minute items to be thrown in.

"Ready for your trip?"

"Yeah, I have a presentation for the executives in Chicago, and I had to extend my trip. I'll be staying over the weekend. Do you mind keeping Winston a few extra days?"

Todd leaned on the doorframe of my bedroom, his hands in his pockets, with Winston at his feet, begging for a pet. "Why don't I come with you? It'll be fun."

I looked up at him. His eyes were bright with enthusiasm. It took me a moment to digest his question.

"Come . . . on my work trip?"

"Yeah," he replied brightly.

"The reason I'm going for the weekend is to work on a presentation. It's not a vacation."

"I know, but we could make it one. We could see some of the sights." He smiled.

"I don't think so," I said hesitantly. As those words left my lips, I felt the air leak from the room.

He was at the foot of my bed now. His eyes fixed on me, nostrils flaring with every sharp breath. In an eerily calm voice, he said, "Don't you want to spend time with me?"

I froze. I wanted to run from him, but he was in *my* house. I squeezed my eyes shut, willing this to be a nightmare I could wake up from. I opened them. He was still there.

Todd erupted into a fit of rage, calling me names, accusing me of cheating with Ryan, never stopping to take a breath. He grabbed items from my suitcase and, one by one, flung them across the room.

"Todd, please calm down," I whispered, my voice trembling. "It's just a business trip."

This went on for a few minutes until he called me what my mom referred to as "see you next Tuesday," and I'd had enough.

"*Just go!*" I screamed. I locked myself in the bathroom.

"*You're such a coward, Kathryn! You know what I'm saying is true. You can't hide from who you really are!*"

I turned on the shower to drown out the noise. I didn't have any experience with this kind of Jekyll and Hyde behavior, nor did I know how to deal with it. After what felt like an eternity, I pressed my ear against the door, straining to catch any sound.

Silence.

I couldn't be sure he was gone. Heart pounding, I quietly turned the lock and inched the door open. I scanned the bedroom and didn't see Todd. Winston was gone, too. Slipping into the hallway, I hugged the wall, every nerve on edge. My breaths came shallow as I crept toward the kitchen, half expecting to see Todd there. Winston's bag by the garage door was gone. My eyes darted to the window above the sink. Todd's truck was gone. I had tolerated enough of his crap to keep the peace, but even I had a limit.

During my trip, I knew in my heart that I was completely done with Todd. There was no going back. Although I was nervous about my network going down, I was thankful to have control over the Google Wi-Fi system.

I tried to focus on work while I was in Chicago. I didn't worry about Winston because Todd had become fond of him. He even took him to the vet for his follow-up appointment after the surgery to be neutered. He wouldn't hurt a poor, innocent puppy. The week passed quickly, and it was time for me to head back. I dreaded flying home to deal with Todd. I had no idea what version of him I would get when I arrived.

The next day, Todd stopped by my house as originally planned. I didn't want to have a conversation inside, so I led him out to the backyard. I braced myself for an ugly scene. I walked to the edge of the patio and waited for Todd to sit down. I was glad his chair was the furthest from the door. If things got ugly again, I could run inside and lock him out.

"After everything that's happened, I think it's time we put an end to this for good." I inched closer to the door.

"I can't believe you're doing this to me again." He threw up his hands. "You're such a drama queen." He continued the tirade I now recognized. I was silent as he called me names, berated me, and told me every reason why no man would ever love me. From his perspective, I was destined to die a lonely old woman with Winston feasting on my carcass.

I held firm in my silence, which infuriated him. Finally, I cut him off. "If you believe I am all those things, then it sounds like this is best for both of us."

That stopped him. He couldn't argue without admitting he was wrong. Instead, he just left. I spent the day waiting for my network to go down, but it seemed to stay intact.

I was thankful when Dylan called, saying he'd be over for dinner. I shifted my focus to making a nice meal for us when my phone started blowing up.

> **TODD**
> We need to talk.

> **ME**
> There's nothing more to say.

> **TODD**
> I'm coming over.

> **ME**
> Do not come here.

I silenced Todd's texts and quit looking at my phone. I flitted around the kitchen, preparing dinner and setting the table. I was in the kitchen, cutting vegetables, when Todd walked into my house through the garage. As he entered, Todd was at a fever pitch, hurling insults at me. I repeatedly demanded that he leave, and when I grabbed my phone, he lunged at me, just as he had done before. I quickly put it down to avoid further escalation. I went back to chopping vegetables, made no eye contact, and refused to respond at all, no matter what he said. This enraged him, and when he came around the counter toward me, I held up the knife.

"You need to leave *right now!*" My face was hot, my knees weak. The knife trembled in my hand. I'd never threatened to harm anyone before.

Our eyes locked fiercely. Neither of us moved. His face grew redder, nostrils flaring, hands balled into fists at his sides. We were in a standoff for what felt like an eternity. Finally, he took several steps back, eyes trained on me. I put the knife down and went to the front porch to draw him outside. As predicted, Todd followed me, stopping in the doorway. I kept trying to draw him away from the door and outside, demanding that he leave, until he finally stepped outside. I rushed back into the house. Before I could close and lock the door, he put his foot between the door and the frame. He leaned against the door, forcing his way in. I didn't want to risk letting the door close with him inside the house, but I was running out of options. I tried to push past him to get back outside. He caught me by the waist. Holding onto the doorframe, I pushed with all my might and forced my way back onto the front porch.

"Dylan will be here any second. I need to finish making dinner."

He paused as if considering whether that was true. "You better promise to call me later," he hissed.

At this point, I was willing to say whatever was necessary to get him out of my house, so I agreed. "Okay."

Todd let go of the door, turned, and walked through the kitchen and out the garage door. I cautiously followed him to make sure he left and to secure the house afterward. As I returned to the kitchen, I picked up the knife in my trembling hands to finish chopping vegetables. But I couldn't. I looked out the sink over the window and watched as he left. Still holding the knife, my knees buckled. I crumpled onto the floor. I sobbed, my hands shaking, breath catching, heart pounding. I'd never held a knife to anyone before. I started questioning the appropriateness of my own behavior—sick to my stomach, dizzy, and on the verge of vomiting.

Winston's collar jingled as he came around the corner. I dropped the knife and pulled him close, breathing in the smell of his fur. He licked my hands and curled against my chest. I took a deep breath. Then another. And another. Soon, I was able to get to my feet. Wiping my face with my hands, I reached for a new knife and resumed chopping vegetables.

I was determined to make a nice dinner for my son.

CHAPTER
TWENTY-ONE

In the days that followed, despite a barrage of calls and texts, I ignored Todd. Knowing just how small our town was and that I'd likely run into him if I left the house, I decided to stay put. One sunny afternoon, I took advantage of the weather and sank into a day of gardening. I moved methodically, pulling weeds and piling them next to me.

Just past the fence was a clearing—a right-of-way the government owned to maintain the pond. Birds swooped over the still surface of the water. I returned my attention to the flower bed when a movement caught my eye. Someone was just beyond the fence—Todd.

"Can we talk?" he asked. His hands were in his pockets, his shoulders sagged, and he looked sad. It was the part of the cycle that had become easy to predict.

I got up, walked toward the house, stepped inside, and locked the doors without a word. His presence terrified me, but I blamed myself for drawing him there. I'd ignored his calls and texts, and in his mind, I had left him no other choice but to show up unannounced. It felt unnerving to see him in my backyard, but I was beginning to understand his triggers. Although I felt there was nothing more to say, he clearly felt otherwise.

Later that day, I ran to the grocery store. I checked out and rolled my cart out to the parking lot. When I look toward my car, I noticed Todd had blocked my car in. I steadied myself and kept walking as if nothing was amiss. As I approached my car to load my groceries, he rolled down his window.

"I just want to talk," he said softly.

My stomach flipped.

My mind raced in a million directions. *Do I talk to him and give him closure? Do I just ignore him? Will he escalate things either way?*

I opened the trunk and placed bag after bag inside as Todd sat in his truck and watched.

"I just want to talk!" he shouted, more commanding.

When I finished, I avoided eye contact, pushed my cart back into the store, and went to customer service.

"Excuse me?" I called out, waving to an associate. "There is a vehicle behind my car, and I can't leave."

"Not a problem." The associate said, then came out from behind the counter to walk me outside. As we entered the parking lot, Todd was gone. The associate turned to me with a glare, and I felt like an idiot.

If stalking is defined as a pattern of behavior that causes a reasonable person to feel fear, Todd's actions certainly fit. I just wasn't seeing it. Todd was a nuisance, sure, but I knew from experience that giving him the silent treatment only caused him to escalate.

Yet I did it anyway.

The grocery store incident became just one of many examples of Todd showing up at places where I was, trying to get my attention. It seemed that any restaurant I went to, any trail I biked on, any store I visited, Todd would appear. Considering the small size of our town, many of these run-ins could have been coincidental. Yet, every time he saw me, he would constantly badger me, saying, "I just want to talk."

Each time it happened, I ignored him or left without responding. Sometimes he would follow me out to the parking lot; other times, he'd just watch me leave. On one occasion, it looked like he was filming or photographing me with his phone as I walked to my car. I felt that, at some point, he'd give up and move on.

I stayed home because I didn't want to run into Todd. I grew tired of sitting at home, so I settled into a comfortable routine with Lauren, going to her house a few times a week to relax and catch up. As soon as I walked into her warmly lit home, I'd take off my shoes and settle into her plush couch or sit with her by the pool, and we'd talk for hours, sometimes about our shared disdain for Todd, but mostly about life. Lauren's home was my safe haven, and I desperately needed to feel safe somewhere.

Then, without warning, Todd changed tactics. I had just turned out of my neighborhood when I saw his truck in my rearview mirror. My phone pinged with a text from him.

> **TODD**
>
> Hey! Just saw u pull onto the main road in front of me. I see you have Winston. Are u taking him to daycare? I miss him so much and would love to pick him up to spend time with him. I can have him back before dinner.

Placating him had worked before, so I thought that if I let him have time with Winston, he might stop showing up everywhere I went and badgering me to talk. I cautiously agreed to let Todd pick him up from doggy daycare and take him to the park. Later that night, I arrived home from Lauren's to find Winston in the backyard, wagging his tail and ready for dinner. I thought maybe this would be the way to appease him until he lost interest.

A few days after Todd's outing with Winston, I received a call from an old friend who'd just bought his first house and needed help decorating. I needed a little fun, so I told him I was happy to help. That afternoon, he came to my house and picked me up. "I can't believe the garage is done," he remarked when he pulled in.

I gave him a quick tour of the garage and the office upstairs. He was blown away by all the work that had been done since the last time he was at my house.

We went from store to store, picking out rugs, throw pillows, blankets, and other decorative items. It felt amazing to have a day when I wasn't constantly looking over my shoulder.

Later that evening, I received an email from Todd. He said a friend had seen me out with a guy, even describing the color and make of the vehicle. He finished by saying, "Since you've moved on and started dating someone else, there is nothing else for us to talk about."

I had complained about Todd to my friend that day, so I called him to tell him about the email I'd just received.

"I mean, I just don't believe anyone would tell him something like that. Do you?"

"I don't. Gosh, I hate to say this, but could he be watching you?"

"Watching me? What do you mean?"

"Don't you think it's strange that the security cameras he installed point toward your doors and driveway instead of out toward the street?"

The blood rushed out of my face. Suddenly, it all made sense. The cameras weren't positioned to catch an intruder—they were placed to monitor when I came and went. I'd been led to believe the cameras were for my safety, but in reality, they were there to watch me.

The next day, I was sitting in the backyard, watching Winston chase squirrels, when Todd appeared at the picket fence, in the path with public access. The proximity made my skin tingle.

"Did you get my email?"

"I did. And I know no one saw me out and reported it back to you."

"What the hell are you talking about? How else would I have known you were out with some guy?" he demanded.

"Just admit it. Admit that you're accessing the cameras at my house."

"That is ridiculous. Just because you would stoop that low doesn't mean I would. I'm a professional. Accessing your cameras is illegal, and I could lose my job over an accusation like that. You're unbelievable."

"Yeah, and *you're a liar!*" I yelled, rising from my chair.

"Don't you dare call me a liar," he said in an eerily calm voice. It sent chills up my spine, but I remained steadfast in calling him out.

"So, who was it? Who told you I was with someone?"

He talked in circles about how I didn't have many friends, claiming it came from someone I trusted. He said he was protecting me by withholding the name.

"That's bullshit." I didn't believe him, but my mind scrambled through possible suspects anyway.

"I'm not telling you," he said, incredulous.

"Right now. Give me a name." I was determined to know if someone had betrayed me.

"Fine. No one told me, okay? I was on my way to the store and was going to stop by to see if I could pick up Winston, and I saw the car in your driveway." His voice shifted to the warm, familiar tone I'd heard so many times before. His excuse was plausible, given I'd seen him driving past my house several times, but he wouldn't have known it was a guy.

I stormed inside, closing my eyes and rubbing my temples, sick of what my life had become. Instead of quiet evenings with Winston, enjoying the life I'd worked so hard to build, I was locked in a seemingly endless battle with a person I simply wanted gone. My only hope was to outlast him, waiting for whatever interest he had in me to fade.

What I didn't realize was that an inevitable collision of fate was just around the corner.

CHAPTER
TWENTY-TWO

The day of Dylan's high school graduation arrived. My family came in for the celebration, but I couldn't relax or enjoy the festivities. I knew Todd was lurking around every corner, waiting for an opportunity to cause a scene. Nobody—except Nathan, Robert, and Lauren—knew what was really going on with Todd and me, and I desperately wanted to keep it that way. I wanted the focus to be on Dylan's accomplishment. He'd struggled in school and deserved to enjoy his moment.

The week after his graduation, Dylan and I sat on the front porch. It seemed to be the only place where we could talk without me being distracted by cooking, cleaning, or laundry. It wasn't long before we saw the familiar truck circle the house. I tried to ignore Todd for my son's sake, but after the third drive-by, Dylan was fed up. He took off running and chased Todd, barefoot, out of my neighborhood.

The next day, Dylan called me from work and launched into a frantic speech about how Todd had come into the store and lodged a complaint against him with the owner.

"I treated him the same as I do any customer. He was just looking to cause a problem."

I knew the owner well enough to call him without making things awkward for Dylan. Before I allowed any emotion to settle in, I dialed his number and explained the situation.

"I'm sorry to hear you're having so much trouble," the shop owner said sympathetically. "He was a real jerk, so I didn't write Dylan up for the complaint. Thanks for letting me know."

I hung up, grateful for the owner's response, and sobbed. Involving my children was inexcusable. I considered asking Todd what it would take for him to stop, but then I remembered that I was not dealing with a sane, rational person. The memory of being pulled by the hair toward his house was enough to keep me from making that call.

One cloudy, overcast morning, I received a call from Mom, letting me know that my grandmother was gravely ill and in the hospital. I immediately took off work and packed a small overnight bag. I called the doggy daycare to see if they could board Winston, but the owner explained they were full—it was a holiday weekend, after all. Lauren had two dogs of her own, so she was out. Nathan wasn't an option either. Desperate for a solution, I reluctantly texted Todd. He was all too happy to help.

Within a short time, I was racing in the car, to my grandmother's bedside. That's when my phone rang. It was James, a co-worker from the Chicago office. We had become friends, often meeting for pub trivia with a few others after work when I was in town. I answered, relieved to take my mind off things during the long drive.

"Listen." His tone was flat. "I've been receiving texts from someone named Todd who claims to know you. He called, but I let it go to voicemail."

A wave of nausea rose from my stomach to my throat. I tried to swallow, trying to push it back down. I could feel the rage building inside me. My fingers clenched the steering wheel, veins throbbing in my hands, and my chest heaved as my breathing quickened.

"Please, James. Don't respond. Just ignore him."

"This guy says you're known for sleeping around and mentions something about your plaid panties. Does your vagina smell?" He burst out laughing.

I certainly wasn't.

"I've gotta go." I hung up before James could respond and angrily dialed Todd.

When he answered, I couldn't even get a word in before he blurted, "You can have your dog back when you can prove to me that you can be a better person!"

"What are you—"

"You're cheating on me, you liar!" he screamed.

"Todd, we are not dating. We are not in a relationship!"

"You're nothing but a liar, and you're never seeing Winston again!"

I forced myself to lower my voice. "Please take him back to my house. I'm turning around."

"No, you're not getting Winston back. You're a horrible person, Kathryn, and you don't deserve him."

"I have nothing to prove to you!" I hung up before he could respond. Simply pressing "end" on a call doesn't have the same satisfaction as slamming the receiver down with brute force, but it was all I had.

There it was—the end of our communication. Forever.

I never made it to the hospital to see my grandmother. I pulled over at the first gas station I saw and called Robert, a friend who occasionally joined Nathan and me for breakfast. He was an attorney, and I hoped he could give me some advice. After I explained what was going on, he offered guidance.

"Mute his messages, but don't block them. You need to collect as much evidence as you can." He made me promise, then continued calmly, "There's not much we can do over the holiday weekend. We'll need to wait until Tuesday—I won't be back in town until then anyway. In the meantime, call the police and file a report. Then go see your grandma."

I filled my gas tank but yanked the nozzle out too soon, splashing gasoline across my hands. I was so focused on getting Winston back that I didn't even notice. I peeled out of the station, heading back home. Hurtling down the highway, I called my local sheriff's department non-emergency line. I finally reached a dispatcher and explained the situation.

"What documentation do I need to get my dog returned?"

"I'm sorry, ma'am. This is a domestic situation, and unless there's a court order regarding ownership of the dog, there's nothing we can do."

"Winston has a rabies tag registered in my name with my address."

"You still need a court order."

"But it matches the address on my license, and I have all his vaccination records from the veterinarian with my name and address on them."

"Court order, ma'am."

"I also have his adoption paperwork in my name, including the canceled check from my payment to adopt him." I tightened my grip on the wheel, my frustration mounting.

"Doesn't matter," the dispatcher said.

As the smell of gasoline on my hands filled my nostrils, it fueled a fire deep within me, illuminating the horror of it all. I kept thinking about how, after our very first meeting, he appeared everywhere I went. I remembered how pushy he was from the beginning about dating. I reflected on how he was there when I left dinner with my dad, talking about buying new exercise equipment, yet never actually exercising. My head spun, blurring the road in front of me. I thought about how trapped I felt riding in his vehicle, knowing he wasn't taking me home. I remembered the fear when I considered jumping out of his moving truck.

My head collapsed into my hand as my elbow rested on the windowsill. Since breaking up with him, he had circled my house, come into my backyard, and followed me to various places.

Then I thought about James. I never spoke about him to Todd, and even if I had, he shouldn't have had the means to contact James. I suspected Todd had cloned my phone, gaining access to my texts—that was the only explanation that made sense. Flickers of each incident from the last nineteen months flashed through my mind. It all started to come together in ways I'd never seen before.

I hated myself for ignoring his toxic behavior. I had to confront the fact that my passive approach had fed the monster Todd was. I thought I could outlast him after everything I'd been through. I managed to rebuild my life as a single mother on welfare. I pulled my house out of foreclosure without selling it. I went from having no formal education and little more than administrative skills to a good job with a master's degree. Never mind the mountain of student loan debt that rivaled my mortgage.

All I knew for sure was that if I spoke to Todd, his behavior would stabilize—until he realized I didn't want a relationship with him. Then, he'd go completely off the rails. It was a vicious cycle.

I finally saw how placating him was a temporary fix. I shook my head as I realized that Todd had been systematically dismantling my life one piece at a time. And now, he was infiltrating my place of employment by contacting James. Everything was at risk—my innocent puppy, my job, my career, my public reputation. And now that I was seeing it, it burned through me like acid.

My thoughts were interrupted when my phone beeped. It never rang, but there it was—a voicemail from Todd. My stomach lurched as his saccharine voice echoed through the car, an attempt to get me to fold.

"Hey. Give me a call when you have a minute, please? You know, regardless of whether a relationship works out or not, I don't tell somebody I love them for us to part ways like this. So, maybe we can talk? If not, maybe we can just get everything sorted out amicably? I actually don't want the nastiness. Thanks. Bye."

Seriously? The nastiness? You kidnapped my fucking dog!

His calm, cool voice was a stark contrast to the thirty-two text messages in three hours, filled with expletives. With each passing syllable, rage flared inside me like wildfire. I wanted to pull over, get out of my car, and scream into the sky. This man was so out of touch with reality, there was no reasoning with him.

Pounding the steering wheel, I cried tears of anguish. I worried endlessly about Winston—if he was being subjected to Todd's vicious outbursts, cowering in a corner, desperate for me to save him. It was killing me that I couldn't be there to protect him. When I finally arrived home, I curled up on the couch like an infant. I learned that the body can produce an infinite number of tears, even if your fluid intake is limited to whiskey and coffee.

CHAPTER
TWENTY-THREE

Around 1:00 a.m., I received an email from Todd demanding a random assortment of items—a socket wrench set, a dog carrier he'd bought for Winston, and a pair of work boots he'd left in my garage—in exchange for Winston. Since he didn't care to see me, he asked that my boys handle the exchange. No way in hell was I going to involve my sons or have them this close to a deranged son of a bitch!

I had not moved from the couch, changed clothes, or even taken a shower when Dylan stopped by after work the next evening. I let him read the email from Todd, and he fumed. He immediately called Caleb, who raced over to the house. My sons, now eighteen and twenty, ganged up on me and convinced me they didn't need to be treated like little boys. They could handle this. Winston was their dog, too, and they were going to get him back. My heart swelled with pride as I realized how capable my sons were. The boys loaded the items Todd requested into the car, and I printed off the email so the boys would have a copy if they needed it. He had never shown aggression toward the boys, so we decided it was better if I stayed behind.

It wasn't long before Caleb called and recounted what happened. He said that when they arrived at Todd's house, they saw him peek through the blinds and the police arrived soon after. The officer told them Todd claimed the boys were trespassing, even though they were parked on the street, and harassing him.

"Mom, I swear . . . we never said a word to him."

"Was it the police department or the sheriff's department?"

"It was the police department—the one Todd works for."

Dylan handed the officer the email from Todd, proving that he had requested they do the exchange.

When the officer looked at it, he shook his head. "You boys go home and let your mother handle this."

As Caleb recounted this over the phone, I clenched my teeth. I could hardly believe what I was hearing. I swallowed hard. The encounter made me wonder if Todd's ties to the police department came with some special privileges.

I called the sheriff's department non-emergency line and told the dispatcher about the email. I requested an escort to make the exchange instead. I ended up speaking with the same dispatcher I'd spoken to hours earlier. "As I advised before, this is a domestic situation, and there is nothing we can do. You will have to seek a court order to have the dog returned."

My vision blurred with anger, everything around me tinged a fiery red. My hands balled into fists, ready to swing at the nearest object. My lips twisted into a snarl as I struggled to contain the raging inferno inside me.

Before the boys arrived back home, Todd managed to contact their father, Mark. He told Mark that I had "involved the boys in my personal drama and nearly got them arrested," and that Mark should speak with me about my behavior. When Mark told me about the call, Todd made it sound as though *he* had done us a favor by not pressing charges. Although I was horrified, I stopped wondering how Todd managed to get in touch with anyone. He'd crossed so many lines, entangling me in messy situations with people—I knew there was no boundary he wouldn't cross.

I forwarded Todd's email to Robert, along with an account of how the boys had attempted the exchange, as Todd requested, but were nearly arrested for trespassing. I desperately needed him to step in legally to prevent things from escalating further. I suggested that Robert contact Adam rather than engage directly with Todd. After all, Adam had brokered a ceasefire once before, and I was hopeful he could help bring Winston home.

As badly as I wanted to sink into my couch and stay there, I knew I had to act. Todd falsely claimed that the adoption paperwork for Winston was in both of our names—an egregious lie. Instead of making Todd produce the nonexistent papers, Robert asked me to gather the documentation proving that Winston was mine.

I dragged myself upstairs to the office. But something was wrong. Todd had installed a forty-inch television screen showing the cameras, so I could see if anyone was at the house while I was working. Now, the screens only displayed an error message. I immediately suspected Todd had remotely disabled my cameras, so I pulled up the app on my phone to check. Sure enough, they were offline. I had no idea how to get them back online—classic Todd. He was trying to bait me into calling him for help. There was no way I was going to fall into that trap—again.

I got down on my hands and knees, fiddling with wires and settings, when my phone rang. It was Robert. He said Todd was claiming he loaned me money and wanted me to repay him. "I have no idea what you're talking about."

"He said that when he was renting office space from you, he paid for some A/C repairs. He sent me a copy of the check. Let me send it to you."

I pulled my phone away from my ear and looked at the image. It was a copy of a check—definitely Todd's. I immediately recognized the amount as Todd's one and only rent check. I looked at the memo line. The word "rent," which I had insisted he write, was missing.

I raced to my computer and logged into my bank account. I retrieved a copy of the check I had deposited—same check number, same amount, with the word "rent" on the memo line, just as I remembered. I also pulled a copy of my bank statement showing the debit card transaction to the A/C company.

I found the email with the invoice that showed the amount for the service was eight hundred dollars more than the check Todd claimed proved he paid the bill. Yet, my bank transaction was for the exact amount on the invoice.

Todd made a strategic error: he altered a copy of his check and was now caught in a lie. My heart raced with vindication. It was a satisfying moment, knowing he was caught in his own web of deceit. I was ready to fight back and reclaim what was rightfully mine—my beloved dog and my life.

Armed with Winston's records proving my ownership, Robert was able to reach an agreement with Adam for Winston's return. There was no more talk about Todd having ownership papers, but I didn't care. Winston was coming home.

Later that day, Todd dropped him off at the doggy daycare, where I was able to pick him up. When Winston saw me walk in, he flew into my arms, nuzzling into my neck.

With Winston back at home, I tried to relax. Instead, a simmering anger coursed through me, impossible to ignore. Winston, once a bundle of joy with a wagging tail and bright eyes, now cowered in the corner and wouldn't make eye contact. He trailed after me like a shadow, always underfoot, seeking reassurance. He moved with a slight jog when going from room to room, tail tucked between his legs, ears pinned back.

I loaded him into the car and took him to the vet. After explaining the situation, the veterinarian said Winston was exhibiting symptoms of doggy anxiety and prescribed medication. He advised me on how to help reassure Winston.

The vet turned to me. "Todd Bennett came in with Winston a couple of months ago, right?"

I hadn't mentioned Todd by name, so I was surprised. "Yeah," I whispered. He'd brought Winston in for a check-up after his surgery while I was in Chicago.

"I thought so. How's he doing?"

"You know Todd?"

"Yeah, he takes care of our network and computers here. He sold me those cameras for the exam rooms during that visit." The vet pointed to a camera affixed to the ceiling.

My eyes locked on his finger. I stared directly into the camera, wondering if Todd was watching. It seemed he was drumming up business all over. This town was already small—now, it felt like it was shrinking, collapsing in on me.

CHAPTER
TWENTY-FOUR

Strategy was crucial. I needed to devise a meticulous plan to extricate Todd from my life—not just one plan, but a series of adaptable maneuvers. Todd's volatility demanded flexibility. I was exhausted by the chaos, and a small part of me hoped that perhaps he was equally weary, ready to sever our ties. Yet, an unsettling fear gnawed at me—that he would take it as a challenge and cling on, like he did in the beginning when I kept declining a date with him.

I was angry that Todd had faced no consequences for kidnapping Winston or altering the check. I hired Robert with part of my bonus to see me through this final split from Todd, once and for all.

Robert advised that the first step would be to issue a "no contact" letter, which is a demand that Todd refrain from contacting or approaching me. "You must have absolutely no contact whatsoever with Todd once I send this letter," Robert said—for the third time—looking me directly in the eye.

"Robert, I am about to lose my shit. I have not contacted him since the day he stole my dog. I am not the one who needs this counsel. Todd does."

"I understand you're upset, but I just want to be certain that you do not contact him under any circumstances," he said reassuringly, but the damage was done. I wondered if he even believed me.

"Also, is he blocked on your cell phone?"

"No, you told me to mute him, but not block him." This was important because if Todd had reached out after the no-contact letter, we'd have evidence of his blatant disregard.

"That's good. And the cameras?"

"They're still offline. I plan on calling to have them removed."

"Don't," Robert shot back. "Have someone get them back online. If he comes by your house, video footage will be important."

"I'm scared this letter will make him angrier than he already is. I have no idea what he's capable of."

"If it does, we'll have the evidence we need for a protective order. Look, Kathryn, this guy is a jerk. I know his type. All bark and no bite."

I left Robert's office with the hope that this would finally bring an end to Todd in my life. The thought of getting the cameras back online made me cringe. The benefit Robert explained made sense, but I didn't want to enable Todd to see or monitor me and Winston.

Robert issued the letter, which Todd took as a challenge. He found loopholes to avoid clear violations. He was clever, and deviously ingenious. In my mailbox, I found my garage door opener and a handwritten letter, which had a stamp on it but no postmark. I was relieved to have my garage door opener back, but I couldn't trust that he didn't program it into one of the buttons on the sun visor in his truck.

I snapped a picture of the two items, then opened the letter.

Dear Kathryn,

I've been doing a lot of thinking lately. I saw a therapist, who helped me see that a relationship with you isn't healthy. I am truly sorry, from the depths of my heart. Maybe one day we can meet for coffee and talk. I like to imagine us laughing together, not as we were, but as the new people we'll have grown into.

I'm not asking for that now. I know I have no right. But I wanted you to know that I am sorry.

With love,
Todd

Coffee and laughter? With him? After everything? The nerve! My fingers itched to crumple his pathetic note and watch it burn, maybe dance around the ashes for good measure. But no—I needed it intact. Evidence of how Todd couldn't follow even the simplest instruction: leave me alone. I snapped a photo and sent it to Robert, my stomach churning.

Todd was clever, and deviously ingenious. Anyone reading the letter would think it was sincere. I'd bought this—hook, line, and sinker—too many times before to believe there was a morsel of sincerity in his words.

It wasn't long before I heard back from Robert. I nearly choked reading his response. He said that was a good sign—Todd was taking responsibility.

Yeah, right. Todd wasn't sorry. Todd was playing chess while Robert was playing checkers. I'd have to wait, and I knew it wouldn't take long. I counted days, not weeks, before Todd's next move.

I was pouring a cup of coffee when I saw Todd's truck in my next-door neighbor's driveway. They were outside talking. About what? Did they even know each other? I pulled out my phone, took a picture from the kitchen window, and sent it to Robert.

"He isn't restricted from going to your neighbor's house. Only your house."

Later that day, I knocked on my neighbor's door.

"Oh, hi, Kathryn."

"Hi there. I saw that Todd stopped by this morning. I didn't realize you two knew each other."

"We don't. Look, I don't want to get involved in whatever's going on." He threw up his hands.

"Can you at least tell me what he wanted?"

He looked noticeably uncomfortable. After a moment, he finally told me. "He suspects you're abusing your dog. Said your dog is even on anxiety medication. Wanted to know if I'd witnessed anything."

My mouth gaped open. The lengths Todd would go to were unconscionable. When I returned home, I called Robert and relayed my conversation with the neighbor.

"It's not a violation of the no-contact letter—"

"But, Robert, he's attacking my reputation. This isn't the first time he's spread rumors about me."

"To make a claim of slander, you need to demonstrate economic loss. Have you been demoted at work? Had your pay cut? Lost your job because of this?"

I deflated. "No."

"I'd advise against that route, Kathryn. You don't want to get tied up in court. It's costly. Just let him blow off steam and keep your head held high. Take the high road."

Then Todd called my work extension. My work phone had caller ID, so I took a picture of his number. I didn't answer. Instead, I texted the picture to Robert, feeling confident that a phone call would be a clear violation of the no-contact letter.

"You said your company hired him to install your home office setup, correct?"

"Yes."

"Then he could claim it was a business call, which isn't a violation."

The knot in my stomach turned into a blazing fire. My teeth clenched, and my grip on the phone tightened to keep from throwing it across the room. I drew a breath.

"Robert, you and I both know Todd is doing this on purpose."

"I agree. But I'm your attorney. I have to consider how I would counter Todd's defense. Right now, our position is weak, at best."

I pinched the bridge of my nose and closed my eyes.

"Look, I'll issue another no-contact letter. We'll document these instances in the second letter. Send me an email with the dates, times, and locations of each incident. Include your neighbor's name and the pictures you've sent so I have everything in one place."

Finally, there was something I could do. Robert had the email within fifteen minutes. Not only did he issue a second no-contact letter, but he had to issue a third one as well. Each time, he documented how Todd disregarded the previous request. Todd's constant attempts were maddening, like the drone of static, but Robert felt they didn't cross enough legal lines to justify a protective order.

One brisk night, Winston woke me in the early morning hours. Since getting him back, I'd kept him in my bedroom. He stood on the bed, barking with his hackles raised—something rare for him. I grabbed my phone and got out of bed to investigate. When I reached the back of the house, I froze—my skin was crawling. Through the breakfast room window, I saw Todd in my backyard, his eyes fixed on the house. He held an object in his hand, down by his side. It looked suspiciously like the night vision scope I had gifted him. The bitter irony sent my stomach into somersaults.

I flipped on the lights and held my phone to my ear as if I was talking to someone, hoping Todd would see and think I was calling the police. As soon as he caught sight of me, he took off. I clenched my chest—my heart pounding, breath caught in my throat.

I considered calling the police, but Todd was gone, and the cameras were still offline. I'd look like a crazy person insisting he was in my backyard. The police had already shown deference to him when they sent my boys home without questioning him about the email.

Instead, I lay frozen in my bed, clutching my phone. No matter how hard I tried to fall asleep, I couldn't shake the image of Todd in my backyard. I turned it over and over in my mind, wondering if he had planned to break in. *What was he doing here? Am I in danger?* Worries raced through my brain like speeding cars. I thought about the conversation we once had about the murdered woman.

I'd rather not know death was coming.

I shuddered.

As soon as sunlight peeked through the cracks in my blinds, I called and reported the incident to Robert. I hoped it would develop into something more than just another letter.

"Listen," he said gently. "There is no proof Todd was in your backyard, so there's not much we can do."

I nodded, even though he couldn't see me through the phone.

"What you need to do is write down the date, time, and location of every incident—every single one. That way, if something happens that we can connect to Todd, we'll have enough to seek a protective order."

"But last night?"

"You said your cameras were down. There's no way to prove he was there."

I wanted to slam the phone down, hear the crack of plastic as it hit the base, but those old phones I had twenty years ago had long been obsolete. All I could do was pull my cellphone from my ear and tap the icon on the fragile screen.

Vicious rumors about me—branding me as an animal abuser—exploded into the community. Old, malicious whispers about my alleged affair with a married man and my supposed financial irresponsibility roared back to life, louder and more relentless than ever. Only now, I was also being branded an animal abuser. The once warm, tight-knit community that had embraced me now seemed hell-bent on perpetuating Todd's lies.

CHAPTER
TWENTY-FIVE

Desperation suffocated me far more than the heat and humidity of summer that had settled in. My social media became a graveyard—people were quick to unfriend me. I told myself they weren't friends to begin with, but it still hurt. Even Carleigh unfriended me. So much for being a bridesmaid. I dodged the board meeting, terrified of facing Pastor Nick, and the thought of leaving my house felt like walking into enemy fire—every glare a bullet of judgment. Isolation clawed at my extroverted insides.

One call to Todd could end this all. That's what this was all about, wasn't it? The thought of speaking to him twisted my stomach with revulsion. I refused to yield—I would not let him savor the taste of victory. I vowed to outlast him, to patch up the wreckage when the storm finally passed. This was my new battle plan.

When Saturday rolled around, meeting Nathan was my lifeline. I craved the presence of someone who supported me. Lauren meant well, but she only wanted to talk about who said what, and I was tired of hearing it. I decided that what I didn't know couldn't hurt me.

We hadn't been there long when Todd showed up and sat at a nearby table. I ignored him. I recounted the incidents to Nathan, and I didn't care if Todd heard me. I lowered my voice when I spoke about the futility of legal action with Robert, since the cameras were dead.

Nathan leaned in, his voice a conspiratorial whisper. "I know a guy." It was the Deep South, and usually a statement like that meant someone was about to get their ass kicked. But Nathan wasn't that kind of guy. He was a fixer, a problem solver.

I was intrigued. "What do you mean?"

"I know a guy who's an expert in surveillance systems. The kid was a Marine, but he works for a DOD contractor now. He could take a look at your setup, see if there's any way to get your cameras working again. Sounds like that's what Robert needs."

I hesitated. "Nathan, you know how small the community is. What if your guy knows Todd?"

"Even if he does, I trust he'll do right by you. I've known him his whole life—his dad and I were buddies in the Army."

I trusted Nathan. If he vouched for this person, they had to be legit. I glanced over at Todd, who was pretending to be engrossed in his phone. The sight of him made my skin crawl. I turned back to Nathan, determination settling in my gut.

"Okay," I agreed tentatively. "I guess it couldn't hurt."

Nathan smiled reassuringly. "Don't worry, he's a pro. I'll give him a call and set something up."

I nodded, trying to muster a grateful smile in return. The following Tuesday evening, a knock at the door startled me from my restless thoughts. I peered through the peephole to see an unfamiliar man standing next to Nathan.

I provided what little detail I knew about the cameras, including how Todd had accessed them when Caleb was home from college and forgot to close the garage door. After poking around on the computer, he informed me that the cameras were operational; however, the feed to the television, the app on my phone, and the connection to the DVR had all been disabled. I was furious. Todd could see me through the cameras, but I had no access to them.

The technician had me change the password before he re-enabled all my devices but warned me that a "back door" could have been installed, and we'd never know it. I could rip out the cameras and replace them, but Todd could still have a back door built into my network to access them.

Before leaving, he recommended that I have my phone checked. "If the stalker has enough technical knowledge to see your cameras, it's possible he's cloning your phone."

This was the first time anyone had actually referred to Todd as a stalker. I was stunned.

"Is there anyone you recommend?"

"Yeah, I'll write down his contact information."

I cringed.

"He doesn't live around here. He's a buddy of mine. You can trust him. Until he gives you the all-clear, I wouldn't do anything on your phone."

The nagging question of how Todd knew Lauren was the one who picked me up that night lingered in my mind. It explained how he knew I was with Ryan that night and how he managed to get in touch with Mark, Jason, and James. If he had cloned my phone, it would explain a lot.

Later that night, I drifted off to sleep, disgusted by the thought that Todd could see me all this time. My eyes snapped open in the middle of the night to the sound of Winston growling—his fur standing on end as he sat up on the bed. Instead of heading to the kitchen, Winston was at my bedroom window, facing the side of the house, barking ferociously. My breath caught in my throat. He couldn't see through the window, and I wasn't about to open the curtains either.

I stumbled out of bed and reached for the lamp. But when I flicked it, nothing happened. The room remained shrouded in darkness. I rushed into the bathroom and tried to turn on the light, but it didn't work.

Pure terror flooded my veins.

Did I pay the electricity bill? Yes, yes, I did. It's on autopay. With trembling fingers, I checked my account online using my cell phone. Balance due: zero. I called the outage hotline: an automated message said there were no outages in my area.

My heart pounded. I dropped my phone onto the bed and fumbled for the gun in my nightstand. My fingers shook as I loaded the magazine and chambered a bullet. Every instinct told me to run, but I couldn't.

The moonlight cast eerie shadows as I crept down the hallway, my body pressed against the wall. My finger hovered above the trigger, ready to shoot. As I reached the corner of the living room, I held my breath and braced myself. With the gun firmly in my grip, right arm straight, left arm slightly bent at the elbow, my eyes couldn't focus on the sights on the barrel. I'd have to rely on my aim. In a swift movement, I rounded the corner, scanning the room. The only sound was the blood rushing in my ears, drowning out any other noise. I forced myself to keep moving.

I cautiously made my way toward the front window overlooking the porch, adrenaline pumping rapidly through my veins. Outside lights were on across the street—safe—while my house remained dark and vulnerable. It confirmed my electricity had been deliberately cut.

I couldn't let fear overtake me—I had to keep going. I took a deep breath and raced back to my bedroom, slamming the door shut. I didn't bother locking the knob; it wouldn't have saved me if Todd was in the house. With shaky hands, I gripped the gun tightly, pointing it at the door. Every muscle was tense, ready to defend myself if it opened.

My phone sat beside me, urging me to call the police, but I couldn't bring myself to do it. By now, Robert had drilled into me that I needed evidence. What evidence would there be that Todd cut off my electricity? Instead, I called the utility company and reported the outage.

"Is anyone medically dependent on electricity?"

"No."

"Okay. Have you checked your electrical box?"

"No. It's outside."

"Check your main breaker and make sure it didn't trip. Do you want me to hold while you check?"

I couldn't. I physically couldn't. But I also couldn't tell her I was sitting in my house with a gun pointed at the door, ready to shoot anyone who entered.

"No. Thank you."

"After you check, if the problem isn't resolved, call us back and I'll put in a ticket for a repair crew."

I considered calling someone for help, but I couldn't. The thought of putting anyone in danger didn't sit well with me. At this point, I only trusted three people—Nathan, Lauren, and Robert. And I could tell Robert was growing weary of my constant complaints about Todd, especially when there was no concrete evidence to act on.

It must've been because of the cameras. If he can't see me, then he doesn't want me to see him coming for me. Oh God! This is it. This is how I'm going to die!

The gun was shaking uncontrollably now. Whether it was nerves or because I was holding it tight with one hand, I wasn't sure. My left thumb clumsily navigated to the app and clicked on the cameras. They were offline. I ran it back to the last recording. Nothing, no sign of anyone. But it was only a partial view—I couldn't see the electrical panel. I clicked on the camera on the front of the house, which Todd had pointed at my front door. I ran that footage back. Nothing.

Yep, the police will think I'm crazy if I call this in.

Minutes turned into hours as I remained in this tense position, my senses heightened for any sign of danger. And then I heard it.

A noise—maybe a door being forced open.

My blood ran cold. I held my breath. Then I recognized the sound: the ice maker dropping ice. I'd heard it a thousand times before, but at this moment, it sounded like an intruder. The fear that had been simmering inside me boiled over. Tears dripped from my chin. I tried to calm down, telling myself that it was just the ice maker, but the rational part of my brain was drowned out by the primal instinct to protect myself at all costs.

I stayed in bed, muscles tensed around the gun, ready to shoot. The darkness outside my window seemed to stretch on forever, amplifying every subtle house noise. My arms ached, and eventually I lowered my gun but kept it in my grip.

The night slowly faded into dawn, but terror still clung to me. Every creak in the house sent my heart racing. I knew Todd would come for me eventually, but when the sun rose, I clung to the hope that he wouldn't.

I reached for the bedroom door, forcing myself into the hallway. The air was thick with fear, but I pushed it aside and made my way to the living room window. Peering out, I saw the usual weekday morning scene—parents walking their children to the bus stop, cars passing by on their way to work.

People who would hear my scream.

For the first time in hours, I put the gun down. Before I did, I ejected the magazine and the chambered round. I remained ready to reload at a moment's notice. Heart pounding, I slowly opened the front door and stepped outside. I moved around to the side of the house. The electrical panel was open, and the main breaker was flipped off. My mind raced with panic—this was no coincidence. It was payback for changing the camera's password.

As soon as I saw it was nine o'clock, I called Robert. He confirmed what I already suspected: calling the police would be futile—they would simply dismiss it as a prank or lack of evidence. But it wasn't.

This was a calculated attack meant to strike fear into my core. And it worked.

CHAPTER
TWENTY-SIX

It was time for another trip to Chicago, and this time I boarded Winston at doggy daycare. As much as I looked forward to getting away from Todd, I knew I'd have to address the situation with James. I hoped Todd's poison hadn't seeped into the water cooler.

Nestled in my seat, I waited until the plane broke through the clouds to breathe a sigh of relief. I closed my eyes, determined to leave Todd and the drama behind.

I got a good night's sleep at the hotel and woke up the next morning to the hustle and bustle of the Windy City. James and I had planned to meet in the lobby for coffee, and I'd ride into the office with him instead of taking a car service. When I made it downstairs, I spotted him at a table with a frothy latte waiting for me. I couldn't look him in the eye, afraid he'd think I was a whore in plaid panties.

"Look, it's only a big deal if you make it a big deal." James sipped his coffee. "I found it hilarious. It's clear this guy is mental."

My shoulders dropped, grateful for James' disregard for Todd's comments. I wanted to ask if he'd told anyone, but I couldn't bring myself to do it. I kept my head down, blowing into my coffee.

As if reading my mind, James volunteered, "And don't worry. I didn't tell anyone at the office about it."

"Can you screenshot the texts and send them to me?"

"No, no can do. I deleted them, then blocked his number after I talked to you. I could tell you were really upset by it."

The evidence Robert needed was lost to the digital world—a world only Todd could access. Not me.

The ride to the office was awkward, but I survived it. I was happy to put the whole thing behind me and focus on work. Between meetings, I texted a colleague, Abby, about happy hour. I *really* needed social time where I didn't have to worry about Todd finding me. Not to mention, a stiff drink.

As the workday ended, Julie, the VP of Human Resources, stopped by my office. We had worked closely together during the mass layoffs, so I was glad to see her. But there was no small talk about the weather or how my trip was. Instead, Julie got straight to the point. She told me about a call she received.

"It was very strange, I admit, but it was someone claiming to have information about you."

My stomach dropped.

Based on her tone, I immediately knew it was Todd. She went into detail about the call, using words like "bizarre" and "creepy." Then she said after their conversation, she received screenshots of what appeared to be my personal text messages. The emphasis on "personal" made my mind wander to the messages James received.

Remain composed. This became my mantra as Julie spoke.

"He claims you've disclosed confidential financial information about our company that isn't available to the public. This has serious implications and could lead to an SEC complaint since we are a publicly traded company."

Remain composed.

I reminded Julie that the company had contracted Todd, and he had installed my home network. I explained that we'd briefly dated—if you could call it that—and that he was having difficulty moving on. "I have an attorney handling this for me, if you'd like to contact him."

Please, Julie, call Robert. Tell him what you told me. Share the screenshots with him. Please, please, please.

"That's okay, but if anything else gets reported the company will have to investigate the accusations." Julie was understanding and sympathetic, and we ended our conversation on a positive note.

I was livid—not just because Todd had contacted my employer and potentially jeopardized my job, but because Julie would have been a perfect witness. The images of my text messages would have been damning, since they were illegally obtained. But I couldn't ask her for them. I had to protect my only source of income.

I left the office, confirming with Abby our plans for happy hour later that evening. Over drinks, I confided in her about Todd. Her heart was in the right place, giving me all the advice I already knew—call the police, keep a log of incidents, destroy any electronics he touched. Of course, if I had unlimited funds, I could've done the latter, but I was already doing the first two, without success.

The next day, Abby approached me in the office. Her face had drained of color.

"Are you okay?" I asked.

She shook her head and turned her phone toward me. On the screen was a social media friend request from Todd.

There was no reason he should have known Abby even existed. He'd never been to Chicago, and I'd never mentioned her in his presence. Todd was supposed to be a thousand miles away, but now I questioned it. The escape I thought I had in Chicago was no escape at all. Like a caged animal, I learned there was nowhere to hide.

This time, Abby sent me a screenshot. But I didn't immediately send it to Robert. Instead, when I flew back home, I had my phone examined by the technician recommended by Nathan's tech. After the Chicago experience with Julie and Abby, I knew Todd was accessing my phone—I just needed proof.

When I handed my phone over, he connected it to a computer while I sat in a chair in the corner and waited.

"Would you look at that? You were right."

"Did you find something?" I jumped to my feet.

He pointed out a hidden app, took screenshots, and asked if I wanted it removed.

"Yes," I said without hesitation.

I immediately called Robert to tell him I had proof that Todd had been illegally accessing my phone via the app. I also sent him the screenshot from Abby's phone. I was certain I had Todd cornered.

He dismissed both.

"Your technician can't be considered a disinterested third party," he said apologetically. "The screenshots can prove there was spyware on your phone, but any good attorney could argue you installed it yourself."

When the technician removed the app, I never fully trusted that Todd's access was cut off for good. And I was right.

I found the numbers for every federal agency that came to mind. I filed online reports with the FBI, Department of Homeland Security, and FCC. I also called the sheriff's department non-emergency line. I was routed to an officer who didn't take a report—she only explained that I could file for a protective order at the courthouse if I felt threatened. With Robert insisting what I had wasn't enough for a protective order, I was like a hamster on a wheel, spinning in an endless loop of hopelessness.

I called Lauren and told her I'd filed reports with the agencies. Most of our conversations now centered around Todd's latest antics.

"Good, they have to do something about it. It's a violation of the law," she said emphatically. But they never did. I even called a local FBI field office to check the status of my report. The woman on the phone explained they had hundreds of thousands of reports and not enough resources to follow up on every single one. I was furious and became confrontational—only to have the call terminated before I could finish my sentence.

I called Lauren back, incredulous that the FBI had hung up on me. I was an American citizen and needed help. Didn't I deserve help?

"If what you're saying is true, law enforcement would absolutely respond because it's illegal to access someone's cameras, the GPS in their car, or to install spyware without consent," she replied.

The reality was, they just weren't concerned with my case. There was no abuse, assault, or homicide—just an unrelenting pest. I felt alone, desperate for someone to help me reclaim my life back. But only dead ends awaited.

I tried to pretend everything was normal, but it wasn't. I drove to doggy daycare to pick up Winston. Todd was at the counter. His calculating blue eyes bored into me with contempt. My breath caught. I noticed the puppy at his feet—one that could have been Winston's twin—the same caramel-colored fur, the same shape of nose and ears. Unbelievably creepy, calculated even, but not criminal. I watched as he filled out forms to enroll his dog.

I quickly got the owner's attention, and she brought Winston to me. I bolted out the door and into my car. Todd knew I took Winston to daycare every Monday and Thursday, so I changed the days in hopes of avoiding him.

The following Tuesday, Winston was full of energy, and I was stacked with conference calls. I made a last-minute decision to take him to daycare, hoping Todd wouldn't be there.

When I arrived, I waited nervously in the lobby with my excited puppy, eager to get to the play yard. Seeing Winston happy to be there always reassured me. I kept an eye on the front door, afraid Todd might show up with his dog. The owner came to the desk and was happy to see Winston, but she didn't look happy to see me.

"I'm sorry to tell you this, Kathryn, but we've had reports of possible abuse of Winston."

"What do you mean?" My face flushed.

"Todd says he has video footage of the alleged abuse, and he turned it over to the authorities."

"Wait, what?" I was stunned.

"I don't want to get into your personal stuff, but we have a strict policy to report any signs of abuse, so we have to be vigilant with Winston."

I felt sick. "I know you mean well, but you have to know I would never hurt Winston. Ever."

I considered not leaving Winston at daycare that day, but it'd make me look guilty. I decided it would be good for us. Let the owner observe him, see that there are no signs of abuse.

Todd was a sick bastard, and I was his target. Battle lines had been drawn. If I could be patient, I believed Todd would incriminate himself. *Go ahead,* I thought, *turn the footage of the alleged abuse you illegally obtained from my cameras over to the authorities.*

Time was my mental enemy but would become my judicial friend.

CHAPTER TWENTY-SEVEN

Instead of celebrating with friends and a birthday cake with candles, I sat on the sofa with a steaming bowl of ramen noodles. I grabbed my notebook and began making a list of every account I had so I could change my passwords. I wanted my life locked up tight—just like my house.

Happy birthday to me.

Whiskey dribbled down my chin as I shot it.

Happy birthday to me.

I poured myself another glass.

Happy birthday, dear me.

The whiskey sent warmth flooding from my head to my shoulders, down my limbs, all the way to my feet.

Happy birthday to me.

I placed some ice in a glass and poured myself more to sip on, but I ended up drinking it in just a few sips. Having become a recluse—a ghost—I was becoming way too familiar with how whiskey numbed the pain. Sometimes, swimming in the depths of a whiskey bottle was my only escape from the grief I felt over the life I was slowly losing to the monster Todd had proven himself to be.

With whiskey in my system, the anxiety was manageable, but I still felt the sting of nerves. The darkened house and the black, starless sky felt like bad omens. As I pulled on my pajamas, I grabbed the remote and put on a movie I'd seen a million times. I needed the familiar voices and swelling soundtrack to drown out the noises of the house. My nerves were so frayed that I jumped at every sound—the ice maker dropping ice, pipes quietly clanging, even Winston's breathing. Every noise I heard was Todd coming to get me.

I let the soft murmur of the movie soothe me as I pulled the covers back and slid beneath them. Thanks to the whiskey, my body relaxed. I turned onto my side, hugging a pillow. The light from the TV danced across the room. My eyes grew heavy, and eventually, I closed them. I took deep breaths, allowing sleep to take me away to a place where I could just be.

Moments later, Winston stood at the window, barking ferociously—his hackles raised, his teeth bared. Between barks, he let out low growls.

My heart pounding, I tossed the covers aside and fumbled for the gun I now hid beneath the spare pillow, since the electricity outage. I held the magazine with the hollow-point bullets in one hand and the firearm in the other. Thanks to Dad, I was quick enough to load the gun, chamber a bullet, and fire—all before an intruder could reach me. I drew a breath. I thought back to the shooting range, to the lessons my dad had taught me—steady yourself.

I clutched the gun at my side. Winston trailed me, pressing his small body against my leg with every step. I moved toward the back door of my house, trusting the shroud of darkness to conceal me. I pressed my back against the wall and craned my neck to peer out the backdoor window. I squinted.

A shadowy figure—stout, short, still.

My heart was a wrecking ball, my breath quickening. I pressed my nose against the glass. The figure came into focus. There, standing in the shadow of the old oak tree, was Todd. I slammed my back against the wall and froze. Had he seen me?

My fear shifted to a steady resolve. I wouldn't let Todd terrorize me—I wouldn't give him the satisfaction of thinking he'd scared me. I wanted him to know I wouldn't back down. My eyes narrowed as I watched him step out of the shadow, now illuminated faintly by the dim glow of the moon. I inhaled sharply as he came into focus.

The moonlight glinted off his belt buckle.

His pants were undone.

His stare was vacant.

His hands were buried in his pants.

He was panting.

Primal fear shot through my body, sending a jolt of ice up my spine. The terror was agonizing. I couldn't blink. I couldn't breathe. I couldn't move. My knees locked. My mind was blank.

I drew a sharp breath.

Feeling the cold steel of the gun against my hand, I forced myself to regain control. I took a slow breath, then another. I widened my stance.

Steady yourself.

I knew my safety was up to me and me alone. I backed away from the window and snapped into action. Winston in tow, I checked the four doors that led into the house, making sure they were locked. I raced back to the kitchen and once again pressed myself against the wall by the back door. Slowly, I reached to my right. My hand connected with the door jamb. I slid it along the wall until I found the switches that control the backyard lights. I placed one finger on the two switches, pressed them up with a click, and bolted into my bedroom.

I raised a single slat of the plantation shutter to peer out of the window as inconspicuously as possible. I craned my neck, scanning the yard, which was now as bright as it could be with the shadows of the trees. It was empty.

Where did he go?

My cell phone was still charging on the nightstand, so I disconnected the cord. I opened the app for the security cameras and pulled up the livestream. I couldn't see any movement on the cameras—certainly nothing that looked like a person. I tapped the phone icon to dial 911. But the conversation was already playing in my head:

What's your emergency? the operator would ask, with an even tone.

Oh, hello. A masturbating man resembling the guy you don't believe is stalking me was in my backyard.

Is he still here?

I don't think so.

Do you have evidence?

Well, no, but he was there.

I deleted the number and began reviewing the events in my mind. Shadows. A dark figure. The glint of metal. A vacant stare. Panting.

Am I losing my mind?

No—the image was burned into my brain. The shock made the memory vivid—indelible. It was him. He was there. He was the hunter. I was the prey.

I re-opened the livestream on the cameras and placed my phone on the nightstand. Still clutching my gun, I shuffled over to the bedroom door and locked it. I knew it wouldn't do much to keep him out if he managed to get inside, but it would buy me a few seconds—enough time to chamber a bullet, at least.

I sat on my bed, leaned against the headboard, and placed my gun on the nightstand. My heart was pounding so loudly that my body felt woozy, the dizziness clouding my vision. I didn't even notice tears streaming down my face until they tickled my nose, ran down my chin, and splattered onto my chest. I looked at my phone, the glow of camera feed shimmering in the lamplight. I tapped the app, rewinding the footage to see if the cameras caught anything. If they had, I'd have proof—and I could make a solid report to law enforcement.

The further back I went on the footage, the clearer it became that I wouldn't find the proof I desperately needed. Todd had installed two cameras in my backyard, and there were blind spots. He knew exactly where they were. When he pulled his car into the right-of-way and slithered into my backyard, he knew exactly where to stand, how to position himself, so the cameras wouldn't catch a thing—even with the yard illuminated.

I locked my cell phone and tossed it onto the bed, frustrated that the cameras had betrayed me by capturing nothing. My tears turned to heaving sobs. I felt like I'd lost my grip on reality. I closed my eyes and repeated to myself:

I know what I saw.
I know what I saw.
I know what I saw.
Happy birthday to me.

That night, I should have kept the curtains drawn or the blinds closed. But I couldn't. I spent hours moving from window to window, straining my eyes to see through the darkness. If he was out there, I needed to know. I had told him that I didn't want to see death coming. I was wrong. I *needed* to see it coming. Fear twisted inside me, coiling like a living thing as I spiraled into an obsession with being able to see out of my windows. My days were filled with dread; my nights were spent in sleepless terror, fully clothed, waiting in silent anticipation.

Focus. I needed to pull myself together. Since Todd might have access to my computer, I decided my belated birthday gift would be a new one. Thanks to a Back-to-School sale, I replaced both my laptop and desktop.

I navigated back to my list of accounts, locking each one down tight. It felt good to regain some control, but that wasn't all I was doing. I was pushing the recent events far from my mind, shoving them toward a cliff that led into a cavernous abyss. His actions were so vile, so beyond anything I'd ever experienced, that I desperately wanted to believe it wasn't real. Things like that only happened in creepy movies or in neighborhoods plagued by crime, to other people, not to me.

As the days passed, I settled into a steady routine—the only way to keep myself safe, keep the monster at bay. I'd wake for coffee and rack my brain for something to eat that wouldn't turn my stomach—I'd fail and forego breakfast. I'd lock and unlock doors as I made my way to the office. I'd immerse myself in work and end the day with whiskey, holding Winston close. His silky ears, my safe place. That's where I lived. Sunken eyes, chapped cheeks, jutting cheekbones. I was slowly losing myself. He dragged my name through mud all over town, making claims and accusations, calling my character into question. Anyone I was connected to on social media became a target for Todd's rumors. Some people were kind enough to check in, others unfriended me. It hurt to see how easily he was able to turn people against me—some I thought were friends.

What really stung was when people who avoided eye contact or made excuses not to talk to me at all.

People were witnessing what he was doing. Yet fear paralyzed them. No one was willing to stand with me. I was living the life of a victim—a recluse.

A woman hunted. A woman haunted.

CHAPTER
TWENTY-EIGHT

I was getting ready to head back to Chicago when Caleb's girlfriend's car had to go into the shop for repairs. I agreed she could use my car while I was out of town.

A couple of days later, I was working when my phone buzzed.

"Hi, Mom," Caleb said, his tone tense.

"Hi, honey," I replied. "What's going on?"

"Annie returned the car to your house today. She won't be using it anymore."

"Oh, good," I replied. "I'm glad she got her car back."

"No, it's not that," he said, his breath hastening. "Anytime she drove anywhere, Todd followed her. At first, she thought it was nothing, but it became too much to be a coincidence."

My breath caught.

"Mom, he followed her to a store, then started circling the parking lot while she was inside. She called me—she was so freaked out. She was petrified to leave the store with him there."

"Caleb, I—" I was too stunned to speak. Words jammed in my throat, a bottleneck of pain and panic.

"It's fine," he said, his tone flat. "We're just not going to use the car anymore. Honestly, I don't think you should either. That guy's a complete psychopath."

I managed to apologize before clicking off the call. He'd followed me before. I knew the panic—the feeling of blood rushing from my face, the tingling in my limbs, the racing heart. To think he'd put young Annie through that made me sick.

The rest of my Chicago trip was a blur. I was working, but my mind was elsewhere. I squeezed my eyes shut as I thought about everything, feeling anger boil in my chest, then evaporate into bursts of fear.

The day after I returned home, I took my car to the mechanic. They searched every inch of the interior and exterior and found no evidence of a tracking device. My guts remained twisted; my heart filled with fear. Of course, they wouldn't find a tracking device. He had set up the app for my car—that had to be how he was tracking it. I changed my password on the app, believing this would revoke his access.

I stretched, rolling back in my office chair, ready to go back inside after a long workday. It was a beautiful day outside, the temperature a perfect 81 degrees. I walked downstairs, poured myself a whiskey, and stepped outside, Winston skittering past me to do his business. Since the night of my birthday, I hated being outside on my patio. All I wanted was to sit outside with a glass of wine and read a book while Winston played in the grass. Instead, I was on high alert—bags under my eyes, chapped cheeks, sallow skin. As I traced the glass with my finger, a sound caught my attention.

Winston heard it, too. He turned toward the pond beyond the fence. My stomach twisted in knots. Up to this point, Todd had randomly appeared in my backyard, but he was careful to stay in the camera's blind spots so I wouldn't get video footage. His appearances were erratic, cautious not to create a discernible pattern. But none of that mattered now. He was here, and I wasn't inside peeking out the window. I was outside, separated from him by just a three-foot picket fence.

Breathe.

I sat up straight, my phone on the table next to my sweating glass. Our eyes locked. Todd seemed shocked that I was sitting there calmly. I had no firearm ready to shoot, but I had an ironclad determination to show him I wasn't afraid—even if I was trembling inside.

Winston's bark pierced the silence.

Todd raised his eyebrows. "If I wanted to hurt you, I would do it right now." His voice was flat, barren.

"Winston!" I said, rising from my chair, walking backward toward the door, keeping my eyes trained on Todd until I was over the threshold, Winston in tow.

I called the sheriff's department, but Todd was gone before they arrived. The deputies stood in my kitchen, their faces blank as they looked over my shoulder at the video footage of me on the patio and the moment I heard Todd's voice. He'd stayed perfectly out of view of the cameras, once again. Since Todd wasn't on camera and there was no audio, they claimed there was nothing they could do.

The glass of whiskey remained on the table for days before I finally went out back to retrieve it. As for Winston, I'd put him on a leash and take him out to the front yard—no matter how many times Todd circled my house in his truck. If his intent was to harm me, he'd have to do it in plain sight.

I was determined not to let Todd get to me. This was my life, and I was going to live it. I resumed my routine around town—ignoring Todd as I went, refusing to speed up when he followed, averting my eyes, escaping to somewhere—anywhere—in my mind. As he followed, circled my house, or showed up anywhere I was, I recorded the exact date, time, and incident. I was building my case, just as Robert had advised.

I had a little extra money and knew I could afford an older model car to run the pup around in—plus, it would be a vehicle untouched and untainted by Todd. For years, I'd talked about getting a VW Bug convertible as a second vehicle, and I came across a good deal on a manual shift. I bought it on the spot and drove home with the top down, my hair swirling in the breeze.

Not long after, as I was driving Winston home from doggy daycare, I stopped at the stop sign outside my neighborhood. A vehicle turned right off my street. I squinted my eyes. It was Todd, but he wasn't in his truck. To my horror, he'd purchased a VW Bug convertible.

Same make.

Same model.

Different color.

There he was, the top down, his hat tipped on his head—his dog, Winston's twin, in the passenger seat. It wasn't just the vehicle or the dog that made me uneasy; it was also the fact that he was coming out of my neighborhood.

What was he doing there? Showing off?

Pulling into my driveway, I decided I wasn't going to stay home and wait for Todd to start circling the house. Instead, I'd run out and get some groceries.

I rolled my cart from aisle to aisle, instrumental music playing on the speakers. I grabbed fresh vegetables, tossed boxes and cans into the cart, and made my way to the dairy section. I felt exposed. Todd had proven he could maneuver around the law, evading critical evidence, like being caught on camera. The thought of an unseen death swirled in my head. With every step, I kept glancing over my shoulder. Every squeak of a sneaker, jostling of a cart, or burst of chatter made me leap out of my skin.

Breathe.

Pay.

Get into your car.

Drive home.

Once I paid, I rolled my cart to the parking lot and double-clicked my remote to unlock the car, just as I had so many times before. I popped the trunk before I reached the car so I could quickly place the bags inside. A movement caught my eye. Todd had come out from between two vehicles and slithered into my passenger seat.

Breathe.

Desperate to show him I wasn't afraid, I held my head high. With one eye on Todd in the front seat, I put my groceries in the trunk and rolled my cart back into the store. My heart pounding, I walked to customer service and waved the manager over.

"Hi there. A man entered my vehicle in the parking lot. I need someone to help me get him out."

His eyes widened. "Okay, let me walk you out there."

With the manager at my elbow, I felt a fleeting sense of safety. We approached my car, and he knocked on the window. Todd cracked the door.

"Sir, this woman says you've entered her vehicle without permission. I need you to exit the car."

Todd rolled his eyes, shook his head—his demeanor casual. "I'm not looking to make trouble." He pulled out his phone and held it up to the manager. "See? Here's a photo of us together. We just had an argument. She's being dramatic."

The store manager turned to me, shaking his head. "This seems like something I shouldn't get involved in. If you feel unsafe, call the police." He then turned and walked back inside, leaving me alone.

I stood next to my car and refused to get in. Todd stayed in place.

"I just want to talk," he said.

I hadn't uttered a single word to Todd since he took Winston and refused to give him back. I clenched my jaw.

"I just want to talk," he repeated.

"Okay," I muttered.

My feigned compliance worked.

He got out of the car, and as soon as he closed the door, I locked it with my remote. He was on the passenger side, and I was on the driver's side, next to the backseat.

He narrowed his eyes, his fists curled, then drew a breath and hissed,

"You are mine." He licked his lips like a predator saving the scent of blood. "And I don't share."

In an instant, I clicked the remote once to unlock the driver's door, jumped in as quickly as I could, and locked the door behind me. I started the car and drove off, not caring if I ran over him. I watched him in the rearview mirror as I left the parking lot. He stood there, stalk still in the space I'd just pulled out of.

Safely home, with all the doors locked and windows secured, I sat at the kitchen table, adding to my record of incidents involving Todd since the first no-contact letter was issued. The entries were single spaced, spilling over two pages—terrifying, considering there were days I hadn't left my house or was in Chicago.

I stared at Todd's relentless campaign to stalk me. In sixty days, I had recorded thirty-one incidents: seven separate times he circled my house (that I was aware of); twelve encounters in public places, including the most recent grocery store incident; four missed calls along with one voicemail, saved for evidence; and three people he had contacted in my life, despite their not wanting to "get involved." Unsavory rumors continued to spread throughout my small community, and I knew they'd made their way to Pastor Nick. I'd already received a voicemail from him, too.

Then there were the six sightings in my backyard, but I only listed five. I was hesitant—embarrassed, even—and didn't know how to put into words what he had done in a place where I had the right to feel safe.

My eyes drifted to the backyard as I considered adding it to the incident log. But Robert was right. There was no concrete evidence that it actually happened, so why trigger myself by recounting this moment?

It's better for me if I don't, I reasoned. I continued reviewing my incident log. *How many times has he been in my backyard or circling my house that I don't know about?*

Frustration bubbled beneath the surface. It was painfully clear that I lacked the solid evidence I needed. Proving stalking against someone as slick and cunning as Todd was going to be no walk in the park, but I was past caring. I was done with feeling helpless. I was ready to roll the dice, even if the odds weren't in my favor. Maybe, just maybe, I'll encounter a police officer who can see beyond the missing evidence and pluck me from this endless cycle.

If stalking was defined as a pattern of behavior, I was certain this fit the criteria.

CHAPTER
TWENTY-NINE

School zones were now in effect, so I slowed down as I passed the elementary school. I decided it was time to take my case to the police. Robert's constant dismissals—telling me I lacked evidence—had pushed me to the edge. I was done listening to him.

Enough was enough. I crossed the parking lot of the sheriff's department, sweat beading on my brow from the oppressive heat and suffocating humidity, each step fueled by determination. I sat in an uncomfortable chair, shifting my weight with a cup of water propped on the table in front of me. I'd been given a form to fill out, detailing the reason I was seeking help. In my lap was the log of incidents I'd had with Todd, along with Robert's three no-contact letters. Finally, the door opened with a creak. The smell of aftershave preceded the officer as he entered the room. He placed a laptop on the table and sat down across from me.

"I'm Deputy Kincade. I hear you've had some trouble with someone stalking you?"

He read over the form I filled out as I spoke.

"Yes." I placed the log on the table and slid it toward him. "I've been tracking every incident since my attorney issued a no-contact letter. It's gotten out of hand, I—"

"I'm sorry to cut you off." He glanced at the log and then pushed it back to me. "There's nothing we can do about this. No crime has been committed."

"What do you mean?" Anger permeated every syllable as it left my mouth. I had done what everyone advised—keep a log of all incidents, record dates, times, locations, and brief descriptions—only to be refused the help I so desperately needed. I showed him pictures I had taken of Todd circling in front of my house, including his license plate, as I feverishly tried to relay my situation.

"And this photo? I took it from my rearview mirror to show him following me. I can show you on my phone the date stamps—these were all taken on different days."

He explained that a defense lawyer could easily argue Todd was visiting a friend in my neighborhood or that he had loaned his car to someone, since the photographs didn't clearly show the driver's face. Todd had the same right as I did to drive down the road and go to public places—maybe he was fueling at the same gas station, maybe he was eating at the same restaurant, or grocery shopping at the same store.

"These run-ins could be anything."

I gritted my teeth. "One is a coincidence, two, maybe even three. But this many? It's a pattern. And stalking is defined as a pattern—"

"Even if some of them were intentional, he never harmed you, correct?"

"That's what I'm trying to prevent. There's a police report I filed about ten months ago." I hung my head in shame. I should've heeded the officer's advice at the time and severed all contact with Todd.

He tapped on his laptop, then rested his elbow on the table while he read.

"Okay. I've reviewed the report, and I see no charges were filed. It appears to be a domestic dispute related to destruction of personal property. Is this the report you're talking about?"

I couldn't tell him it was an attempted kidnapping, but I withheld that information because I was scared. I couldn't reveal that the night was about more than just a broken cell phone. I only nodded.

"What was or is your relationship with Mr. Bennett?"

"I met him through a friend two years ago, next month to be exact. Four months later, we started casually dating. It only lasted about five months. We broke up three months before that police report was filed." I nodded toward his laptop.

"That report is almost a year old. That's a long time for this to be going on."

"It's complicated," I wanted to say. How could I ever explain that I kept in contact because it was the only way to make him stop? That appeasing him was the only thing that worked?

"You can seek a protective order. If he violates it, that's a crime. But even that requires more than what you have here."

He wasn't seeing the bigger, criminal picture unless there was physical harm—the very thing I desperately wanted to avoid. I felt deflated. Todd had stolen my freedom, my liberty. How was that not a crime?

I propped my elbow on the driver's door as I navigated home, running my hand through my hair. Todd was a fixture at the police department. While he wasn't wearing a uniform or flashing a badge, he was very much part of that close-knit brotherhood—the kind that runs deeper than blood. The ties that bind them are woven from courage and sacrifice, with each member ready to lay it all on the line every time they clock in. But Todd? Danger wasn't part of his job description. Nope—he was the guy in the back, eyes glued to a computer screen, fingers dancing over the keyboard.

It was Todd's technical wizardry that earned him the respect of those street-hardened officers. They counted on him, leaned on him, to piece together the evidence they needed—unearthing data, resurrecting deleted files, even using facial recognition to identify suspects, sometimes even when the image looked like it was shot through a foggy window. In their eyes, Todd was a hero—albeit of a different kind—wielding a mouse instead of a gun.

I thought more about what the officer said. He was right. What I had was a log of incidents that, when considered separately, weren't criminal. It wasn't a crime to buy a dog or a VW Bug convertible. But stalking is a pattern, and this officer couldn't—or wouldn't—see it.

I just needed proof.

Thinking about the cameras installed at my house, I contacted an audio-visual company and asked them to rewire my system. It would be a bonus if they could also confirm whether Todd was accessing them. Days later, as the technician examined my house—wires and small tools hanging from his belt—he furrowed his eyebrows, turned to me, and asked, "How many cameras do you think you have?"

My heart sank into a pit of dread. "Four," I managed to choke out.

He shook his head and held up six fingers.

"Where are the other two cameras?" I demanded, my voice rising with desperation.

He explained that he traced the cables but couldn't say where the additional cameras might have been installed—the wires had been cut. It made me sick to think about where they might have been. He offered to rip out the entire system and reinstall it, which would cost thousands of dollars. My savings were already running thin, so I asked if there was another solution—some way to change things so Todd could no longer access my system.

"I'll install a new DVR, but there are no guarantees he won't still have access," he said, eyes sympathetic. "If he installed your network, he could have put in a back door."

The possibility of unknown access to my system left me feeling exposed.

That evening, I sat at the bar at Café Calais with Nathan, swirling my glass of wine. "I can't stop thinking about where those other cameras could have been." I dabbed at my eyes to keep tears from spilling over.

Nathan patted my back gently. "This is scary stuff, kiddo." He shook his head in disbelief. "You need to rip them out."

I nodded. "It's a double-edged sword. I know Todd can see me—I can feel it. But I need *them* to catch *him*. Which is worse? Ripping out the cameras so I have no evidence, or leaving them up and assuming the risk?"

Brandi, working behind the bar, placed our glasses in front of us. "Excuse me?" She leaned in, her voice lowered. "I'm sorry to interrupt, but I heard you talking about Todd and your cameras." She gestured toward a camera in the corner of the room. "He just installed our system, too."

I felt sick. I stared directly into the camera overlooking the bar. Todd knew this was where I met my friends on Wednesdays for happy hour. I tentatively brought my glass of wine to my lips, trying to calm my racing mind. I was already overwhelmed by the thought of two hidden cameras in my house, and now this?

Despite the urge to leave, I stayed and tried to enjoy my evening with Nathan. If Todd was watching me, I was going to show him that I wouldn't cower. I looked at Nathan, the restaurant's soft lighting dancing in his kind eyes. I felt safe with him and chose to push the bartender's comments out of my head. I took another sip of wine, letting the warmth relax me. I changed the subject and let the evening carry me along gently.

For a moment, I felt a flicker of normalcy.

As Brandi delivered another round of drinks, I spotted John, an acquaintance, walking out of the main dining area with his girlfriend. I'd seen on social media that they were recently engaged.

"Congratulations, you two. Have you set a date?"

"Thanks, Kathryn. We're planning a spring wedding next year." The lack of a smile immediately concerned me. "I have to say, though, I know Todd. He reached out to me. I'm sorry to tell you this, but—"

"I'm sure it's not true, but oh my God!" Shelly added, her enthusiasm betraying how tipsy she was. She went on to vomit every morsel of gossip Todd had spread about me in front of Nathan. And she didn't hold back—about my supposedly overactive sex life with random men, my infested vagina, and the vile things Todd claimed I allegedly asked him to do in the bedroom. Of course, Todd insisted he refused and broke up with me over my "abhorrent sexual behavior."

I pasted a smile on my face and nodded, pretending this was all old news. But beneath the surface, I was seething with anger and humiliation. Nathan was hearing things he shouldn't about me. Worse, I worried these rumors might reach my kids.

"Is there any possible way you'd sign an affidavit attesting to what Todd told you?" I'd grown used to people not wanting to get involved, but perhaps this time would be different.

"I'm sorry, Kathryn, but we can't. I just thought you should know."

Days later, I logged into social media. I'd been avoiding it, but was curious. I typed in John's name and wasn't surprised to see the "add friend" button. My shoulders sagged as I sighed. It felt like everyone but Nathan and Lauren was jumping ship. And I was sinking. Todd was making sure of that.

With the sting of the hidden cameras still fresh, my mind raced. I was a rat in a maze with all exits sealed. I clawed desperately—digging, scraping, scratching—for a way out. I needed to regain my footing. For hours, I searched online for any help available. Websites about stalking kept emphasizing that documenting events and timelines was crucial. But I was already doing that—and still, nobody was listening. With my phone, I had taken pictures of Todd's car following me, videos of him circling the house, but law enforcement officers I spoke with said the driver was not identifiable in the photo.

Dead end.

I called hotlines and victim resources, only to hear the same generic advice: "Keeping a log of activity is key to establishing stalking as a pattern of behavior."

Dead end.

Each time I failed to obtain help, I sank into a lower state of depression. I went back to my house. It was no longer the sweet, loving place that I raised my boys in. It was a prison. I'd sit on my couch, my legs crossed beneath me, and stare at the particles of dust that waltzed in the air. Every sound made me jump, sending me into panic attacks so intense that the room swirled, my throat closed, and I ended up in a heap on the floor, certain I was about to die.

After yet another backyard incident, I no longer recognized myself—I was a zombie, a shell of a person. I'd once had a beautiful life, vibrant and luminous like stained glass with dreamy light streaming through. Now, I was living a monochrome nightmare. I found it hard to get out of bed, much less bathe. The fear oscillated between debilitating and energizing, leading me to develop an obsessive-compulsive disorder. I had a certain cadence of checking my locks, checking for Todd in the backyard, and watching to see if he was circling out front like a shark. I performed rituals —rinse and repeat—trying to regain control.

My days alternated between work, binge-watching TV with Winston at my side, and obsessively cleaning the house. I scrubbed the tiles with fury, unleashing my anger on the surfaces. When my boys visited, I cleaned every surface they touched. Not because I wanted the house to shine, but because I needed clean surfaces to hold any forensic evidence Todd might leave behind if he came to kill me.

The dead woman—it was no accident.

I wrote instructions on how to access the video recordings from the cameras and placed them next to the computer that feeds them. Beneath the instructions, I handwrote a note stating: *I would never harm myself*, in case Todd tried to make it look like a suicide.

No accident, indeed.

For many restless, fear-filled nights, I slept in jeans and a shirt, with socks and shoes on, ready to bolt at any moment. My pistol lay under the spare pillow, the magazine chambered to fire in a split second. I'd wonder whether I'd shoot Todd or myself if he broke into my house. Would I take another's life to save my own, or would I choose to end my life before he could?

In my gut, I knew this nightmare wouldn't end until one of us was dead. And I was determined it wouldn't be me.

CHAPTER
THIRTY

Exhausted, I decided I needed to get away, so I went to visit my parents. After a quick 'hello' to them, I walked into my childhood room and dropped my bag on the bed. I sat on the mattress and looked around. Reminders of my innocence stared back at me.

Where did I go?

I needed to hit the pause button on the life I saw spiraling out of control into an inky abyss. I needed clarity. I needed to think and formulate a plan to get past this.

How did he go from the charming, charismatic man who so eagerly wanted to date me to a masturbating madman in my backyard? I sat staring in disbelief, clutching one of my most cherished childhood possessions—a teddy bear from my childhood.

My phone pinged, and I fished it out of my bag. It was a text from a friend—a picture of him standing next to Todd at a restaurant near my house, both smiling wide. Below it was the phrase, "interesting conversation." I felt sick. He was yet another casualty of the war I was fighting. I wanted to throw the phone and shatter it into a million pieces, to tear down the house, the trees beyond, and destroy the earth.

This was the moment I hit bottom. I finally broke.

Curling up into a ball on the bed, I sobbed, crying for myself, for the part of me that was dead and gone, for the part of me that would remain if this ever ended. Would I even recognize myself?

I wiped the tears from my eyes and shuffled into the living room.

"What's wrong?" Dad asked.

Mom looked up, her head tilted.

I sat down on the couch and brushed tears from my cheeks as I started telling them what was going on with Todd. I deliberately left out the incident the night of my birthday. I told them about the rumors, the contact with everyone I'd ever known, the circling of the house, the cameras—everything. When I finished, my breath caught as I rubbed at my bright red eyes.

My dad leaned forward in his chair. "Well, that's too bad."

"Yes," Mom agreed. "What a mess."

Without another word, I stood and walked into the kitchen. They didn't understand the hell Todd had put me through for two years now. I poured myself a whiskey, shot it, then poured another and shot that one, too. I drank—a lot. I let the burn of the alcohol anesthetize my pain as I hid the bottle and walked into my room. The darkness clung to me like a shroud, suffocating me. I lay in bed for hours, my body numb from lying motionless, unable to escape my thoughts. I had reached the edge of the cliff, and all that lay before me was an inky abyss—seemingly endless and unfathomable.

I picked up the glass of whiskey, swirling the amber liquid before bringing it to my lips. As I took a sip, I couldn't help but wonder if this would be the last time I ever tasted it.

I wondered if ending it all—on my terms—would bring me the peace I longed for. An image of the life that once filled me with joy crossed my mind. I thought of my children and my parents in the next room, then quickly dismissed the thought. As I fell asleep, I dreamt of a death I wouldn't see coming, carrying me away. It was the only sure route to ending this nightmare.

The next morning, I was nursing a hangover, horrified that the thought of suicide had even crossed my mind. I'd never contemplated it before, but I felt like the whole world was conspiring against me, and it was the only way out. Hitting rock bottom was the rocket fuel I needed. I found a new sense of empowerment—a fire lit inside me, fueled by fury. My mission was to seek justice. To expose Todd as the stalker he was. To protect others from this monster of a man.

With my new resolve, I set my sights on the very thing Robert and the police said I needed: evidence. Although I had my log of dates, times, locations, and witnesses, it was useless on its own. What I needed was something concrete. Indisputable. Irrefutable.

I remembered a former co-worker of mine, Brad, who had left the company to start a private investigation firm. I sent him a message asking for help. He was quick to reply, explaining that this wasn't the kind of investigation work he usually did, but he agreed to meet me for lunch to see if we could come up with a solution.

That day, we sat at a table at a local brewhouse—I don't typically drink beer, so it wasn't a place I usually visited. I had my incident log in front of me, sharing every detail except what happened the night of my birthday. Words caught in my throat as Todd walked through the door and slid into a chair at a nearby table.

"Is that him?" Brad glanced at me, concern etched on his face, sensing my discomfort.

I nodded.

Todd was alone. He sat with his back to us, talking loudly. "You should know, man. She's a whore."

Brad and I locked eyes. I looked like a portrait of fear and desperation as he scanned my face.

"I'm telling you, she's nasty. You don't want to touch her because you'll catch something."

I looked down at the table, ready to burst into tears, but not wanting to give Todd the satisfaction. Instead, I leaned toward Brad and whispered pleadingly, "I have one chance to get this right. If I don't, I'm certain I'll end up dead."

"Do you really believe that?" His eyes widened as he whispered the words.

"I do."

Brad tossed cash onto the table and walked me outside. As we stood on the rutted asphalt, the October air rustling my hair, he placed a hand on my shoulder. "I'm going to help you."

My knees went weak. At that moment, those were the five most precious words I needed to hear. Without thinking, I threw my arms around him and sobbed uncontrollably.

Later that day, as I worked at my desk, my phone rang. It was Brad. He said he had run a criminal history check on Todd and read the list of previous arrests, which spanned three different states, all involving domestic violence, abuse, and breaking and entering.

"How did he get a job working at the police department with that kind of history?"

"It's a small department—low budget. Their background checks might only pick up convictions. If that's what they did, I don't see any convictions here."

"Can you send me what you have?"

"Sure, I'll email it over to you."

"Wait. Don't." I gave him Nathan's email address, then called him. Within half an hour, we met at a gas station. I felt ridiculous topping off my tank—it was nearly full. Nathan pulled up on the other side of the pump and passed the printed copy through the driver's window.

"I read through it, kiddo. You need to get as far away from him as you can."

As soon as I got home, I contacted the courthouses where Todd's arrests took place and requested all publicly available documents. After paying the fee, they emailed them to me. I sat in the soft glow of my computer screen, wide-eyed, scrolling through page after page. The similarities between these cases and mine were uncanny—like reading a stalker's playbook.

It turned out Todd had been arrested for an altercation with a woman he'd been dating, and broke her phone when she tried to call the police. In another case, he'd been harassing a woman he'd been seeing and was arrested for breaking into her house. The narrative was chilling:

> *... victim arrived home one evening to find the defendant in her house ...*

After reading this, I knew I would never feel safe in my home again. The vivid details in the police report replayed mercilessly in my mind, especially at night before bed. And then there was the chilling memory of seeing him lurking in my backyard—a predator waiting to strike. I couldn't shake the fear that he would break into my house and find me defenseless in my bedroom. If Caleb or Dylan weren't spending the night, I would gather my pillow and gun and retreat upstairs, knowing I had to stay one step ahead to give myself a fighting chance.

Although I'd always preferred to fall asleep with the television on, since the night of my birthday, I'd stopped. I needed to hear every noise in the house, especially after reading Todd's previous police reports. For the same reason, I quit taking showers. The rushing water made me feel vulnerable, so I took baths, with a gun on the sink, within easy reach.

In the days that followed, Brad and I made a plan. He tasked me with arranging dinner with a male friend at Oskar's to see if he could catch Todd in action. It made sense to ask Ryan, whose wife Todd had contacted.

"I don't want to get involved with this," he said. I couldn't blame him. He had his own family to protect.

I then asked my neighbor, Patrick, and he agreed. But he didn't exactly know what he was agreeing to. Brad had warned me against explaining the situation, emphasizing that we needed to behave naturally. Anything less would diminish the value of the evidence.

Leading up to dinner, I was a nervous wreck—drinking was the only way I could quiet the "what ifs" that haunted my mind. An overthinking problem that I've had since childhood.

What if I incur this expense and Todd doesn't show up? After all, it was a lot of money upfront, and my savings were growing thin.

What if Brad, like law enforcement, thinks I'm just a crazy person?

What if I really am?

Arriving early, I sat at the bar and ordered a drink to help calm my nerves. A few sips in, Patrick appeared. I motioned him over, and he joined me in a glass of wine. He asked if I wanted a table, but I shook my head. Sitting at the bar offered better visibility.

We enjoyed casual conversation before ordering dinner, but I couldn't concentrate, no matter how hard I tried to play it cool. With my back to the door, I didn't know Todd had walked in until I heard his voice.

"Whore." Todd hissed, then disappeared into the bathroom.

"Did you hear that guy?" Patrick asked.

"Yes." I felt a flush of embarrassment. Patrick was upset, but I put my hand on his arm. "Ignore him."

Todd emerged from the bathroom. "Stupid bitch," he said as he walked past us again. When he did, I spun around on my barstool, glaring at him. A man at a nearby table caught my eye—I recognized him as one of Brad's investigators.

Brad had explained that since Todd had seen us together, he wouldn't be with me tonight. If Todd recognized him, he might figure out what we were up to.

"He's smart. We'll be smarter."

Brad advised me to ignore Todd if he showed up, but I couldn't. I nervously glanced over my shoulder—his back was to us. What was he doing? Was he just going to stand there all night?

Patrick was talking about the vacation he was planning. "Would you mind getting my mail while I'm out of town?"

I nodded, then looked back at the investigator. He shook his head, so I turned my attention back to Patrick. When I looked over my shoulder again, Todd was gone.

Patrick and I finished dinner without further incident. He was kind enough to walk me to my car. Alone in the quiet of the vehicle, the gentle hum of the engine calmed my nerves. I drove the familiar route home. In my rearview mirror, I saw the investigator following me.

Normally, an incident like this would send my mind into chaos—fear, anger, frustration, and anxiety blending into a cocktail of debilitating madness. But not tonight. This was a win. We caught Todd in action. I hope.

CHAPTER
THIRTY-ONE

Once safely inside my house, I called Brad. He told me the other investigator was still watching Todd.

"Okay, can you tell me what you got from the dinner with Patrick?"

Brad explained that he filmed Todd arriving at the restaurant after I had settled in at the bar. Todd walked up to one side of the restaurant and managed to wedge himself between some bushes to peer through the window. My throat tightened as I imagined his face pressed against the glass.

Todd then returned to his vehicle, sitting with the door open and fiddling with his phone. Suddenly, he got out, locked his vehicle, and walked inside. The other investigator was already inside and filmed Todd walking past Patrick and me, but was too far away to get any audio of the comments he made. Apparently, Todd met a woman whom he greeted overly romantically—almost as if he were putting on a show—before heading to another restaurant.

I grimaced. The evidence would show Todd had done nothing more than go to the bathroom, and once he saw me there, he left. The police would never see it as stalking. Brad agreed. He felt strongly that I needed more proof to strengthen my case. Given the issues I'd previously experienced with Todd at the grocery store, Brad and I decided that would be our next move.

∼

Visions of Todd standing outside the restaurant, looking in, kept running through my mind. How many times had he done that? What could his defense possibly be for peeping into a restaurant? I didn't understand why it wasn't enough; why I had to go through this all over again. But I was grateful to have Brad's help. I trusted him.

I was in my routine of wiping down surfaces when Dylan came home. He startled me because I wasn't expecting him.

"Sorry to scare you, Mom. I just thought I'd stop by and see what you're gonna do for dinner later?"

"I ate a late lunch, so I doubt I'll be hungry. Sorry about that, sweetheart." I knew he didn't understand, but I wasn't about to subject him to Todd peering into a restaurant window at us.

"Okay, well, I was actually going to ask if you wanted to drop me off for basic training?"

I'd completely forgotten that he was leaving in a few days, but I wanted to play it cool. "I was going to ask if I could. Of course, I'll take you." I didn't bother asking if Mark was coming with us—the tension between us was still high from his call the night the boys tried to get Winston back.

We chatted a bit longer, but I was on edge with Dylan at the house. I was anxious for him to go to Mark's, when I should've been cherishing every minute with him before he left.

"I'm starving, so I'm going to head over to Dad's."

The moment he walked out the door, I grabbed a disinfectant wipe and meticulously cleaned every surface his fingers had grazed—the doorknob, the kitchen counter, even the back of the chair he briefly leaned against. My chest tightened with each swipe. Guilt gnawed at me, a heavy weight pressing down on my conscience. What kind of mother was I to be so consumed by fear? I agonized over the possibility that Dylan might see my actions as indifference, when in truth, my love for him and Caleb overshadowed everything else.

The next day brought a cool front. Fall temperatures carried a slight breeze, the first sign of relief from the summer heat. I thought about calling Brad to delay the grocery store outing, since I'd forgotten the date Dylan was to report for basic training. It was Sunday and we'd planned to do the store tomorrow afternoon. Dylan was leaving on Tuesday, so I decided not to cancel with Brad.

On Monday morning, I received an email from Todd.

Instead of reading it, I pressed 'print.' The printer groaned on and on. Seven pages came out—seven pages I didn't have the stomach to read.

I walked down to Patrick's house as though I were taking an afternoon stroll, thankful to see him working in his garage.

"Hey, neighbor," I said in my most friendly, cheery voice.

"Hi, Kathryn."

"What're you up to?"

"I'm just tinkering. The line is caught in the weed eater."

"I see that. Looks ugly."

"That's what I get for using thin string on thick weeds." He reached for a screwdriver.

"Would you mind if I borrow your phone?" I held up my old, broken phone. "Mine fell down the stairs."

"Talk about ugly. Sure, you can use mine."

Brad had suggested I memorize his number in case anything happened. I was grateful for the advice as I dialed his number.

"Tanglewilde Investigative Services."

"Brad? It's Kathryn," I turned my back to Patrick and lowered my voice. "I'm calling from a neighbor's phone. I just received a seven-page email from that guy."

"What did it say?"

"Dunno. I don't have the stomach to read it."

"I'm not far from your house. I've got another investigator with me. I'll swing by and take a look at it. Things might be escalating. Do me a favor—cover your cameras with sticky notes so he can't identify me."

"I don't think I can reach them."

"Okay, open your garage door as soon as we arrive and close it right after we pull in. If he sees us on camera, it'll be impossible for us to follow him later without being recognized."

"Thanks so much. I'll see you in a bit."

I handed the phone back. Patrick looked up "Everything okay?"

"Yeah." I made small talk with him before saying I needed to get back home.

It wasn't long before Brad and his partner arrived—the man who'd been inside the restaurant with me. Brad looked ridiculous. He wore a bandana under a baseball cap to hide his hair color and sunglasses. He covered the cameras with sticky notes while his partner set up a noise machine to obscure our conversation in case Todd had a listening device inside the house.

We sat at my formal dining table near a large bay window overlooking the street. Within ten minutes, Todd began circling the house. I suspected he was investigating because he couldn't see the camera footage anymore.

Brad read the email while the other investigator started filming. I was glad they were here. "I can't believe this guy. At least he's gone now, what, twenty minutes later?"

I shook my head. "He's not gone. He's going to my backyard." Usually, whenever Todd circled the house, he went to the backyard. I hoped this time was no different.

Brad grabbed the video camera, put his cap and sunglasses back on, and bolted out the back door.

"Stay here, Ms. Caraway," the other investigator instructed. He stood at the door, watching Brad's back. I stood behind him, looking over his shoulder. We watched Brad walk quickly toward the fence. The camera and his attention were focused on the left, toward the entrance to the right-of-way.

My phone rang. I looked down and saw it was Dylan. "Hello?"

"Hi, Mom. Just wanted you to know I'm almost there. I didn't want to scare you again."

"Great, I—"

In a sudden motion, Brad sprinted back into the house. "Open the garage!" He looked at the other investigator and pointed at me. "Stay with her."

My jaw dropped, but I could hear Dylan talking. "Wait. What's going on?"

"I—"

"Mom! Todd was in an accident. He hit someone. I'm at the stop sign around the corner, by the right-of-way."

I pulled the phone away from my mouth and I called out to Brad. "My son is there. Todd hit a car."

Before Brad could answer, Dylan was already talking. "I got a picture of him. I'll be there in a second."

Dylan and I hung up and I turned to the investigators. "My son got a photo of Todd's accident. He'll be here any minute. What happened, Brad?"

"When I got close to the fence line, Todd was sitting in his vehicle slowly rolling toward your house. As soon as he saw me, he reversed and hit the gas. That's when he hit a car. I got the whole thing on camera, but I don't know how well you can see Todd's face."

Dylan burst through the door, his phone extended and the photo on the screen. Brad was the first to see it. Dylan swiped, and another photo appeared. It showed Todd's vehicle in relation to the entrance to the right-of-way, with my picket fence and the house in the shot. Todd would never be able to explain this.

Brad nodded his head. "That photo has everything you need. It clearly shows Todd's face, his license plate, and the entrance to the right-of-way. When you put these pics with my video footage, along with what we got the other night, I think you have enough."

I have evidence. The thing I've needed but couldn't get. I wanted to be excited about it, but I was afraid to trust it. I couldn't help but feel skeptical.

I called Robert on the speakerphone and introduced him to Brad. Robert was surprised I'd hired a private investigator, but once Brad explained what had happened, he was glad. "It sounds like we have the evidence to get law enforcement to listen. At minimum, we have enough for a protective order."

Incredible! I couldn't help but feel skeptical.

After hanging up with Robert, Brad turned to me. "Let me get back to the office and type up a report." He looked to the other investigator. "You download the footage and save what we got today and from the other night. How many copies do you think you need, Kathryn?"

I cocked my head in contemplation. "Let me have three."

"Okay. I'll text you the code—one, two, three, four—when I'm on my way to the sheriff's department."

Hours later, Brad and his partner met me at the station. We sat at the large oak table where I'd felt the sting of disappointment when I tried to get the police to listen to me before. When the officer entered the room, I remained composed and tried to be factual rather than emotional. I explained the situation, which Brad corroborated. He played the videos and showed the photos. I provided the incident log.

"I need each of you to fill out this form. Be as detailed as possible." He handed one to each of us with a pen.

My stomach sank. I'd filled out this form before, only to be told no crime had been committed. I stared at the form, its words jumbling in my mind. I explained to the officer how I'd filled out the same form, only to be told to go home.

I pushed the form back across the table and said, "I'm not filling this out. It won't do any good."

The officer looked at me kindly. "Here's the thing. The law defines stalking as a pattern of behavior, so an isolated incident doesn't merit law enforcement action. I need to speak to my supervisor, but with the incident log, your first-hand accounts, the photos, and the video surveillance footage, there might be enough to establish a pattern. If so, we'll be able to file a stalking charge. But that all starts with you filling out this form."

I hoped he was right.

I handwrote my statement, detailing everything from the incident log, then added the day's events—the email, the house, the accident. When I finished, the officer left the room. Brad and his partner had to go, too. He made me promise to update him as soon as I could. I waited in silence—agonizing silence. But at least I was safe—for now.

An hour later, the officer returned and said, "Great news. My supervisor agreed. A warrant for Todd's arrest is being prepared."

Less than a week earlier, I'd had lunch with Brad. Now, a warrant? I should've reached out to him a year ago! The rush of relief was temporary. Fleeting. The reality of what a warrant for Todd's arrest could mean sank in almost immediately. I remained silent, my eyes fixed on the officer.

"After the warrant is issued, we will attempt an arrest, but you need to be vigilant about your safety. The time between issuing the warrant and making the arrest is the most dangerous. Do you have somewhere safe to stay?"

I nodded.

My sneakers squeaked on the linoleum as I left the station, the cool air breathing life into my weary body. I texted Lauren, telling her I'd be staying over and staying with her for the night—I didn't tell her why. I called Dylan as I pulled out of the parking lot.

"Are you still at the house?"

"No, but I'm heading back. What's going on?"

"Listen, a warrant has been issued for Todd's arrest. I'm going to stay with Lauren until he's in custody. Can you take Winston to your dad's with you for the night?"

"You don't need to stay at Lauren's. I'll stay with you, Mom."

"We'll talk about it when I get there, but please be extremely careful."

"I will, I promise. I'm headed that way now."

I focused on the road, steadying myself as the double yellow lines sped by like ribbons on a kite. I didn't feel the relief I thought I would. Instead, I felt scared—especially after remembering one line from a prior police report, in particular:

> *... victim arrived home one evening to find the defendant in her house ...*

I was afraid Todd's behavior would escalate—and now, that fear had grown into an overwhelming sense of dread, nipping at my heels. Halfway home, my phone rang. Dylan's voice burst through my car's speakers in short, urgent sentences.

"Mom! I'm at the house. I just pulled up. Todd's parked behind the house. It's dark. I can't tell if he's in his truck or somewhere else."

My guts twisted into knots. "Go to your dad's. Do not go inside."

"I'm not scared of Todd. I'm not leaving." Dylan was nineteen now, and I'd be taking him to basic training in the morning. There was no point arguing with him. I pressed harder on the gas and told Siri to dial 911.

"911, what is your emergency?"

"Hi, my name is Kathryn. I just left the sheriff's department. A warrant is being issued in my case. My son was going to meet me at my house, but when he got there, the offender was parked nearby. Can you send someone?"

"Is he still there?" the operator asked.

I'd just entered my subdivision. I slowly rolled past the entrance to the right-of way. Of course, Todd's truck wasn't there anymore. "I don't see the vehicle now," I responded.

"If you see it again, call back."

"Okay, thank you," I said, and tossed my phone onto the passenger seat. My adrenaline was high, and I focused on getting to Dylan.

When I arrived, Dylan had turned on the outside lights and opened the garage door. I rushed into the garage, eyes darting in every direction in case Todd was inside. I pulled in, then bolted into the house, locking the door behind me before the garage door even closed.

CHAPTER
THIRTY-TWO

I kept vigil at the kitchen table throughout the night while Dylan slept soundly upstairs. I gazed across the wooden surface, staring at the swirls and knots, letting the silence envelop me. The doors were locked, the lights were off, and I was alone with my thoughts.

The world would be a better place if you just weren't in it.
You are mine. And I don't share.
If I wanted to hurt you, I would do it right now.

My stomach tied in knots as my mind flashed to the murdered woman —his connection to her. The way he disparaged her. The way he obsessed over the crime. What did it all mean?

I chewed my lower lip as my eyelids began to droop. I was exhausted, but I knew I needed to fight the urge to tuck into bed and burrow beneath the covers. I shuffled around the house, performing my nightly routine— moving methodically, checking doors, and scanning the front and back yards for Todd. I finished the downstairs loop, then went upstairs to make sure Dylan was asleep. As I cracked the door and peeked past the jamb, I let out a sigh. No matter a child's age, a mother still needs to see their chest gently rising and falling as they sleep.

I walked back to the kitchen table and sat down in the moonlight. I spun my phone, willing it to ring. I desperately needed to hear the words—*he's in custody*.

The weight of sleep pressed down on my shoulders. I made my rounds again, checking the locks on the doors and windows, then peering into the backyard, scanning for his form. I remained on high alert, certain not to overlook a lock or miss anything that might be out of place.

I finished my loop by peering into the backyard. I stared at the mature trees swaying in the gentle breeze, the long grass, and the stars hanging in the sky. I willed them to bring me peace, but I could see him in my mind. Beneath every shadow was Todd's stocky form. The more I stared, the more vivid the image became:

His stout figure.

His fixed gaze.

His flared nostrils.

Him.

∽

I awoke to the sun breaking through the window, my head resting on the hard surface of the table. I blinked hard as I wiped the drool from my cheek with the back of my hand. I reached for my phone, desperately searching the screen for any signs of a missed call that Todd had been arrested.

Nothing.

My body was stiff as I stood and stretched. Winston scrambled to his feet to do the same. I hated that I'd fallen asleep, but I was grateful we'd made it through the night unscathed. I let Winston outside by himself before pouring a steaming cup of coffee and wandering into my bathroom for a quick shower.

Even with the deliciously hot water cascading over my body, my mind resisted any measure of relaxation. I toweled off, threw on some clothes, gathered my things, and hurried Dylan into the car. I knew that, for him, this ride didn't mean much. It was something I'd given him countless times in the past—to practices, play dates, and school events. Yet, to me, this ride was different—significant. I felt a mix of sadness and anger. The warrant for Todd's arrest cast a shadow over what should have been a joyous, momentous occasion. While I dreaded seeing him leave, a part of me felt relieved. He'd be safer in the hands of the military than within the walls of our home.

We breezed through the security gate at the base and made our way to the building where I was to leave Dylan. I couldn't help feeling both pride and sadness as I watched him fill out his paperwork. My son was about to become a soldier.

When I left the base, I dialed the sheriff's department non-emergency line, hoping that Todd had been arrested. *Maybe the call to me had slipped through the cracks?* The phone crackled to life, and I explained the reason for my call. The dispatcher confirmed no arrest had been made. I hung up with a pit in my stomach and tears prickling the backs of my eyes.

Less than two miles from home, a vehicle in my rearview mirror caught my attention. There, hanging about two car lengths behind, was Todd. My heart slammed against my chest as I fumbled for my phone.

Did he know about the warrant?

Was he coming to hurt me?

Todd was following me turn for turn. Stop for stop. Brake for brake. My hands trembled as I desperately snapped a photo then dialed 911. My voice shook as I explained what was happening, and the warrant for Todd's arrest. Instead of dispatching a car to intercept him, the operator instructed me to drive to the nearest police station.

Just as I reached the final stoplight—the police station in sight—Todd made a sharp right turn. Once I pulled into the parking lot, his truck was out of sight. I quickly got out of my car and hurried inside. I rushed to the receptionist's desk, breathless. "I was just on the phone with 911, and the operator told me to come here. The man who's stalking me has a warrant out for his arrest, and he was just following me!"

"I'm sorry to hear that," she responded flatly, as if this wasn't the first time she'd heard a desperate woman claim she was being stalked. It felt like, even with a warrant, the police weren't helping me. My adrenaline surged. My voice rose. Tears streamed down my face.

An officer emerged from a side door. "Calm down, ma'am. Tell me what's going on."

Words spilled from my mouth like rapid fire. He peered past me into the parking lot, squinting as he scanned. "I don't see a vehicle out there matching the description you gave."

I took a deep breath and tried to calm myself, but my mind screamed—*of course, you don't!*

"I told the dispatcher on the phone that he went straight after I made the U-turn on High Street at the Oak Street light."

The officer cocked his head. "That's not our jurisdiction. You need to go to the sheriff's department."

Exasperated, I sped to the nearest sheriff's substation—one I'd been to before. Because I'd been documenting all interactions, I noted the surname on the chest of the first officer I saw. My breath caught, and tears welled in my eyes as I stood there in stunned silence. The officer was the widowed husband of a friend I'd lost years ago. They had been married just a month before her cancer diagnosis, and she didn't live to see their first anniversary. In that moment, I felt like she was with me.

"Shane? It's me, Kathryn. Lisa's friend!"

His eyes lit up. "Kathryn, yes, I remember you. What are you doing here? Is everything okay?"

After a brief exchange about Lisa, I calmly shared the details about Todd. Shane led me into a small, sterile room. He motioned for me to sit at a table facing a mirror—I knew it was one-way glass.

"Do you need anything? Coffee, water?" he asked.

I shook my head.

I sat alone, glancing at my watch repeatedly. The longer this took, the more time Todd had to get away. Ten minutes later, the door swung open. A deputy entered, sitting across from me with his back to the mirror. "Okay, Ms. Caraway. Can you tell me what's going on?"

I explained everything—the stalking, him showing up in my yard, the constant following, the harassment, the warrant. I tried to stay measured, worried that if I was too calm, he wouldn't believe me; if I was too emotional, he might think I was being dramatic. I had to walk that line carefully.

When I finished, he sat back, expressionless and stoic. I was struggling to keep it together.

"Okay," he said with a sigh. "I'll need your driver's license and a list of any identifying information—full name, date of birth, address, etc.—on this guy. I also need the type of vehicle you saw following you."

I provided everything he asked for, including Todd's license plate number and the photo I'd taken from my rearview mirror. The photo didn't show the driver, but with the warrant issued, I held onto hope.

"What else can I give you?" I asked.

"Do you have any idea where he might be headed?"

"It's Wednesday, so I assume he's headed to work—at the police department. He works out of the investigations building on Second Street."

The deputy looked skeptical at that. He opened a laptop and started typing. "Do you know anyone he works with?" he asked, avoiding eye contact.

"I only know Peanut." I was embarrassed to utter the nickname, as if I knew the detective personally, but I couldn't remember Peanut's real name.

"I know him. Actually, I have his number. Let me give him a call." He handed me the familiar form to fill out.

"Hey, man," I could hear the deputy's side of the conversation, and it was clear they knew each other well. He asked if Todd worked for the police department. He nodded and said, "Interesting, okay. Do you think he's on his way there now?"

The deputy was silent for a moment before telling Peanut there was a warrant for Todd's arrest. Peanut must have asked what the charge was, because the next thing I heard was "stalking," then silence.

"Yeah, I'm sitting with her now—Kathryn. The warrant was issued yesterday. She says Todd was following her just now, and she's filling out a statement." He looked at me, and I held up the form showing I'd completed my part.

"Uh-huh . . . I hear ya, brother . . . okay, take it easy." The deputy hung up. "I'll be back. Sit tight," he said, walking out with his laptop and my statement tucked under his arm. I leaned on the table, trying to relax in the sterile room.

I looked up eagerly as the door opened again. The deputy returned, shook his head, and said, "I know you saw his truck behind you, and that spooked you—which is totally understandable—but this was likely a coincidence. No crime has been committed."

Unable to contain the rage boiling inside me, I yelled, *"Are you kidding me?!* This man has been stalking me—he has a warrant for stalking—and you're seriously calling this a *coincidence?!"* Tears streamed down my face. Exasperated, I gave him the name and badge number of the officer who issued the warrant. "Please, just call him," I begged.

"Look, I know who took the report—I can see it in the system." He pushed the form I'd filled out back across the table. "There's nothing more I can do."

I snatched the form, grabbed my purse, and stormed out of the building. My head ached as I sank into the driver's seat, blasting the air conditioning to help me regain my composure. Once again, law enforcement's inaction only increased my frustration. And I feared that this would give Todd the confidence to grow bolder and more dangerous.

CHAPTER
THIRTY-THREE

My heart felt like it was trying to break free from my chest as I sped down the road toward the courthouse. With the warrant issued, Robert said I had enough to file for a protective order. The clock was ticking, and I was certain he was still tracking me. Every moment outside my house made me feel exposed.

"Fill out this form," the clerk said, handing me a document. I hated these forms, but I sat down and filled in the blanks quickly. I retrieved the slip of paper with the police report number from the warrant issued last night. I pulled out a copy of the handwritten statement I'd given, along with a document Brad had sent on his company letterhead with his findings, and made my way back to the counter.

"Please," I begged, "help me. I'm scared, and I don't know what else I can do to protect myself."

She flipped through the papers, tracing each page with a fire-engine red fingernail. "Oops, looks like you missed one," she said, handing me a pen. "Sign here."

I scribbled my signature on the line. She reviewed the rest of the documents, then retrieved the paper I'd just signed and jostled it into a neat stack.

"This'll take a few minutes. Wait here."

I sat on a plastic chair nearby, tapping my foot anxiously as I waited. I knew I was safe inside the courthouse, but I couldn't help but think about what would happen after I left—how I'd be back out in the open. And always in my mind, like the constant drone of static—how might this enrage Todd?

The clerk returned after about twenty minutes. She called me over to her desk, and I pulled up a chair across from her. She held a stack of papers, peeled one away, and slid it toward me. "Okay, a Temporary Restraining Order has been granted—signed by the judge. You'll be protected until a hearing can be held, where a judge will decide whether a civil protective order will be issued. You are to always keep this certified copy of the order with you."

I nodded.

"And I mean at *all* times. Never, ever leave home without it."

I nodded again. The tears felt cool on my chapped cheeks as I was engulfed by a halo of relief. It wasn't just because this piece of paper alone would protect me, but because it would lend credibility to future police reports. And I knew there would be more. I was certain the arrest on the stalking warrant wouldn't make Todd stop.

In fact, I worried it would cause his behavior to escalate. He would become infuriated—his nostrils flared, his chest puffed out, his eyes black, flooded with vitriol, laser-focused on me.

I stared at my phone, willing it to ring with news of his arrest. My body felt heavy as I dragged my feet across the creaky wooden floor, checking the locks on the doors and windows. Winston followed close behind, his gaze fixed on my every movement. The late afternoon light trickled through the window, dimming with the setting sun. I exhaled slowly, knowing I needed to sleep while it was still daylight, so I shuffled upstairs to the guest bedroom I'd been using. There was no way I could sleep in the master bedroom tonight—he'd be looking for me there. I'd hear him, and I'd be out the window using the flimsy fire escape ladder I'd bought on Amazon. With my gun, of course.

I made my way to the bed, sliding beneath the sheets, the rubber soles of my running shoes catching on the covers as I pulled my knees into my chest. Winston threw himself onto the coverlet beside me, curling into a ball and pressing against me.

I lifted the pillow next to me, placed my gun beneath it, and tucked the newly issued Temporary Restraining Order beside it. I turned to face the door, trying to get comfortable. I placed my hand on the pillow, closed my eyes, and began to drift off. But even as I snuggled under the blankets, I couldn't escape the memories of that horrific night on my birthday.

Then, I heard it—

A familiar laugh, rising and falling like ocean waves, mocking my terror.

Gasping for air, I bolted upright.

The nightmares were always the same: someone was trying to kill me, and I was fighting for my life. I clutched my chest, feeling as if my heart were about to rip through my flesh. I took slow, purposeful breaths as Winston whined and pawed at my lap. It was still early evening, but already dark outside.

I packed a bag and texted Lauren:

> ME
> I'm coming over to spend the night.

> LAUREN
> I just put away dinner. Think you'll be hungry when u get here?

> ME
> Yes!

> LAUREN
> Food and whiskey will be waiting.

I retrieved my gun and the Temporary Restraining Order from under the pillow, then fixed Winston a bowl of wet dog food, with a bowl of dry kibble next to it. It was more than he needed to get through the night, but I couldn't bear the thought of him being home alone and hungry. I topped off his water bowl, apologized profusely for leaving him behind, and set out for Lauren's house.

Pulling into her garage, I was greeted by the aroma of seasoned roast beef, mashed potatoes, green beans, and corn. Since I received Todd's email, time had passed in a haze of exhaustion—all I wanted was to sit, eat, and not think about anything else.

"What the hell is going on?!" Lauren yelled as she raced toward me. "I talked to Nathan!"

I'd planned to tell Lauren about the arrest warrant, but if she'd talked to Nathan, she already knew. She peppered me with questions while I ate. I recounted everything that had happened in the past twenty-four hours, sipping my third glass of whiskey.

"I want to read the email!" Lauren blurted.

I knew I'd have to face the seven single-spaced pages of Todd's hateful words someday, but today wasn't it. I didn't offer to let her read it, and thankfully, she didn't press.

She opened the door to the guest bedroom, motioning for me to go inside. I removed my pajamas from my bag and relished slipping into them. Since learning about Todd's break-in at a previous victim's home, I'd been sleeping fully clothed, with one eye open, my shoes laced tight in case I needed to make a quick escape. The thought of him lurking in my backyard filled me with an unshakable dread—I didn't know when or how his behavior might escalate. I couldn't bear the idea of being caught off guard, and every night was a restless battle between sleep and hypervigilance.

At Lauren's, I didn't worry—maybe because Todd never tried anything there, or perhaps because of the comfort of having someone else nearby. Whatever it was, for that one night, I slept in soft pajamas and barefoot again. I sank beneath the billowy comforter, my body melting into the mattress.

The next morning, I awoke and began what would become my routine—calling dispatch to check Todd's arrest status; letting Winston out; getting some work done; then letting him out again; and returning to Lauren's for the night. The relentless dread was like a stone tied to my neck, dragging me further and further into the depths of my personal hell.

PART TWO
AFTER THE ARREST

CHAPTER
THIRTY-FOUR

Seven days.

That's how long it took between the warrant being issued and Todd's arrest. It was a Tuesday afternoon when I received the call, approaching 4:00 p.m. My phone vibrated across the desk—an unknown number.

"Hello?"

"Sheriff's department. Is this Kathryn Caraway?"

"This is Kathryn. Is Todd in custody?"

"Yes, Todd turned himself in. He came in with his lawyer. It seems they're pushing for bail to be set and a quick release."

My mind immediately went back to the day after the warrant was issued, when I was told to drive to the police station. I imagine the deputy who made the call to Peanut was how Todd was tipped off.

"Okay, but he's in custody now?"

"Correct."

"And I'll be notified if he's released?"

"Yes, ma'am."

"Thank you. I appreciate it," I said.

After hanging up, I jumped up from my desk and ran into the house. I poured a tall glass of sweet tea, and Winston and I walked outside to sit on the front porch swing. As we swayed, I closed my eyes and let myself feel the warmth of the setting sun and the cool breeze tousling my hair. I allowed myself to be lulled into a state of tranquility by the gentle rocking.

Todd was in jail.

I was safe.

It was like I was seeing the world in color again. I could hear the birds singing, the leaves rustling, and Winston's soft panting as he nestled beside me. That brief, euphoric feeling of relief, however, quickly vanished. My throat tightened as my mind grappled with the words: *quick release*. I wondered how long it would be before Todd stormed out of jail, jumped into his car, and barreled toward my house to do God knows what. I couldn't allow myself to get too comfortable. I needed to stay alert, always two steps ahead of him.

When I called Lauren to tell her Todd had been arrested, I had to hold the phone away from my ear as she erupted in a half-dozen shouts of, "Hallelujah!"

As night fell over my small town, I made my way into my bedroom. I changed into clean, comfortable pajamas, happy to sleep in my own bed again. I even allowed myself the familiar luxury of falling asleep with the TV on.

Early the next morning, I sat up in bed and checked my phone. No missed calls. Whatever "quick release" meant, I was glad it included a night in jail. I smiled as small particles of dust danced playfully in the light streaming through my window. Winston followed me into the kitchen and sat beside me as I sloshed coffee into my mug and took a slow, deliberate sip. The serenity of my peaceful morning was interrupted when my phone rang.

I held it to my ear. "Hello?"

"Ms. Caraway? This is the sheriff's department—"

My stomach clenched. It had happened: Todd made bail.

I swallowed hard. "I wasn't notified there was going to be a hearing to set bail," I said awkwardly into the phone.

"You'll have to talk to the district attorney's office, ma'am. We'll call you once he's been released. We're still processing his bond paperwork now." Then, he clicked off the line.

My stomach was in knots. I thought I'd at least have an opportunity to attend the bail hearing to plead my case for not letting Todd out of jail.

I felt his anger burning in my bones, a hole blazing through my flesh. It emanated from his jail cell; his rage was that of a caged animal with its back against the wall. I called a new boarding facility for Winston that I'd recently toured, and packed a few essentials to take with me to Lauren's. I gripped the kitchen counter as I contemplated what to do next. I loved my house more than anything—in the fourteen years before Todd, it had been my fortress, my safe haven, and now I had to leave to stay safe in the days following Todd's release.

I looked down at Winston, who had tucked himself between my legs. He'd been through so much with me that his eyes reflected the exhaustion I felt. I patted my thigh. "Come on, boy," I said, leading him toward my bedroom.

With morning light streaming through the window, I climbed into my still-warm bed. Winston jumped onto the foot of the bed and snuggled against me. He looked up at me with sleepy eyes and let out a yawn before curling into a tight ball and dozing off.

I turned on the television and waited for the call—he's been processed out of jail.

As the sun traveled across the sky, casting long shadows into the room, I worried that maybe the jail had forgotten to call me back to let me know he was released. And just like that, I was back where I started—checking the doors, listening for noises, slipping my hand under the pillow to feel for the gun and my Temporary Restraining Order, over and over again.

Once the sky turned a dusty blue, my phone rang. I squeezed my eyes shut as I listened to the dispatcher's matter-of-fact tone, telling me Todd had been released. I leapt from the bed and sprang into action. Our bags were packed, and all I had to do was put Winston's leash on and walk out the door. We sped out of the subdivision as if Todd had already found me.

Life after Todd's release became brutal—the days seemed to drag on endlessly. No matter where I was, my head was on a swivel. The rest of me was stuck in the past or panicking about the future.

Todd's constant stalking, humiliating me in public, and the expletives and vulgarities from his old texts had burrowed deep into my mind. It seemed like too much effort to end there. No. I was certain he had something more sinister in mind, and I felt paralyzed.

I stayed with Lauren for nearly two weeks until my monthly trip to Chicago approached. It seemed my entire life was about Todd and the case, as if I had ceased to exist as a person. I welcomed the opportunity to get on a plane, soar into the clouds, and land in a city where I was anonymous.

The trip was uneventful—just the way I liked it. I'd leave the building each day and find myself among the throngs of people hustling home from work. At the office, it seemed like word had spread. There were no more invitations to happy hour or dinner with colleagues. My nights in the hotel room were lonely, but at least I could rest, knowing Todd wasn't outside.

It wasn't enough to humiliate me publicly. It wasn't enough to jeopardize my job by contacting Julie. It wasn't enough for him to suffocate the safety I felt in my own home. And now, it seemed my reputation at work—specifically at the corporate office—was stained. James was no longer inviting me to pub trivia while I was in town.

When will it be enough for him? I kept asking myself over and over.

Despite the troubling nature of being treated as a leper at the corporate office, I returned from my trip feeling refreshed, having slept like a baby in the hotel. I knew I couldn't stay at Lauren's forever, and it wasn't fair to leave Winston in boarding. He'd been there for three weeks now. I picked him up as soon as I returned and made my way home, pulling into the garage. I stayed in the car with the engine running until the door touched the floor. When I walked inside, the familiar scent of home hit me—a smell I'd never noticed before. It was lilac and lavender, with a hint of coffee and cream. Winston bounded through the house, happy to be home. I placed my bags on the bed and then began my familiar routine—checking windows and doors.

I wasn't home for long when Lauren called. Before I could say anything, she blurted out, "You need to come over tonight!"

"Okay," I replied. "Is something going on?"

"Are you kidding? Tonight, my favorite show is on—and they're doing an episode about the murdered woman in our town!"

It had been more than a year since the murder, and the case remained unsolved. But the promotional clips promised juicy details that Lauren couldn't wait to dissect. In a strange way, hearing about someone else's drama was a good distraction. I was glad her case was getting national attention, putting pressure on the police department. Given my dealings with them and the fact that the case was still unsolved, I was curious to see how the media would spin it.

"Alright," I said. "I'll be there."

When I arrived, Lauren hurried me inside, handing me a glass of whiskey.

"It's on!"

We settled in to watch the episode—Lauren reclining in her chair and me sprawled out on the sofa. It was dramatic and intriguing, but then it took an ominous turn. After going through a list of suspects and clearing them, the episode focused on an unknown stalker. Before the murder, the woman had told friends she was being stalked and provided details that I found myself nodding my head to. Whoever it was had also left evidence of it near her front door, undetected by her security cameras.

My stomach flipped. I thought of my own situation. Todd had installed my cameras and knew where the blind spots were. His intimate knowledge of my system was why I could never catch him on video.

As if we were thinking exactly the same thing at the same time, Lauren paused the episode and blurted out, "That sounds like Todd!"

I hadn't told her that Todd said he installed the security cameras at the murdered woman's house, and now I wondered if I should. I simply nodded.

Later, we sat at her table with heaping plates of her homemade lasagna, dissecting every minute of the episode, drawing parallels to my situation, and forming our own theories. I shared every thought I had, but I kept quiet about the fact that Todd had installed the victim's cameras. I don't know why, but maybe I just wasn't ready to go there yet.

The next day, sitting behind my desk, I took a deep breath. I reflected on my conversation with Lauren the night before and realized that every conclusion we'd drawn was likely fueled by overactive imaginations, possibly amplified by alcohol. My life wasn't an episode of a juicy TV show. Todd was a monster, but a murderer? No, surely I would've known. The more I thought about it, the more I was able to distance myself from the idea that he could be involved. I had to think this way—I couldn't get lost in the narrative that Todd might be the killer, because I needed to hold onto whatever fragments of sanity I still had, despite the anxiety, fear, and panic threatening to consume me.

The line between paranoia and vigilance had already been blurred beyond recognition, making it impossible to distinguish which was the true emotion.

CHAPTER
THIRTY-FIVE

After Todd's release, my brain spun in confusion. I felt adrift, not knowing what to expect. Brad had referred me to an attorney, Gina, who specialized in representing women in domestic violence situations. Although I had Robert, I felt like I needed someone who understood the intricacies of criminal law. Gina seemed eager to take my case. After the bail hearing, I didn't trust the judicial system to keep me informed. With Gina, I had someone I could rely on. With the upcoming Civil Protective Order hearing, I knew I would need her.

The incident log had started with Todd kidnapping Winston, but Gina asked me to expand the timeline back to when I first met him. Not only was this a massive undertaking, but it was also an emotionally intense experience to see his insidious behavior from a forensic perspective.

It was painful to revisit the beginning and watch it unfold; hindsight is 20/20. I cringed at all the ways I had naïvely responded to Todd's attention. I had been so flattered by his relentless pursuit that I allowed him further into my life when I should have been pushing him away. I was forced to recognize the role I had played in all of this. But I also realized there was no benefit in beating myself up over the red flags I had missed or dismissed.

What happened, happened.

My new timeline began with the night I met him nearly two years ago. I used emails, text messages, and any other available documentation to make it as accurate as possible. I took screenshots to avoid the risk of messages mysteriously disappearing and printed them.

Everything I used for the timeline went into what would become known as The Black Binder. It was two inches thick, neatly organized with dividers. The timeline itself detailed each event and referred to supporting documentation tucked between the tabs, so it was easy to read the timeline and locate the corresponding evidence. Now that I'd compiled it all on paper, I felt like my life was on display, open to judgment. But I didn't mind. I knew I was my own harshest critic.

I arrived at Gina's office, clutching The Black Binder tightly.

"I've read over the report from the P.I., including Todd's prior criminal history, and I've familiarized myself with the stalking timeline," she said, leading me into a private room. "Let's go over this together, line by line."

We sat in the conference room, and I flipped open The Black Binder.

"The screenshot here confirms my phone lost signal as soon as Todd was about twenty feet away," I said, pointing to the corresponding page. I flicked pages. "And this is a picture of him standing nearby, looking at his phone. It may sound absurd to say someone was jamming my cell phone signal, but he works in IT for the police department and has technical knowledge." I had already researched online and printed a copy of how easy it is to get a cell phone jammer. "And here is a copy of a company that sells jammers to anyone."

"Well, the language you use here is very general—can you explain this?" she asked.

I sensed she was preparing me for testimony, challenging me on even the smallest details.

The process took nearly three hours. Three *excruciating* hours reviewing how Todd had tried to destroy me from the outside, using others in my life to break me from within.

When we finished, she turned to face me. "Listen, Kathryn. I have something about all this—about Todd."

She piqued my curiosity. "Okay."

"I'm friends with the last woman who filed charges against him. I believe you've read her report—it's about six years old. She had broken up with Todd and was having dinner with another man when Todd approached her, yelling obscenities and calling her names. He followed her home, but she wouldn't let him in, and when she called 911, he broke her phone."

"Sounds familiar," I said, thinking back to the night he nearly kidnapped me and broke my phone in the process.

"Yes. Assault and property destruction charges were filed, and Todd was arrested in that case."

"How did it end for your friend?" I asked, chewing on the inside of my cheeks.

"Well, she won a Civil Protective Order and reported being repeatedly harassed afterward. So, another charge was filed for a violation of the order, and Todd was arrested again."

My throat tightened. If her protective order hadn't stopped him, mine wouldn't either.

"The charges were dropped, but I spoke to her to see if she'd be willing to testify about her experience with Todd at your upcoming hearing."

"What did she say?" I nervously tapped my foot.

"Well . . ." Gina leaned forward, placing a hand on the table as if to brace me. She spoke slowly and seemed to be guarded. "She said she dropped the charges because she was scared. It seemed to be the only way to get him to leave her alone. Now, she's on friendly terms with him to avoid further escalation. When she tries to put distance between them, he starts harassing her again. It stops when he's seeing someone else."

"He's been doing this to her for the last six years, and she's just placating him?" Tears brimmed my eyes.

"I know. She said she once saw you and Todd at a restaurant. She felt bad for you and thought about warning you, but she didn't want to risk pissing him off."

"I guess I can't blame her for that."

"Also, she said Todd called her before he turned himself in, so she knows about the stalking charge."

"Hold on. That confirms Todd knew about the stalking charge before he was arrested. So, he deliberately evaded arrest."

"It doesn't matter. My friend urged me to advise you to drop the charges and meet with him to smooth things over. What are your thoughts?"

Without hesitation, I said, "That's bullshit. He's used to women backing down. Someone has to stand up to him."

A bright smile burst across Gina's face. "Exactly! I'm so glad to hear that, Kathryn. Don't let any of this deter you. Stay strong."

Despite tears sliding down my cheeks, I smiled back. Gina was a litigator at heart—powerful and commanding when she wanted to be—but with me, she always showed her softer side.

"But will she testify about her experience with Todd?"

"Unfortunately, no. She's too scared of him," she said apologetically, pausing briefly. "I'll need to keep The Black Binder so we can make a few copies of it."

I hesitated. The binder weighed heavily in my hands, a reminder of all the mistakes I'd made. Despite my reservations, I had to trust Gina, but I was still afraid of that kind of information leaving my sight—and she knew it.

As I closed it and slid it toward her, she placed her hand on mine. "I'll take good care of it. I promise." Gina rested her elbow on the arm of her chair and drew a breath.

"There's one thing we haven't discussed yet. The email."

I knew instantly she was referring to the seven-page email that had prompted Brad to come to my house the day the warrant was issued. My eyes dropped, already humiliated just thinking about what must be in it.

"Have you read it?"

I shook my head, shoulders slumping.

"I'm sorry, Kathryn, but I need you to read it before the hearing. I'll warn you—it may stir some emotions, but just stay strong. It's repulsive, and there's some crazy shit in there."

My mind immediately went to the plaid panties comment sent to James. I didn't know what the message said, but I knew it wasn't good, given the rumors Todd had been spreading. I felt emotionally bankrupt and dreaded reading the awful things he'd written. "Do you really think that's necessary?" I asked.

"I do—and here's why. The email reads like a blueprint for Todd's defense. They may introduce it into evidence, either for this hearing or for the stalking charge. You need to be ready."

"Okay," I replied, wiping away tears.

"I will help you, Kathryn." Her hand extended to my arm, my bottom lip quivering. "We'll get through this—as a team. You can even read it here. I can sit with you, or I can leave you alone."

"Thank you, but I can't," I sniffed. "I'm sorry. I promise I'll read it soon."

Days later, with The Black Binder back in my possession, I sat at my computer with Winston at my feet. In the warm glow of the screen, I scanned document after document—copies given to me by Gina. She'd obtained police reports and attachments from other states, which hadn't been available through my public records request.

One in particular caught my eye. It contained new information related to the case from six years earlier. I read it, hoping to understand why Gina's friend would placate such a monster for so long.

The charges spanned five months, ranging from simple criminal damage to property and domestic battery to two arrests for violating a protective order. I was surprised to see a familiar name listed as a witness for Todd's defense: Tricia. Her oldest son was Dylan's best friend, and we'd spent years carpooling and socializing. I knew her well enough to pick up the phone and call her directly.

"I know you're calling about the charges against Todd," Tricia said curtly.

I was stunned by her response, but she was right—I wouldn't have called otherwise. "I'm sorry it's been so long since we last spoke. It took everything I had to get the boys out of high school, and now Caleb's getting married next year, and Dylan's in the military," I added feebly. "You understand, right? You know how it is."

Tricia ended the call before I could ask her anything. When our boys were in the Boy Scouts, I shared a tent with her. We had taken the boys to fairs, festivals, and parades together. And now we were not only not friends, but it felt like we had become enemies. This turned out to be the last time we'd ever speak, despite our fourteen-year history.

I continued going through the documents and another name jumped off the page. It was Raymond, the attorney who represented Gina's friend. He was someone I knew, thanks to his generosity to the nonprofit board. I called his office and shared an abbreviated version of my story.

"Man, I'm sorry for what you're going through. The girl I represented was absolutely terrified of Todd. I begged her not to drop the charges against him. But, as you know, she dropped them anyway."

"Help me understand how a victim can decide to drop the charges when the case is the State versus the defendant."

"No cooperating victim, no conviction. It's that simple. As soon as a victim refuses to cooperate, the district attorney, the prosecutor will elect to drop the charges. It happens more often than you know."

I muttered a shocked "Thanks" before ending the call. I was seething with frustration that this woman hadn't put up a fight. If only she had, maybe I wouldn't be trapped in this nightmare. But who am I fooling? I didn't even bother doing a simple Google search, let alone a background check on Todd. Why would I? When I first met him, I had every reason to trust him and no reason to believe he would morph into a monster.

CHAPTER
THIRTY-SIX

The next evening, as constellations hung in the sky, my fingers trembled around my mug of chamomile tea. The hearing was three days away, and I needed to read Todd's email in solitude. I glanced at the clock: half-past eight. The world outside seemed so tranquil, but I refused to be fooled by a false sense of serenity. Todd was out on bond, and I was certain he was waiting for his opportunity to strike.

I took a deep breath, absorbing the aroma from my tea, then wiggled the mouse. I printed off the email I was dreading to read so I could annotate it, keeping the one in The Black Binder pristine. I reached for the sheets of paper that were spitting from my groaning printer, one by one. I steeled myself and began reading.

The beginning was filled with words describing me as beautiful, smart, and funny. Bile rose in the back of my throat.

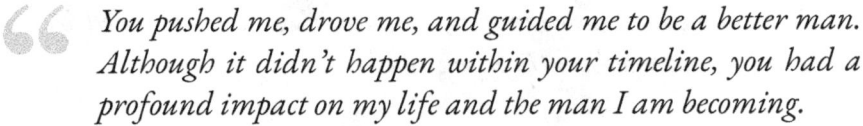

You pushed me, drove me, and guided me to be a better man. Although it didn't happen within your timeline, you had a profound impact on my life and the man I am becoming.

> *There were moments in which I didn't handle things in a manner that was respectful, kind, and gentlemanly.*

I shook my head in disbelief—unbelievable. To an outsider reading this, he'd seem genuine in explaining what he had learned about himself. Yet, I'd heard—and naïvely believed—a variety of versions of this over the past two years. Knowing Todd as well as I did, I saw beneath his words a mountain of sadistic lies.

Todd's monologue continued, recounting his version of events from the moment we met until the time he wrote the email at three o'clock in the morning. Of course, he omitted many of the incidents I had documented in my incident log. He made excuse after pathetic excuse for others, explaining away all the "coincidences" and expressing surprise at how often we happened to be somewhere at the same time.

Lies! All lies! I forced myself to keep reading.

> *Speaking of coincidences, a funny thing happened. I was on Facebook one day and your friend Abby popped up as a "People You May Know." I guess the algorithm connected us because you're a mutual friend. Anyway, I clicked "Add Friend" on accident.*

My jaw clenched so hard I thought my teeth would break. I ditched the hot tea for two fingers of whiskey neat.

He went on to describe how he coincidentally ran into a man I'd been involved with before my marriage to Jason, and the unfavorable remarks he supposedly made about me.

> *It saddened me to hear that, because it's a feeling echoed by me and many others from your past.*

Todd expressed hope that I would reflect on my mistakes and behavior so that someday I'd be in a healthy enough place to have a lasting, loving relationship.

As if to lend credibility to his statements, he claimed I once told him Lauren said I shouldn't act like a whore—which never happened and would be easily refuted if she were called to testify.

Of course, he never mentioned sneaking into the passenger seat of my car at the grocery store—an incident that still haunts me to this day.

I finally reached the end of what turned out to be a lengthy, desperate rant—where he painted himself as a helpless victim and me as a heartless woman who left behind a trail of discarded men. I stared at the email, and doubt crept in like a poisonous fog. He'd use the same charisma and charm in court—evidenced by this disgusting email—that he'd used on me in the beginning. I could feel justice slipping through my fingers.

My whole body shook with anger—an anger, a hatred I'd never known before. He had decimated my life, and now I feared I'd never see justice. My hands clenched into fists, fingernails digging into my palms. I had to find a way to expose Todd's true nature, to peel back his carefully crafted mask and reveal the sociopath lurking beneath.

Todd wasn't seeking self-improvement or forgiveness, as the email implied. No, he was looking for a way to escape his guilt. And I was determined not to give him that.

On the day of the hearing, Gina and I met at the courthouse. I stayed close by her side, trying to appear confident but failing miserably. Our heels clicked in unison on the polished marble floor as we made our way to the second level. Sitting side by side on a bench outside the courtroom, Gina and I carefully went through the list of incidents to ease my nerves. I was grateful she didn't ask me about the email.

As Gina's perfectly manicured finger traced down the page, I looked up—my breath caught. There, across the atrium, standing in a dress shirt and khakis, was Todd. He looked respectable—nothing like the image of a stalker in a hoodie pulled low over his eyes.

He was animated as he spoke with his lawyer, his eyes sad, shaking his head as if in despair. He was playing the part of a man whose name was being dragged through the mud by a crazy ex. His lawyer was eating it up.

My stomach lurched as Todd ran his hands through his blonde hair, his face flushed, his ice-blue eyes wild.

You are mine. And I don't share.

"Hey, just focus on me, okay?" Gina urged, her hand on my knee.

I nodded.

Once we'd gone over everything, Gina stood up and walked across the atrium, clutching her copy of The Black Binder. She kept a line of sight on me while she spoke with Todd's attorney. They talked at length—Gina gesturing wildly, the attorney snapping back. Then, Gina turned on her heels and walked back to me.

Lauren and Nathan arrived just as Gina was relaying her conversation with Todd's attorney. She said he thrust a folder at her and told her I needed to "drop the charade." She opened it and found Todd's seven-page email inside. As she shuffled the pages to see if there was more, she realized the email was Todd's only defense—no additional documentation, no log, not a shred of evidence. Just the email.

Gina held up her copy of The Black Binder. She didn't open it for him to see its contents but explained that I had a significant amount of documentation to support my claims—including two witnesses ready to testify—and that the email was bullshit. She also added that I had video footage and an independent report from a private investigator documenting Todd's stalking behavior.

"I told him that if all he has is an email his client wrote, which, by the way, falls under harassment given the three letters from Robert demanding that Todd refrain from contacting you, then he should rethink his client's position going into the hearing."

Lauren's eyes lit up. Nathan remained stoic, absorbing it all. But all I could do was focus on the email. If Todd's email was introduced at the hearing, it would become part of the public record. The thought of my children seeing it someday was unbearable. My hands shook uncontrollably as I fought back tears, overwhelmed by shame and humiliation.

Gina added that Todd's attorney assured her he wanted no contact with me. "I told him that if Todd felt that way, he should have no issue agreeing to the protective order. Believe it or not, he agreed!"

Gina explained that, procedurally, we would still have a hearing even if Todd consents to the protective order. The judge would ask us both to confirm on record that we understood the terms, conditions, and consequences before he would issue the Civil Protective Order.

We made our way back to the bench where Gina and I sat and stared at her laptop as she typed up the terms of the agreement and sprinkled in a few stipulations of her own. Every once in a while, she left me, balancing the laptop in the palm of her hand as she got Todd's attorney's attention. They would have a discussion, and she'd come back and relay the information to me.

After one such conference, Gina smiled and said they didn't want to agree to two of our terms:

- *The Defendant is to remove or disable any vehicle tracking devices which may be on or connected to Petitioner's vehicle; and,*
- *The Defendant is to disable any access he has to cameras at Petitioner's residence or on Petitioner's cell phone.*

Gina said they claimed it would damage Todd's professional reputation as an IT worker to have this on public record. I had the evidence we needed to support these terms and I'd just hold out for a hearing if they wouldn't agree. I would show him as much professional courtesy as he showed me in contacting the vice president of human resources at my company and supplying her with my personal text messages.

After an hour of back-and-forth, Gina finally emerged with an agreement that included the two terms I insisted on. My eyes landed on Todd across the courthouse. He was squatting against the wall with his head in his hands.

When our case was called, we filed into the courtroom. Nathan and

Lauren took seats on the bench, and I settled into a chair next to Gina in the front.

Gina informed the judge that an agreement had been reached. She handed the terms to the bailiff, who brought them to the bench. The judge reviewed it, asked a few questions, and made some notes before passing it to the clerk, who filled in some details and handed the document to Gina —the official Civil Protective Order.

The order would be valid for eighteen months, which should be enough time to prepare for the trial on the stalking charges. If Todd is convicted of stalking, Gina said I would automatically receive a longer-term protective order.

I read it carefully, making sure I understood every word. I noticed the judge had handwritten the terms Gina typed, as if to confirm they came directly from him. All other terms and conditions were either checked or crossed out.

Then I saw one term that was neither checked nor crossed out, and I knew I wanted it.

- *The court finds the Defendant represents a credible threat to the physical safety of the petitioner. Therefore, the Defendant is prohibited from possessing a firearm for the duration of this order.*

Gina motioned for the bailiff. Casually, as if the judge forgot to put something in his grocery cart, she said, "The judge forgot to check this box," and handed the form back.

The judge looked at it and asked Todd's attorney if they agreed to a firearm prohibition. The attorney, of course, said no, arguing that Todd didn't own a firearm and, therefore, it wasn't necessary. I quickly flipped through The Black Binder and handed Gina a photograph of Todd shooting a firearm.

Seeing the photo, Todd's attorney again claimed Todd didn't own a firearm. But Gina was quick to respond: "While that may be true, the photograph indicates he has access to one."

The judge motioned for Gina to bring the photo to his bench. He grimaced as he looked at it. Without further discussion, he checked the box prohibiting Todd from possessing a firearm. My heart pounded—furious that I had to fight for even a basic measure of safety from such a clear and present threat.

When I took the photograph from Gina's hands, my eyes locked on the date—the weekend before the woman's murder. The same woman who was shot in the back of her head and didn't see death coming.

I had been with Todd that day at the shooting range. I had taken that photograph. A wave of dread washed over me.

My blood ran cold.

CHAPTER
THIRTY-SEVEN

A week later, I received news that a prosecutor had been assigned to my case. Gina also found that when Todd posted bail, the judge had issued a Criminal Protective Order. This Order existed in addition to the Civil Protective Order, providing two avenues of relief if anything should happen. After feeling so desperate for so long, I finally felt validated.

"Just remember," Gina advised, "these Orders are only going to protect you after the fact. You have to remain vigilant at all times. Never let your guard down."

I had a partner in this. I was no longer going it alone. Despite limiting when and how often I left the house, knowing Todd was out of jail, I was determined to get my life back on track. One of the major steps I took was resuming Saturday breakfasts with Nathan. We decided to stop meeting for breakfast the day he brought Brad's email to me at the gas pump.

With the charges pending against Todd, I had been consumed with the case. I looked forward to seeing Nathan and having a normal conversation. A new routine emerged—I'd circle the parking lot for any sign of Todd before I parked. Then, once in the restaurant, I'd sit with my back against a wall where I could see the door. And breakfast went beautifully.

Finally, a taste of normalcy! We lingered at the table over mugs of coffee long after our last bites. That simple meal—one I'd had many times throughout the decade we'd been meeting—was empowering.

The number of times I left the house increased, as did the number of incidents in my log. The protective order clearly stated that if one party arrived at an establishment first, the other must leave, including me. If Todd was there first, I would have to comply with my own protective order and leave the establishment. That's when it became a cat-and-mouse race to see who could get where first.

One Saturday, while I was on my way to meet Nathan for breakfast my heart raced as Todd's truck sped up from behind. I accelerated, but he gained on me. We blew through red lights, dodging traffic so we could say we were there first. Somehow, I arrived in the parking lot before he did and raced inside.

Todd came in just as I lowered into the chair across from Nathan. And he didn't stay quiet.

"Y'all just lost my business because I refuse to eat anywhere near that piece of shit," he loudly told the hostess. He turned, and stormed out of the restaurant.

I sank in my seat, embarrassed. "I'm sorry, Nathan. I can't continue to meet you for breakfast. I'll reach out when I feel safe enough."

He looked at me sympathetically. "I hate what he's doing to you, kiddo. Why don't we try again tomorrow morning? Change up our routine?"

"I can do that."

Nathan waved the waitress over to pay for his coffee. "Sorry, but we're going to go. We'll be back tomorrow. Can I just get the check?"

She smiled sweetly. "You only had one cup of coffee. It's on the house. See you tomorrow."

I was glad to see there was still kindness in our small town.

Nathan and I met for breakfast the following morning, an hour later than our usual Saturday time. We were lost in conversation over fluffy pancakes, crispy bacon, and scrambled eggs. My heart shattered at the sight of Todd walking in. He strolled up to the young hostess with a smug, devilish smirk on his face.

Our eyes locked. His face tightened. "I won't eat anywhere near that whore!" His voice boomed, and his finger pointed straight at me.

A sea of heads snapped in my direction. I fought the urge to crawl under the table.

"I've lost my appetite," he added before storming out.

My cheeks burned with humiliation as I looked around the restaurant. Patrons were wide-eyed; some whispering to one another, others stunned into silence. The only movement came from large fans lazily spinning overhead. Nathan reached out and touched my arm. "These theatrics make Todd look like the ass he is. Hold it together, kiddo."

Soon, the young hostess approached the table to ask if I was okay. I wasn't, but I told her I was.

"Listen, I'll talk to the owner and see what we can do about stopping him from coming in here and making a scene every time you're here."

I nodded and thanked her. Inside, a part of me died. This was my life, my future. There would never come a day when I could just be at peace. The protective order was clear: whoever arrives first, the other must leave. And that's exactly what he did. There was nothing to report to the police—no charges to be filed.

But I knew differently. Todd was an animal teasing his prey, taking any opportunity to rattle me. And it was working.

"He clearly has some way of tracking you, Kathryn. You need to figure out how."

"I think it's the app he set up for my car."

After breakfast, I drove straight home. I pulled up the app, but I couldn't figure out how to delete my account. I had never used the app except to change the password to lock him out. A few days after the race to the restaurant, I went to the dealership where I purchased the car to see Jim, my service provider. I breezed through the glass doors, walked up to the counter, and smiled.

"Welcome in, Ms. Caraway. Not time for an oil change already, is it?"

"No, no. I have a question for you. When I bought the car here a few years back, I was told there was a smartphone app to pair with the car—do you know about that?"

"I'm not much of a tech guy, but I'll see if I can help. Are you trying to set it up?"

"No. I'm actually trying to delete my account."

"Oh, I see. I'm sorry, it's a third-party app, so you would have to contact them."

"Really? So, what do you do when a car is traded in and you resell it?"

"As far as the app goes, nothing," he said, shaking his head. "We're not required to let the third-party know when a vehicle is traded in," Jim said, stiffening.

"You're kidding me," I replied, astounded. "I'm asking because I had an IT guy set up the app for me, and I think he's using it to stalk me. I have a Temporary Restraining Order where the judge specifically wrote that he's not to access the GPS on my car."

"An ex?" he inquired, with one eyebrow raised.

It was more complicated than a simple, binary response. I hated admitting I'd dated him. Slept with him. But I couldn't deny it. I nodded to satisfy Jim.

Jim's face softened. "One thing you should know," he said, leaning over the counter and lowering his voice, "even if you get your account removed, you only need a VIN number to set up another. Lots of people have raised this as a security concern, but so far, it hasn't changed."

I brought my hand to my mouth. "Could he know my VIN number or have a way of finding it out?"

Jim nodded and said slowly, "It's etched on the windshield of your car."

Dead end. Not only was it frivolous to pursue deleting my account, but there was no way to prove Todd was accessing the GPS on my car in direct violation of my protective order. By now, my expectation that anything would work in my favor was low, if it existed at all. While I was confident this was how he was following me, I would never really know.

Thanksgiving was fast approaching, and I wanted nothing to do with the holiday. My boss invited me to the company feast—a collection of dishes from local workers—to be held in the office the week before Thanksgiving. I politely declined. After all, my job was to cut costs and save the company money. The expense of my travel couldn't be justified for a meal, I explained. He scoffed at the notion and said it was about building rapport with colleagues. Maybe he'd noticed that nobody invited me to lunch, dinner, or happy hour. Maybe he hadn't. Either way, I declined.

The week of the company feast, I read every article I could find on the internet about the murdered woman and rewatched the TV episode, this time without alcohol. I wanted as much information as I could find to put my mind at ease.

Flipping on my lamplight as the sun slowly disappeared beneath the horizon, I turned to my computer and constructed a timeline using all the information I'd gathered. I added in dates from my own history with Todd and highlighted these connections in blue.

What emerged was astounding.

The day we'd gone to the shooting range—the day of the picture used at the protective order hearing—was a month after Todd had dropped the L-bomb on me, and I didn't reciprocate. I thought he had backed off and was respecting my boundaries. Could he have been stalking her, planning her murder?

A narrative swirled through my head—compelling, terrifying, and possibly completely fabricated. Had Todd courted her the way he'd done me? Showered her with attention until she felt special, until she trusted him enough to let him install cameras "for her safety"? Had she seen through him like I eventually did? No. I was making this up. Wasn't I? I couldn't tell anymore if I was connecting dots or just desperately trying to make puzzle pieces fit where they didn't belong.

I needed a second opinion. While I loved Lauren, I needed someone level-headed. Nathan. This time, we met for dinner at a small Mexican restaurant tucked into the corner of a strip center north of town. The walls were painted yellow, with faux cracks to mimic a hacienda in Mexico. The atmosphere was festive, but the mood in our booth was somber.

I waited for the waitress to take our orders before pulling out the murder timeline, with my blue text woven into it. I placed it on the table and launched into my suspicions about Todd while Nathan pecked at the tortilla chips.

Saving what I thought was the most damning piece of circumstantial evidence for last, I pulled out the photograph I'd used at the hearing.

"Remember this picture of Todd holding the gun?"

"Uh-huh." Nathan dragged a chip through the red salsa. "What about it?"

"It's the same caliber this article said she was shot with. This photograph was taken four days before her murder. I was there. I took this photograph," I whispered, keeping my voice low to avoid anyone overhearing our conversation. "Nathan, what if this is a picture of the murder weapon the police are looking for?"

The waitress approached with our plates. I could hear Nathan's fajitas sizzling on the cast iron skillet, the smoke billowing through the air. I snatched the photo and the murder timeline from the table, turning them face down on the vinyl booth next to me.

"Be careful. Hot plate."

"Thank you," Nathan said.

When she turned and left, I went right back to it. "He'd told me he was in love with me, and I didn't reciprocate. He stopped coming over every single day, which seemed like a normal response to me. Now I wonder if he directed his anger and obsession toward this woman. You watched the episode—you know she was being stalked. Does the white truck sound familiar?"

Nathan scratched his head. "I don't think he could have done it. I'm sure he's harmless. Remember when you hit him that night he broke your phone? He ran away."

Nathan had a point. But he hadn't experienced what I had. He had not seen what I had seen.

"Todd *invited* me to go shooting that day. It's too coincidental."

"I think it's a stretch, kiddo. You need to focus on your case."

Nathan's response was just as I feared. With no tangible evidence, I'd hit a dead end. I sounded like a crazy person seeking revenge. Confirmation bias, they'd call it—interpreting things only in a way that supports your thoughts or theories.

We rode back to my house in silence, except for Nathan's belch, which he blamed on the refried beans. I think he was trying to lighten the mood, but my mind was reeling. If I'd imagined Todd's connection to the murder, what else had I imagined?

CHAPTER
THIRTY-EIGHT

A slight breeze played with the leaves, blowing my hair into my eyes. Although it was November, the winter chill had not yet arrived. My heels clicked on the pavement beneath me, carrying me into the courthouse, where I felt small in the hallowed halls, holding The Black Binder by my side. I eventually found my way to a set of glass doors that gave way to a bright, sleek office on the second floor. I was greeted by a smiling receptionist who asked me to take a seat until the prosecutor was ready for me.

I sat in a chair closest to the glass window, which ran the length of the lobby. My eyes wandered over the central atrium that had separated me from Todd at the hearing.

After a few moments, a blonde woman emerged from a door with controlled access. "Kathryn! It's nice to meet you. I'm Elaine, the prosecutor handling your case." She extended her hand, offering me a firm handshake.

"Hello. It's nice to meet you."

I followed her back through the door into a large conference room that held an impressive oak table. "Take a seat," Elaine said with a smile as she changed the sign on the door from "Vacant" to "Occupied" before closing it. Just then, a middle-aged man wearing a suit stepped into the room, followed by a waft of spiced aftershave. The chair rattled as he pulled it toward him and stuck out his stocky hand. "I'm Jacob, the district attorney investigator assigned to your case."

Time had not been gentle to him. His tired, wrinkled shirt matched his crow-footed eyes. Sitting next to Elaine, polished and perky, Jacob seemed out of place. My stomach dropped at his presence, and I wasn't sure what it meant or what a D.A. investigator even does. *Is he investigating me to see if I'm telling the truth?*

After Jacob and Elaine provided some background about themselves, Elaine piped up. "We've been through all of the information provided to us, including the binder of documentation you compiled."

"Yes," Jacob added. Then came the dreaded statement: "We need to ask you a few questions."

I grasped the armrests of my chair. Elaine began the interview with simple questions—about my job, how long I'd lived in the area, and how many children I had—basic things to orient them to my life.

Then Jacob asked more difficult questions about my relationships, whether I had ever been a prostitute, my alcohol and drug use, and if I had ever been diagnosed with a mental health disorder. I knew these questions were necessary, but they were still offensive and unpleasant.

I hadn't exactly been celibate in the eleven years between my divorce from Mark and my marriage to Jason. On days the boys were with their father, I was guilty of casual flings and at least one friends-with-benefits arrangement. But a prostitute? No.

Drugs? No.

Alcohol? *Hmmm.* Before this, I was a social drinker.

Mental health disorder? Debatable in my current state, but diagnosed? No.

As I nervously answered, I felt an overwhelming sense of vulnerability.

When Jacob finished, he leaned back in his chair and folded his hands over his belly. "So, let me make sure I have this right—tell me the story from beginning to end. You're at the bar with a friend and you're introduced to this guy . . . start from there," he prompted.

I took a deep breath to calm my racing heart and asked for some water. Elaine left the room, leaving me sitting in silence with Jacob. He studied me, and I ached to itch my arm—but what would that mean to him?

Should I make eye contact or avoid it completely?
Does he see me breathing rapidly?
Can he see my pulse racing in my neck?

My knee bounced uncontrollably beneath the table. I was deathly afraid that any nervous energy or hesitation could be misconstrued as fabrication. This is what a lack of support does to you. When you're dismissed again and again, your confidence fades into the ether.

Finally, Elaine returned with a smile and placed an unopened bottle of water wrapped in a napkin in front of me. I hesitated to take it because I had seen this tactic on television crime shows. They give you a bottle so you'll pick it up and leave your fingerprints behind. Why else would Elaine have wrapped it in a napkin? She was keeping her fingerprints off the bottle. Even though I had committed no crime, I felt like I was being interrogated as a criminal.

"Kathryn," Elaine said softly. "Are you able to begin?"

I took a deep breath and nodded, dragging my gaze away from the napkin-wrapped water bottle to meet hers. I reached for the water, my fingers brushing against the cold condensation, and took a shaky sip.

Jacob's stony demeanor hadn't changed, so I looked at Elaine as I explained how I met Todd a little over two years ago when I was at Oskar's with Monica. I used my timeline to walk them through everything from that moment up until the recent Sunday breakfast with Nathan. I paused occasionally to make sure neither of them had questions. As the words spilled out of me, I felt my apprehension melt away. I sat upright, using hand gestures on the table as I described the incidents. I could tell my voice reflected confidence rather than emotion.

"When Todd took my cameras offline this last time, I hired a company to help me get them back online and discovered two I didn't know about. The technician traced the cables, but they were cut, so I think Todd may have accessed my house at some point without my knowledge and removed the additional, hidden cameras. Isn't that illegal?"

"It is illegal for him to have installed cameras in or around your house without your knowledge," Elaine said. "But the problem is proving it. If the cables were cut, that doesn't necessarily mean a camera was ever there."

"Much less one we could trace back to Todd," Jacob quickly added.

Elaine nodded in agreement. "Is there anything else you haven't shared with us or the police? It's important we have all the information," she said softly.

My heart raced as I thought of the secret I'd kept buried deep inside— the one I hadn't told anyone. The one that weighed heavily on my heart and held me back from moving on.

Todd's thick form in the moonlight.
His nostrils flared.
His belt buckle glinted in the light.

I felt torn between wanting to keep it hidden and wanting to get it off my chest. I sat there, struggling with what to do next.

"Take your time," Elaine said, sensing my hesitation. My eyes darted back and forth between Elaine and Jacob, searching for a safe place to land.

Jacob's face was stern and serious. Elaine's was passive and expressionless. Both waited silently for a response.

"Kathryn, you can trust us," Elaine said gently.

Jacob studied my expression, seemingly trying to read my mind, before finally speaking. "You can trust us with your story. You can tell us anything, and it will remain between us—unless the three of us decide to use it in the case."

His kind words, which contrasted with his tough demeanor, brought me a tiny spark of hope. A wave of relief washed over me as I finally found the courage to speak.

Slowly, I began unraveling the story of seeing Todd in my backyard on the night of my birthday. Fixated on a tiny spider making its way up the wall to my left as I spoke, my cheeks flushed bright red as I used words like fondling and masturbating. My face was streaked with tears. I felt utter shame.

Elaine and Jacob remained silent throughout, their eyes never leaving me. When I finished, understanding dawned in their expressions. I knew I had finally been heard.

"Are you okay to continue?" Jacob asked.

I nodded and forced a smile. I knew what question was coming next.

"Why didn't you report this to the police?" he asked.

The two of them stared at me, waiting for my answer. The room was eerily quiet; I could hear myself breathing as I tried to think of what to say. I felt like I was in the belly of a creature that had swallowed me whole.

"I don't know," I said, slowly shaking my head. "I was so shocked I didn't believe what I had seen at first." I caught myself, realizing that such an explanation might cast doubt in their minds as well. I swallowed hard and sat up straight, trying to project every ounce of confidence I could muster. "I know what I saw, without any doubt whatsoever. But that night was just so terrifying that I didn't *want* to believe it."

"You said it was your birthday?" Jacob asked.

"Yes."

"And what day is that?"

"June seventeenth."

Of course, Jacob knew my birthday. I sensed he was easing me back into questioning.

"You said you didn't celebrate it?"

"That's right. I stayed home by myself to avoid any incidents with Todd."

"Uh-huh."

A pause.

"And you said earlier that you routinely drink alcohol?"

"Yes."

"Did you have anything to drink the night this happened?"

"Yes."

"How many drinks?"

"At least three, maybe more. I don't remember."

"Would you say you were intoxicated that night?"

Suddenly, I realized where he was going, and my humiliation shifted into anger. "I know what I saw," I said firmly but quietly, daring him to contradict me.

Elaine scribbled something on her notepad, and I instinctively knew each piece of my narrative was being scrutinized and passed through some algorithmic sieve in Jacob's mind.

Jacob stared at me for a long moment and finally spoke. "Kathryn, I believe that happened. And I'm sorry it happened to you."

"I'm sorry, too," Elaine said gently.

I appreciated Elaine's words, but hearing them from Jacob brought me the most comfort. Here was a man trained to tell the difference between truth and lie, and he had used the words "I believe you."

"I see how tough it was for you to share that. I promise it won't go further than this room. We won't be using that for the trial," Elaine said, her brows furrowed.

"I'm sure I can keep it together on the stand. I want to testify about the whole experience—to show how Todd has completely unraveled."

"We can't use it," Jacob said. "It's your word against his, with no physical evidence, no police report, and you admitted to being possibly intoxicated."

The way he said it was clinical, yet definitive, and I dared not challenge him. Jacob looked deep in thought before finally speaking again. "Do you have anything else to add? Anything else you may have noticed during your interactions with Todd?"

"No," I said firmly, looking directly into his eyes, determined not to waver in my story.

"Okay. Thank you for your time. Again, I'm sorry this happened," Jacob said, rising from his chair and extending his hand. As I got up, he handed me an official looking document along with his business card.

"If anything happens, call 911, and provide them with the information on this sheet. Then text or call me—anytime, day or night," he advised, moving Gina to the third rung on the notification ladder.

I knew that if I had made it this far without going off the deep end, then surely there was hope that things would turn out okay in the end.

CHAPTER
THIRTY-NINE

Todd's taunting remained within the lines of the protective orders, so that any report I tried to file fell on deaf ears. It was no different than when Robert issued the first no-contact letter, so all I could do was wait. He screwed up once before; maybe he would again.

Since the day Todd slid into my car at the grocery store, I had been getting my groceries delivered—a practice I'd keep for years to come. Despite Gina's advice to go about life normally, I withdrew. Instead, I made it my mission to restore order to parts of my life I had previously neglected. It was my way of regaining control.

I started with my consulting business. I'd done nothing with it that entire year except pay government fees to keep it open. It was time to shut it down. I'd only ever had that one client who had put me on a monthly retainer just a few months before Todd attempted to kidnap me. After that, I dodged their emails and calls. I lied that I was on vacation. They reached out with a polite thank you, and my services were no longer needed at the end of last year. "Send me a final bill, and I'll get you paid."

Putting together my profit-and-loss statement for the accountant should be easy, so I started with that. The company had a bank account, which I kept track of in my head. I rarely used any funds from the account, and with limited income, the balance was low. The debit/credit card had long sat on my desk collecting dust so I wouldn't forget about it, but I didn't have any expenses.

I logged into my bank to download my year-to-date transactions. The balance was far lower than what I had in my head. At the beginning of the year, I received my last payment, which I confirmed matched the monthly retainer. I checked the handful of debits from the account, mostly for software and professional dues, and began matching them to receipts. I found all but two.

I racked my brain trying to remember what I might have purchased from an Internet-based computer wholesale supplier, and then it hit me—Todd. I pulled out my black binder and cross-referenced the dates of the transactions. They were just days after Todd returned Winston. The cameras at my house had been disabled. Either he was at my house while I was on the road the night he stole Winston, or he'd recorded my debit card information somewhere because he knew I wasn't keeping up with the account.

I found the company's website and called, asking for Accounts Payable, since they had no physical location. I explained that I was missing two receipts from earlier in the year to finalize my year-end transactions and asked if she could help. She asked for my name and the name of my company, but came up with no records.

"I contracted my IT work out. Can you search under the owner's name or his company's name?"

"No, ma'am. You'll have to contact the company you contracted with directly."

Dead end.

~

My mission to get the receipts was derailed when Dylan called to say he'd be home for Christmas. This was the longest I had ever gone without seeing him, and I longed to hold him in my arms. I steeled myself and tried to shut out the hum of anxiety—above all, I was a mother, and it was Christmas.

I stared at an empty corner—the spot where the Christmas tree usually stood. I felt so defeated, so broken, that putting up a tree seemed all wrong. Winston nudged my leg as if to tell me I needed to put it up for Dylan.

I called Lauren for backup, and she showed up in a red, ugly Christmas sweater and green yoga pants, ready to decorate. She had Christmas music playing, and it was impossible not to feel cheerful as we worked together, laughing as we pulled each ornament from the box, pretending they were earrings or big bulbous noses.

Dylan's presence was the temporary solace I needed. After seeing him off to see his dad, Nathan invited me to a restaurant across town.

We were seated at a table near the bar when Todd walked in and joined a group of people not far from our table. Even though we were there first, we paid our bill, and as we were walking out, I heard Todd's distinctive southern drawl growl to the man next to him. "That's the bitch I was telling you about."

Nathan stopped dead in his tracks. I grabbed his arm and pulled him toward the door. "He's not worth it," I whispered.

I wanted to dig my heels in and call the police to report the violation, but I didn't. I just wanted to go home, add it to the incident log, and get the rest of the boys' presents wrapped.

Once the holidays were over and Dylan was back in training, I had a chance to revisit the mystery charges on my business bank account. I contacted the Accounts Payable department again, praying I'd get a different person than before. I explained that my IT contractor had charged the items directly to my card, and I had paid separately for the labor. I added that I'd heard he had been arrested, so I didn't want to contact him for the receipts and wondered if she could help me obtain them so I could finish reconciling my transactions for the accountant.

I sensed her hesitation as I provided Todd's name, his company's name, and the last four digits of my card. She asked for the address, and I hesitated. If I got this wrong, she might not help me. Most equipment Todd purchased had been shipped to my house since I worked from home full-time, but I wasn't sure if that was the case if he was stealing from me. Fingers crossed, I gave her my home address.

"Thank you for confirming the address we have on file."

"Great. Can you email me the receipts?"

"Unfortunately, no. Your email address is not in our system. What I can do is mail you a hard copy to the address we have on file."

"I understand. Yes, please put them in the mail—I will wait for them."

I anxiously waited for the mailed receipts. They were slow to arrive, but eventually, I received them. As I flipped through, I learned that he'd used my card for the purchase of IT equipment for the police department, according to the customer reference line on one of the receipts. I reached out to Gina, who didn't hesitate.

"I want to see those receipts. If Todd is convicted of theft, that means the police department is using equipment criminally acquired."

By this time, two months had passed since I first saw the charges. Even so, the purchases were dated five months before his arrest on the stalking warrant, so I was concerned the police wouldn't believe me.

"That doesn't matter," Gina explained. "Contact the police right away."

That same afternoon, I went to the sheriff's department, and a deputy took my report. I had little hope that anything would come of it, based on my previous experience with reports that went nowhere.

Yet, a week later, a detective contacted me and asked me to walk him through the details. He asked the same questions four or five different ways to see if my answers would change. Just like with Jacob in the conference room, I felt like I was being interrogated.

"Thank you for your time, Ms. Caraway. If you think of anything else, feel free to call me. In the meantime, I'll continue my investigation."

"Thank you, Detective."

"And Ms. Caraway? I'd strongly advise you to change your passwords."

"Yes, sir."

Sitting on the couch, I started going through all the apps on my phone. I flicked from screen to screen when an app caught my eye. It was a Google Search app that I'd never realized was there. I was so accustomed to using Safari for anything I needed that I'd never even looked for another.

Curious, I opened it and saw that it was signed into Todd's profile. I opened the settings and was alarmed to see that all his search history was about me. From what I was seeing, he was obsessively scouring the Internet for information on me. Even more alarming, several searches related to content in my personal text messages. For example, Dylan had texted me the address where I could send care packages while he was in basic training. There was a Google search in Todd's history with the same address and even the name of the military base. I felt sick at the sight—why did he need to know where Dylan was? Instinctively, I worried he had something sinister in mind for Dylan if he couldn't get to me.

As I continued to look through Todd's history, I noticed he was searching for information on a flight number from Chicago. Using the date of his search, I checked my work-related travel file, and the date and flight number matched up. He'd managed to figure out what flight I was on when I returned from a trip. I was completely stunned. *How was he getting this flow of information after the spyware was removed from my phone?*

Once again, I created a tab in my binder with screenshots of Todd's search history. I also took a screenshot of my texts from Dylan with his address to show how the dates matched up, and repeated the process for other linked events. Finally, I logged into my work computer and printed out my flight itinerary, showing the date and flight number that matched Todd's search.

As I thought about that flight, I remembered participating in a special airline promotion. If you posted a photo to social media and tagged the airline, you received a free in-flight drink. Coming home, I needed a whiskey, so I met the promotion's requirements. It may sound far-fetched to say Todd got some data from the selfie I posted, but not when I remembered what he told me about extracting information from a photo taken with a smartphone.

This would become the last photograph I ever posted on social media.

Armed with the new tab in my binder, I met Gina at her office. "Look, here's the app signed into Todd's profile. You can see here that he's searched for Dylan's address, and here—this was my flight number when I returned from Chicago!"

"How did your app get logged into Todd's account?" Her question hung in the air.

I bit my lip, realizing I had no good explanation. "He set up a Google Wi-Fi system at my house," I said slowly. "When he took down my computer network after I filed the first police report, he came over to fix it. He used the app on my phone to show me how to reset the system. I guess when he set everything up, he connected it to his Google account."

Gina frowned as she continued scrolling through my phone, piecing together Todd's Google searches with my texts.

"I'm worried Todd will accuse me of illegally hacking his account. I don't even know how to do that, but Elaine and Jacob might not believe me."

Her eyes widened. "I'm scared for you, Kathryn. We have to report this to the police." She picked up her phone and dialed the sheriff's department non-emergency line. Soon, two deputies arrived at her office, and we sat with them in the conference room.

Even with all this information, the deputies said no crime had been committed. No charges would be pursued, even with my Criminal *and* Civil Protective Orders.

"He's getting the information from her phone!" Gina said, incredulous.

"You can't prove that." One deputy shook his head. "Google searches aren't enough. They don't really mean anything."

Gina pressed him further, and then it came—the familiar statement form, slid across the table. They would never have filed a report if I had spoken to them alone.

With the report number in hand, I went straight home and up to the office. I emptied the binder Caleb used in high school, and set about organizing the Google searches with the corresponding text messages—Binder No. 2.

I was ensnared in Todd's digital web of surveillance. He seemed to be everywhere—in every corner of my life. Nothing was sacred.

CHAPTER
FORTY

Two days after filing the Google police report, I was on a conference call when my phone chirped, alerting me to a social media message from an unfamiliar name. I held my breath, dreading what I might find when I tapped on it.

Social media had been the source of so much of my suffering throughout this ordeal. Todd had posted numerous inflammatory statements about me. He never mentioned me by name, which rendered me helpless to stop him. His posts always concluded with *Y'all know who I'm talking about*—and everybody did. I had blocked him on social media a long time ago, but well-intentioned people had either shown me or texted me screenshots of his posts for over a year. The same well-intentioned people who wouldn't testify on my behalf.

My heart raced as I opened the message. More messages came in as I started to read. The sender was a woman who claimed she had recently dated Todd. He told her about the stalking charge, but she believed the lies he spun about his innocence. That is—until he revealed his inner monster to her.

Because of the time she spent with Todd, the woman was able to detail my recent movements—dates, times, and places—with accuracy. It chilled me to the bone, especially when one particular date stood out. She was there the night the private investigators filmed me at dinner. I remembered the investigator mentioning that Todd had left with a woman after peeping through the window from the bushes. She was that woman.

The woman's message deepened my unease. She had been with Todd at places where I was, without my even knowing he was there. As I read on, an acid taste rose into my throat.

> *One night, Todd picked me up and was supposed to drive me home. Instead, he took me to his house. I was terrified. He refused to let me leave for 2 days.*

She concluded by saying she hoped I would win a conviction.

I ended the conference call as my printer hummed to life, churning out a copy of the messages. Snatching up the printed sheets, I raced out of my house. The only thing I could think of was that I needed to get this message to the sheriff's department. I clutched the pages in my white-knuckled hands while driving. I hurried into the station and asked to see an officer. I was taken into the small room I'd been in several times now—the one with the one-way mirror.

I told the story to a clean-shaven deputy, and he raised his eyebrows. "How do I know you didn't make this profile yourself?"

My mouth gaped open. I was stunned. "Because you investigate it. Why on Earth would I—"

"And, I mean, even if this woman does exist, she might be seeking revenge because this guy broke up with her. I can't do anything for you." He shook his head.

"Please—"

"Has he physically harmed you in any way? Threatened you?"

"No. That's what I'm trying to prevent."

"I can't help you," he said flatly.

I left the sheriff's department devastated. If I was fragile when I arrived, I was shattered when I left. Climbing back into my car, I realized my clothes were rumpled and my hair disheveled—a stark contrast to the polished officer who seemed to have already made up his mind about me before I even opened my mouth.

Defeated, I retreated to my fortress at home. I wanted whiskey so badly I could already taste it, but I couldn't let alcohol taint this moment. I needed to think clearly, rationally.

Once safely inside, I curled up on the sofa with Winston by my side and just sat, staring at the floor. Alone with my thoughts. Even though it was now after hours, I grabbed my phone and messaged Gina. She responded immediately. I hated that I was taking time away from her family, but this was important, and I didn't know who else to turn to.

Gina asked that I send her the messages. My phone rang a few minutes after I sent them. It was Gina.

"Kathryn, are you okay?"

"The police won't even look into the messages."

"This is bullshit. Do not, I repeat, do not respond to the messages. The minute you respond, the prosecutor won't be able to use them. Do you understand?"

"Yes, of course."

"Call Elaine first thing tomorrow morning. I know it's tough, but you have to sit tight. And don't tell anyone about them, okay?"

"Okay."

"Are you alone tonight?"

"I have Winston with me." I tried to be light-hearted amidst such a heavy day.

"Can you go to Lauren's without telling her about the messages?"

"I could, but honestly, I just want to be alone."

"Please make sure you are safe. Doors locked. Outside lights on."

I moved through my house like a woman with nothing left to lose. I didn't bother checking the doors or windows. I was resigned to the notion that I'd rather Todd hurt me, so they'll have to do something about it. Walking through the kitchen, the printouts of the social media messages were on my kitchen table—taunting me. I shoved them in The Black Binder so I didn't have to see them. Even with them out of sight, I couldn't let it go. The messages corroborated my timeline. I just needed someone to check out the sender.

The next morning, I called Elaine's office, but she was in court. Instead, I asked for Jacob.

"Hi, Jacob. It's Kathryn. I'm sorry to bother you, but—"

"You're never bothering me, Kathryn. I said you could call anytime, and I meant it."

I explained the message I received, reading its content to him verbatim, my voice shaking as I battled emotion. I paused after finishing, trying to catch my breath.

"Did you report this to the police?"

"I tried. They wouldn't take a report." I sniffled. I gave him the date, time, location, and name of the deputy I'd spoken with.

"Thanks for keeping me updated. Send me a copy of the message as soon as you can. I'll be back in touch," Jacob said before we said our respective goodbyes.

To my surprise, Jacob called back a few days later. As he spoke, I crumpled onto the cold kitchen tile beneath me. He had spoken to the woman who sent the message and confirmed she was legitimate. He'd also compared her message to my incident log and matched up the dates and places she mentioned with the entries I'd cataloged. After sharing his findings with Elaine, she was so distressed that she said she would be filing a Motion to Revoke Bond.

"What does that actually mean?" I asked.

"There will be a hearing, and the judge will decide if there is sufficient evidence that Todd is a credible threat. If so, he will be remanded back to jail until trial."

Now I understood the purpose of a D.A. investigator—and this was the person I needed most.

"And Kathryn?"

"Yes?"

"Do you have Todd blocked on social media?"

"Yes. And I know he has me blocked."

"How do you know that?"

"I can't remember who unfriended whom, but I started hearing from people about posts he was making about me, though not naming me. I tried to find him, but his profile wouldn't come up. Screenshots I've been sent are included in The Black Binder I turned over to the sheriff's department the night the stalking warrant was issued."

"If I were in your position, I wouldn't post anything on social media. I'd stay off it completely. We are monitoring his posts."

The call ended. I slumped against the kitchen cabinet, my eyes squeezed shut. Emotions swirled around me. The Motion to Revoke Bond was promising, so I decided to focus on that. I was anxious to tell Gina, so I called her right away.

"Praise Jesus!" she shouted into the phone. "Okay, as soon as the date for the hearing on Elaine's motion is set, we'll schedule some time to go over your testimony."

"Thanks, Gina. Jacob also suggested I stay off social media. I haven't posted since we linked his Google searches to that one social media post I made on the flight home from Chicago. I changed all my passwords, but should I just delete the accounts?"

I grimaced. I'd only posted on social media to get a free drink. And I only needed a drink because I was flying back into the hurricane named Todd. Now I realize that a free drink cost me so much more than if I'd just paid the damn money.

"No, do not delete the accounts. There might be more women out there who only have this way of reaching out to you. But I agree with Jacob—don't post anything on social media."

"I wish someone would tell Todd that."

"I know it's hard, Kathryn. But maybe he'll slip up and post something that we can use to incriminate him."

As Gina spoke, I scrolled through my profile. I'd set it up in the early days of social media to stay connected with loved ones back home. My page was full of pictures and posts about the boys' childhood—the boys who are now men.

After we hung up, I didn't want to dwell on it. Instead, I focused on the potential that Todd's bond would be revoked, and he'd have to await trial in jail.

This would be the first time I'd have to face Todd in criminal court. And I was terrified.

CHAPTER
FORTY-ONE

As I sat at my desk in the mid-morning sun, a detective called to follow up on the Google police report I had filed two weeks prior. Things were starting to happen, and I was having trouble keeping everything straight. The detective offered to come to the house, but I told her I didn't think that was a good idea because of Todd's access to the cameras. Instead, we agreed to meet at the sheriff's department.

I made sure I entered with confidence, dressed impeccably. The last time they had seen me, I was a mess. Now I was dressed up, with makeup on, hair meticulously curled, and two binders of documentation tucked under my arm. I was ready for any questions the detective might have. When I walked through the door the receptionist led me into a conference room where the detective was waiting.

"It's nice to meet you," she said. "Please sit." She had the police report and printouts of the Google searches, which showed Todd's profile picture in the upper right-hand corner.

"Kathryn, show me where you believe his searches coincided with items on your phone," she requested.

I complied. I went through the information I'd received via text and was able to show her exactly what Todd searched for, often right away, feeling more confident than I had before. After I showed her the final search, I handed her my phone. "Take a look."

After reviewing the items on my phone and asking me a string of clarifying questions the detective asked if I would be willing to leave my phone at the station for a few days. With Dylan away, I hesitated, but I needed my suspicions about Todd having access to my phone confirmed, so I agreed.

She handed me an affidavit indicating that I voluntarily provided my personal property for use in an investigation, and that anything found may be used against me. I paused.

She looked at me sympathetically and said, "Remember, we're not looking for anything on you. We're looking for evidence against Todd. You do want him to be held accountable, right?"

I was incredulous. Of course, I did. But she failed to see that it was *my* freedom to move about the community that Todd had infringed upon. It was *my* right to privacy that he had violated. Yet, I was the one under the microscope—no one had gone to his house, checked his phone or his computer to find the evidence I was certain existed.

I didn't ask for any of this. Sure, I made mistakes, and I have paid dearly for them. It seemed law enforcement was so focused on me that Todd faced no consequences. That was why he continued. Why couldn't anyone see that?

I signed the form and disabled my password—a bitter pill to swallow. Anyone with my phone would have complete access to my entire life. The detective kindly explained how the chain of custody works, which gave me some small measure of comfort as she sealed my phone in an evidence bag.

Without my phone, I felt barren and disconnected. Many times, I thought about getting a burner phone that Todd couldn't track. Now that I didn't have mine, I stopped off and picked one up just so I wouldn't be without one. I returned home, a fragile shell of my former self. Over the next few days, the only times I left the house were to check the mail or let Winston out for a bathroom break. Although Winston wasn't on anxiety medication anymore, he still stuck close by—and still does today.

A notice arrived in the mail about a pre-trial hearing on the stalking charge. I had no phone, no email communication from Gina or the prosecutor's office, but it was scheduled for the next morning. I pulled myself together and arrived at the courthouse twenty minutes early. The pews were uncomfortable—wooden and stiff. The courtroom was crowded, and neither Todd nor his attorney was present. I wondered if a no-show would lead to a contempt of court charge, like I'd seen on TV shows.

After some time, Elaine asked to speak with me in the hallway. "Todd has changed attorneys, so a Motion to Continue has been granted."

I pressed my lips together. "What does this mean?"

"It means the pre-trial hearing will be rescheduled, and you'll be notified of the new date. I'm aware of the pending police reports, and I'm closely monitoring those. I will be filing a Motion to Revoke Bond based on the incidents you've documented. If we're successful, the longer the trial gets continued, the more time he'll have to wait in jail."

"Okay." I nodded, my mind racing. Jacob had said Elaine was going to file the motion weeks ago. *Why is she waiting?* I wondered but didn't ask.

I borrowed Lauren's phone and texted Gina as I was leaving the courthouse with the update. She confirmed that this was good news. In fact, she wrote, *We want this.*

The next day, the detective emailed my work account to let me know my cell phone was ready to be returned. She offered to meet me at the sheriff's department again to go over the results. When I was finally seated across from her, she got straight to the point.

"We did a forensic analysis of your phone. The items you have that coincide with Todd's Google searches are concerning, but we can't find anything concrete to tie them to him."

My shoulders sank. I was crestfallen.

"I'm going to leave the report open for a while. We'll see if anything else comes up that we can build a case from."

While disappointed that the search had been unproductive, I appreciated her offer. I couldn't help but wonder if having a female officer on my side worked in my favor. All the other officers I'd worked with had been male.

As I stood up to leave, the detective said, "One more thing. You need to log out of his Google account."

I placed my phone back on the table and, under her watchful eye, I logged out.

∼

One wintry February day, I impulsively decided to take Winston to the dog park. The only park with a large, open field where he could run off-leash. It was closer to Todd's house than mine. Thinking about it made my stomach flip, but I reasoned that since I didn't have to drive directly past his house to get there, I would be okay.

Winston and I hadn't been at the park very long when Todd's truck crept by, his window down and arm casually hanging out. I froze as it circled the park, gliding along like a shark circling its prey. Disconcerted, I looked around. There was only one way in and one way out. I was trapped. A handful of people were in the park that chilly winter day, and I knew no one would come to my rescue if Todd decided to storm through the gate.

Armed with my Civil Protective Order and Criminal Protective Order, I dialed 911. As the phone eased to my ear, Todd slammed on the gas and sped away, leaving a cloud of steamy exhaust behind. The operator instructed me to call back if I saw him again.

My senses heightened; my heart pounded as I continued to scan the surroundings for Todd's vehicle. Then it occurred to me—he could be waiting at the park exit for me. Even though it was a huge complex spanning 488 acres, there was only one way in and out of the park.

Suddenly, his truck reappeared. I was prepared. I didn't hesitate to call 911 again, describing Todd's movements with urgency that rattled my bones. I begged the operator to send help quickly before he got too close.

"Hold, please."

What the hell?!

They told me a unit was on its way and asked me to stay on the line.

As Todd passed again, the back passenger window rolled down, and Winston's twin stuck his head out. I was certain that after seeing me at the park, he had driven to his nearby home, picked up his dog, and used him as a cover story. Todd was masterful at creating enough doubt so law enforcement would see it as a coincidence. I feared this time would be no different.

His truck inched forward like liquid silver, circling the dog park until he reached my car. "He just pulled into the parking lot and is stopped at the rear of my car!" I exclaimed to the operator.

I called Winston over and clipped his leash on.

Where are the police?

Todd accelerated quickly into a U-turn and sped out of the park. I was left standing there, with the cackle of activity on the other end of the line. Despair and confusion clouded my judgment as I realized there was no sign of a crime being committed.

It seemed like an eternity before the police car finally appeared, and the operator ended our call. I led Winston out of the park and crossed the street to the parking lot where the police car had stopped. The officer approached me but kept his distance from Winston.

"For the safety of the officer, please put the dog in the car," he said firmly.

With Winston in my car, the officer approached. "I'm Officer Daniels. Can you tell me what the problem is?"

I could sense this was going nowhere, but I willed myself to comply. The officer asked for my driver's license and handed me a statement form to fill out. As soon as I finished writing, I snapped a photo of my statement for The Black Binder and gave it to the officer.

"Thank you. Another officer on patrol was able to locate Todd."

"Really?" I almost shouted with relief.

"Yeah, he was driving away from the dog park." Apparently, the officers with Todd relayed his story—and just as I thought, he claimed he had simply taken his dog to the park, saw me there, and left, then rerouted to a nearby nature trail.

"I made two 911 calls. He circled once, left to pick up his dog and create this cover story, then came back. I have both a Criminal and Civil Protective Order against him. How is this not stalking?" I said, anger rising.

"I am aware two calls were made. You told the operator he didn't have the dog on the first drive-by, correct?"

"Correct."

"How do you know the dog wasn't in the vehicle?"

"Well . . ." I stammered. "I couldn't see into the vehicle, but on the second drive-by, he rolled down the backseat window for his dog to stick his head out." I sounded ridiculous, but to me, it was clear what Todd had done to muddy the waters. And the police seemed to be letting his calculated, manipulative plan work.

"He told the officers on scene that he did not drive by the first time. Could you be mistaken it was his vehicle?"

I rattled off his license plate number, which the officer wrote down to verify.

The officer explained that he would file a report to be on record. He knew I had other open reports and he would send the detectives a copy. In the meantime, he told me to "Remain vigilant." Sensing my frustration, he empathetically advised me not to be discouraged.

"Give the judicial process time to work," he said.

Even with two protective orders, I still couldn't get law enforcement to protect me from Todd's incessant stalking.

CHAPTER
FORTY-TWO

By now, it had been over a month since I filed the police report for the fraudulent debit card charges, three weeks since the initial Google police report—which was followed by the social media message Jacob investigated—and a week since the hearing that never took place. Jason was still making a lot of demands, which essentially delayed the divorce further. The dog park incident was still fresh, and I was obliterated. When I looked in the mirror, something akin to a zombie stared back at me.

I was barely keeping my head above water at work and still trying to decide whether I should resign from my board position. It filled my heart with warmth to know I'd contributed to improving the lives of children in our community. But I knew there was still work to be done, and I had more to contribute—if I could make it past Todd.

I resigned myself to the thought that, like with the other police reports, the dog park incident would go nowhere. To my surprise, a few days after it was filed, the detective handling the theft case called with more questions.

"What was your relationship with Todd at the time of the charges to your bank account?"

"He was someone I had been seeing—we'd broken up before the transactions." I bit my lip. It felt like judgment day had arrived.

"Uh huh. Would you say he was your boyfriend?"

"No, I never considered him my boyfriend," I snapped, staring at the ceiling. "But he was renting office space from me. At my house."

I felt defeated, and his patronizing tone only made it worse. When I explained the breakup and how I involved Adam to mitigate Todd's demands for money, the detective's tone changed completely.

"There's more. When my attorney issued a no-contact letter to Todd, he asserted another claim—that I owed him money. This time, he presented an altered check that he supposedly paid on my behalf." The detective prodded for more details, which I was happy to share.

"Okay, I see. Are you at your computer?"

I hurried up the stairs to my office two at a time.

He provided me with his email address, and I forwarded the communications I had regarding Todd's demands for money, including a copy of the altered check and the original check cashed by my bank. As I clicked off the line, I stared out the window at a cotton ball cloud sailing across the sky. I felt a flicker of hope.

Three days later, the detective called again.

He had obtained the serial number of the equipment purchased on my debit card from the vendor. He then went to the police department and verified that the equipment had been sold to them and installed by Todd. Given my refusal to comply with Todd's demands for money, the detective was convinced this was theft. A warrant was issued for bank fraud—a more serious felony than theft.

I knew it was a stretch, but if convicted, it carried up to ten years in prison, whereas felony theft carried a maximum of five. The detective took a breath and said, "Honestly, Kathryn, this isn't the first time I've investigated Todd, but it's the first time I've been able to bring charges. Thank you for your cooperation and for the excellent documentation you've provided."

A smile instantly spread across my face at the irony—a law enforcement officer was *thanking* me. I couldn't believe my ears.

"One more thing," the detective started, then hesitated, as if he was debating whether to continue. "I would advise you against posting anything on social media. Especially pictures."

"Why?" I asked, curious despite not having posted anything since the Google police report.

"Seeing the information on your case, and knowing what I know about him, he could be using social media to get information on you and who you're associating with."

I'd already figured this out, but it was good to hear from an authority figure.

"Stay alert at all times," the detective warned. "The most dangerous time for a victim is the period between the warrant being issued and the arrest."

Hearing this again sent my anxiety into overdrive. After printing out all the information I'd provided the detective, I assembled the documents into Binder No. 3 and slipped it into the bag with the others.

I headed downstairs to my bedroom, Winston trailing me. I pulled the covers down and slid beneath them.

I felt for the gun.

I felt for the protective order.

I placed my hand on Winston's head. Here we were again—in danger. I believed he wouldn't stop until I'd been eviscerated, consumed, and left bone-weary and hollow.

My heart pounded. My stomach churned. My chest bore the weight of the world as I waited for word that he had been arrested. Paranoia, anxiety, and depression raged like wildfire. I refused to leave my house, convinced that Todd would find a way to hurt me. But even at home, I didn't feel safe.

... victim arrived home one evening to find the defendant in her house ...

I knew this second charge could escalate into physical violence, especially since it was a felony. What did he have to lose?

I settled back into my reclusive state, pacing the same familiar pattern, sleeping fully clothed with my gun and protective orders tucked beneath my extra pillow. I hid The Black Binder, which had been accumulating more documentation with each unfolding event. Lauren knew where it was hidden, and she had the passcode to the camera DVR, just in case something happened to me. I checked in with her regularly via text as part of my safety plan. On my phone, she was given an "emergency bypass" to ensure I'd never miss her call, even if my phone were on silent. I also told her that if she called and I didn't answer or immediately texted back, she was to call the police. She also knew not to come to my house under any circumstances. If I went missing—or worse, if I ended up dead—I didn't want her to contaminate potential evidence.

Four emotionally taxing days.

That's how long it took for them to arrest him. It then took another twenty-four hours for the jail to notify me that Todd had been arrested and released. There was no momentary reprieve where he was in jail awaiting arraignment and bond processing. One call that he was in and out. It seemed I was stuck in a never-ending cycle of unimaginable fear.

Later that day, I learned Elaine had finally filed the Motion to Revoke Bond. Since I hadn't heard anything more, I assumed she had decided against it. Gina surmised that Elaine was likely waiting to see what the police reports revealed.

So here we were: Todd had bonded out for the second time and the Motion to Revoke Bond on the stalking charge was pending a hearing. I was living like a rabbit trapped in a cage—not knowing when a predator might strike again. All I knew for sure was that I wouldn't see it coming.

CHAPTER
FORTY-THREE

After a long wait, a date for the hearing on the Motion to Revoke Bond was set. It would be the first time I had to face Todd in criminal court from the witness stand, and Gina prepared me to testify. The lack of information from Elaine and Jacob had been disheartening and only heightened my anxiety. *What aren't they telling me?* It seemed Gina and I were funneling bushels of information to them in exchange for an acorn.

On the morning of the hearing, I was a nervous wreck. I couldn't bear the thought of being in the courtroom with Todd. I asked Nathan and Lauren to come with me for support, and they agreed. Lauren offered hugs, and Nathan offered encouraging nods—they were my tiny, perfect army.

The docket was called in the morning, and the hearing was set for the afternoon. With the court in recess, Elaine met with me in her office. She was one of the top prosecutors in the office; her résumé of criminal prosecutions was impressive. This was her time to shine.

As Elaine began reviewing the incidents with me, a woman entered and handed her a piece of paper. She peered over the top of it. "Who's Jason?"

My brows furrowed, and a knot formed in my stomach. "He's my estranged husband. We're getting a divorce. Why?"

"He's on the witness list for the hearing this afternoon."

My palms began to sweat. "I don't understand. What could Jason possibly testify to?"

"Let me see what's going on." Elaine left the office for a few minutes and then returned. "Okay, well, your divorce from Jason is still pending. That means anything Jason testifies to could be discredited as 'revenge testimony.' I know this is emotional, but I'm not worried about him at all."

If she wasn't worried, I certainly wasn't. Still, it drove me crazy to think that these men—who had once professed their love for me—were now working together against me. Now I understood why Todd reached out to Jason in the first place. It wasn't just to destroy me; it was to gain an ally.

"Okay." Elaine closed her binder and tidied a stack of papers into a neat pile. "Don't talk to Todd or go anywhere near him. Stay with Nathan and Lauren at all times. If you need to go to the bathroom, take Lauren with you. While you and Todd are both in the courthouse, you should not be alone."

"I understand." I nodded.

"I'll be honest, Kathryn. This is the worst case of stalking I've seen where the victim is still alive." Her eyes were sympathetic. A wave of nausea passed over me. I was both sickened and relieved to hear this from a seasoned prosecutor. Finally, someone understood—and not just anyone. I was thankful Elaine was prosecuting my case.

Leaving the district attorney's office, I ran into Jacob. He came up close and asked, "Did Elaine get a chance to talk to you?"

"Yes, I just left her office. I'm headed to the courtroom."

"Okay, good. I just got back to the office, so I'll touch base with her. I just finished a nice conversation with your witness, and I think things will go smoothly today."

"A witness?" I was confused. Elaine had said she didn't need Lauren or Nathan today.

"Yes—the woman who sent you those social media messages. She was hesitant to get involved, but I talked her into it. She's sequestered in a witness room, and it's important that you have no communication with her."

"Oh, I didn't know any of that. Thank you." I smiled.

"I wish she would have agreed to press kidnapping charges, but she was too afraid. I see that so much." He paused, looking me in the eyes. "It's admirable what you're doing."

Tears welled in my eyes as I thought about everything I'd been through—the winding, terrifying road that had led me to this day. I was grateful for the brave woman who would speak louder than any of Jason's lies, but I also felt a deep sadness that she, like me, had been subjected to Todd's horrors.

Nathan and Lauren looked just as perplexed as I was about what Jason could possibly contribute to Todd's defense. As Gina advised, I kept my mouth shut about the social media messages and the witness. I pondered whether this courtroom moment might resemble something out of a TV show. I envisioned Elaine's booming voice: "We'd like to call a witness to the stand." Mouths would gape open, whispers would swell, and the witness would step forward to testify.

I thought about the look of disappointment on Jacob's face when he said the witness wouldn't press charges. Having lived this nightmare, I understood a victim's refusal. I'd seen firsthand the tragic duality of the system. Sometimes, it can provide safety, but too often it fails those who need help the most. Even when assistance is offered, those in desperate need may refuse—they know that the system they turn to for protection could leave them feeling betrayed, criminalized, helpless, and even further victimized.

We sat for hours on the courtroom bench, my knees bouncing and my toes tapping. I kept drifting back to Elaine's comment—*This is the worst case of stalking I've seen where the victim is still alive.* As much as I appreciated her acknowledgment of my situation, her words haunted me.

Nathan held my seat and guarded The Black Binder as I stepped into the corridor to meet Gina. My words spilled out as I filled her in on my meeting with Elaine. It felt good to get it off my chest. Gina's eyes widened as her mouth gaped open.

"Alright, let's go over this again. Let's take it one thing at a time," she said.

As I recounted each item, starting with Jason, Gina peppered me with questions. Then I saw him—Todd—out of the corner of my eye. I spun around so fast my necklace was briefly pinned against my collarbone. His belly hung over his pants, fastened with a dingy belt, his shirt tucked in, and his hair neatly combed.

Gina grabbed my arm. "Don't look at him," she commanded in a tone I'd never heard before.

My eyes widened, and I fixed them on Gina. *Breathe. Hold. Release.* Still holding my arm, she pulled me toward the elevator. We went to another floor to finish our conversation privately. She reassured me that all of this was good news—except for Jason.

"What a slimeball," she said.

It felt good to have her by my side. Gina escorted me back to the courtroom, where I nestled between Lauren and Nathan. Lauren started a game of Hangman, and Nathan joked about playing it in a courtroom. Their back-and-forth jokes eased the tension in my stomach. Occasionally, I opened The Black Binder to refresh my memory on various details, but most of the time, I stared blankly ahead, trying to organize my racing thoughts.

Finally, Elaine came in and motioned for me to step outside, where Gina was waiting. We entered the corridor, and she explained there would be no hearing. Todd's attorney had agreed to an ankle monitor to track his location instead of revoking his bond. I was frustrated that the hearing had been scheduled and then canceled, but Elaine assured me it was a win.

"We can now monitor his movements and let him incriminate himself."

I wasn't as convinced. Todd had been so devious, skirting the protective order, that I feared the ankle monitor would be no different.

"One last thing," Elaine said. "And this is a big one, so brace yourself."

I pressed my lips together, and Gina shifted closer.

"Todd claims you are stalking him. His attorney asserted that the system shows deference to women and that you beat him to filing criminal charges."

The words ripped through me like bullets. My eyes bulged like a deer caught in the headlights. My throat tightened as I fought to contain my boiling fury. I clenched my fists, a familiar heat rising in my chest. I said nothing, but I felt Jacob's eyes locked on me, analyzing my reaction.

Elaine warned, "You are not to go anywhere near him or his house. If you do, it will destroy your stalking case."

The woman who had just told me this was the worst case of stalking she'd seen where the victim was still alive was now warning me not to stalk the stalker. Any comfort I'd found in her belief in me dissipated.

I was shattered.

Shortly afterward, court resumed, and the agreement was entered into the record. The judge signed the order to have Todd fitted with an ankle monitor, which he would have to pay for himself. I felt a small sense of relief that he was finally sharing the financial burden of his criminal antics.

However, the monitor only provided a one-hundred-yard perimeter around my house. But one hundred yards doesn't give me much time to get to safety, much less for police to arrive.

Rather than the sweet taste of victory, the stench of his accusations forced me to swallow the vile words echoing in my mind: *I'm stalking him?! Incredible.*

Though this small victory should have been comforting, all I could feel were the seeds of doubt Todd's deception was sowing.

My hope for justice rested on the frail wings of truth.

CHAPTER
FORTY-FOUR

Todd's ankle monitor wouldn't prevent him from causing me physical harm, but it would give my family a lead to follow if something happened to me. I was certain that, if given the chance, Todd would kill me. I chose to take the small victory of imagining an ankle bracelet on him. Hopefully, he would be seen with this court-ordered monitoring device by everyone who had believed his repulsive lies.

Determined to get out of the house, I planned a gathering of four women—the refreshing break I desperately needed. I texted Carleigh, who'd unfriended me on social media. I was certain she, like everyone else, had distanced herself from me to avoid Todd's wrath.

As we gathered at the restaurant, the chatter rising and falling around us, Carleigh arrived shortly after me. She looked surprised to see me as I made my way over to her.

"Hi," she said tentatively.

"Hi!" I reached for a hug, which she met with a soft pat on the back.

"I'm actually meeting someone here." She looked around.

I laughed. "I know, we already have a table. I invited a few others."

She looked confused and raised her phone. "Did you text me from a new number?"

I forgot that I had texted her from the burner phone I picked up when I turned my cell phone over to the police. I explained to Carleigh it was a temporary number.

"Oh, I'm so sorry—my mistake." She laughed. "I thought you were someone else. Listen, something's come up. I need to run."

Before I could respond, she turned on her heels and left. I didn't realize it then, but this would be the last time I would ever see or hear from her. The twisted betrayal of those I once called friends was like a knife to my already broken heart.

As we sipped our mimosas and savored the flavors of our Southern breakfast, I listened gracefully to everyone's opinion on what I should do and what law enforcement should do about Todd. Some women shared their own stories of stalkers. Their cases never went to court because they handled it themselves. I felt judged and uncomfortable, but managed to plaster on a polite smile anyway. At least I had gotten out of the house.

Arriving home a little tipsy, I remembered a detail from the TV episode about the woman's murder. Investigators had attempted to access the ankle monitor of a family member they suspected might be involved. He was local, in the same court system as Todd, but they found out his ankle monitor had never been activated. He was wearing it, but no data was logged. Eventually, he was cleared as a suspect. But the fact that he had been released from the same jail as Todd haunted me. I couldn't risk Todd's ankle monitor slipping through the cracks.

I dialed the district attorney's office to see if I could confirm whether Todd was actually wearing it. I was routed to someone I hadn't spoken to before.

"Hi, Kathryn. This is Sharon. I'm the victim advocate in your case."

Although we'd never met, I recognized her name from the letters I'd received from the district attorney's office. "Hi, thank you for taking my call."

"Of course. How are you doing?"

It felt good to speak with someone in a position of authority who displayed real compassion. We briefly discussed the hearing. I steeled myself. "Is there any way to confirm Todd has been fitted with the ankle monitor?"

"You'll need to call probation about that," she advised, providing a phone number.

I called them, only to learn that they handled monitors post-conviction. Since Todd hadn't been convicted yet, I was advised to check with the court clerk to see if a confirmation of the monitor had been filed.

I then called the clerk's office, but they said nothing had been filed and directed me to speak with the judge's assistant, providing me with a phone number. I called, but was told their office couldn't have direct contact with me and that I should speak with the district attorney's office.

My ear now hot from pressing my phone against it, I called the district attorney's office again and asked to speak with Elaine. I was routed back to Sharon. I gave her a summary of the calls I'd made.

"I'm so sorry. I'll look into it and get back to you as soon as I can," she said.

Without the monitor, Todd could be anywhere. I was back in the cycle of fear. I jigged the handles, checked the windows, and scanned the yard. I slept with my shoes tied tight.

Same jail.

Same court system.

The ankle monitor wasn't activated.

Todd had proven how adept he was at manipulation, and no matter how hard I tried, I couldn't trust the system. My only option was to become my own advocate.

I waited a few days before texting Jacob to see if he could confirm the ankle monitor was in place, but he directed me to speak with Sharon.

What's happening here?

I sat at my kitchen table with my laptop, put a piece of electrical tape over the camera, and searched for ankle monitoring companies. I contacted a nonprofit organization, which was of no help. I reached out to another who advertised victim assistance; they sent me a copy of our state Victim's Bill of Rights, which offered no answers.

Finally, I called Gina to see if she could find out which company provided the monitors, explaining that it was for my peace of mind. She shared my frustration about the lack of information. "I'll help you figure this out. Just give me a couple of days."

But I didn't want to wait. I needed to know now.

The next day, the local women's shelter came up in my search, and I decided to call. The woman on the line proved to be a wealth of information. "Ankle monitors are contracted out to third-party vendors, and there are two local ones that I know of." She provided me with their phone numbers and wished me luck. Finally, someone at one of these organizations was actually helpful.

I called the first number. A man answered, and when I explained the situation, he replied, "It's against company policy to divulge any information."

Although he couldn't release the details to me directly, I was making progress. I could have Gina, or better yet, Sharon, request the information.

I decided not to give up and dialed the second number. Instead of answering with the company's name, a man answered and gave his full name. I was stunned. I knew him! He was my divorce attorney's husband, and I'd met him at her office one afternoon when I stopped in to sign some papers. Knowing that my divorce attorney had recently gone out on maternity leave, I used that as my opening.

"Hey, there! It's Kathryn. We met at your wife's office. I'm a client of hers and have a quick question about ankle monitors. Ironically, I was referred to you. How's the baby?"

They were first-time parents, so that was an easy in. He rattled off the stats—gender, weight, length—before launching into stories about sleepless nights. It made him yawn. "So, you said you had a question about ankle monitors?"

"Oh, yeah. I do. Sorry I got caught up in the baby talk. My kids are grown, and it reminds me of how a baby is like a breath of fresh air."

"She will be when she starts sleeping through the night." We both laughed.

"So, there's a criminal case . . . it's complicated, but it's someone I dated after Jason and I separated who is stalking me. I'm the victim on record in the case, and he was ordered to wear an ankle monitor last Thursday. I'm just trying to get confirmation that he's actually wearing one."

"What's his name?"

I offered it without hesitation.

"Listen carefully, Kathryn." He paused. "I am not allowed to give out any information about our clients. But I am *familiar* with that name," he added cautiously.

"Understood." I inferred from his tone that the ankle monitor was, in fact, in place. "I wouldn't want to put you in a difficult position."

"Let me explain how our ankle monitors work. One of the best features, in my opinion, is the victim notification."

I perked up.

"In, say, a stalking situation, it's helpful for the victim to receive a warning when the suspect is in proximity."

Yes!

"If his device comes within a hundred yards of a fob the victim carries, a text alert will go to her phone. The fob looks just like one for a car, so it's not noticeable."

Yes!

"If the victim fails to deactivate the alert on the fob, our system will automatically notify law enforcement."

Yes!

"It sounds like your system is top-notch. How would a victim get one of these? Asking for a friend," I joked.

He laughed. "Generally, it's court-ordered, but if the district attorney reaches an agreement with the defendant, we will provide one."

He wished me luck, and I asked him to send my best to the new mom. Now I just had to work on obtaining a victim notification fob.

In the meantime, I gazed out over my backyard, where I'd once shared my first kiss with the devil himself. The grass seemed to sag under the weight of my fear, tainted by his memory, and stained with my shame.

CHAPTER
FORTY-FIVE

It had been a little over two months since I received confirmation that Todd was being tracked. My tiny legal army—Gina, Elaine, and Jacob—now knew about the victim-fob available and we were waiting until the next hearing to request it from the court. I hadn't seen Todd in my backyard at night since before the ankle monitor was ordered. I still occasionally saw him in my rearview mirror, but I appreciated its effectiveness.

Now I was sitting in a church pew in front of my parents, looking up at the altar where Caleb stood in a tuxedo, anxiously awaiting his bride. Dylan, who had recently returned home after basic training, was standing next to him in full uniform. He looked like a toy soldier—resolute and polished—but I couldn't have been prouder of both. Caleb looked the happiest I'd ever seen him, and, for one brief night, I allowed myself to return to normal. It was a night I didn't want to end, with a beautiful reception filled with delectable food, chilly drinks, belly laughter, and music.

Dylan was back at home with me while waiting for his Advanced Individual Training to start. It comforted me to know he would be here at night. I felt guilty for feeling safe with a soldier in the house. A mother shouldn't have to rely on her young son to feel protected. But just as I knew he would protect me if Todd managed to break into the house, I knew I had to protect him.

I'd always kept firearms in the house, even when the boys were young. I'd taken them to the shooting range many times, taught them firearm safety, and made sure they never had access to my guns. Even with Dylan back home, trained by the military, I still made sure the gun that was once under the extra pillow on my bed was now in my nightstand, hidden beneath the protective order, out of sight.

On Mother's Day, I heard Dylan thundering down the stairs, and I met him in the kitchen to see where he was going. It was Sunday, so it was unusual to see him up mid-morning. He kissed me on the cheek, sweetly wished me a Happy Mother's Day, and said he was going to surprise me with donuts but had overslept. It was a sweet gesture I appreciated in a way only a mother can, and I asked to ride with him to the donut shop. After explaining he was low on gas and planned to use his gas money for donuts, I offered to drive.

The best donuts in our small town came from a little shop at the end of a strip mall. It was family owned and operated. It was the place I'd taken the boys since they were little. We chatted on the ride over, and soon we were in line at the drive-thru. Dylan suddenly interrupted me, pointing out Todd passing by. Todd had his window rolled down, and even though he was wearing sunglasses and a ball cap, we could see it was him. I didn't raise my kids to poke fun at others, but I admit, we made fun of Todd and his feeble attempt at being incognito. We took turns bantering, and it felt good. Then, the laughter subsided when we noticed Todd coming back from the other direction, as if he had turned around and was passing by again.

I reasoned that maybe he had just run to another store, but even I didn't buy it. A few minutes later, Todd passed by again. I thought about snapping a photo since his face was visible, but I didn't want to ruin the moment with Dylan. Shortly after, Todd appeared from the opposite direction again. Once we had the donuts in hand, we drove off. When we arrived home, I added the receipt to The Black Binder and noted the drive-bys.

I settled back into my Saturday breakfasts with Nathan, but I wasn't yet confident enough to go back to the grocery store or Café Calais, where Todd had installed cameras. If Dylan was up early enough, he'd join us, and I would sit back and enjoy listening to them talk about military stuff.

One Thursday, I received a letter from the district attorney's office notifying me that a pre-trial conference on the stalking charge was set. I looked at the date and gasped—it was for the following Tuesday! I felt blindsided by this notification, so I reached out to Gina, who was supposed to be monitoring the court case. She looked it up in the system and confirmed it. "I don't know anything about this. I'll reach out to Elaine. In the meantime, prepare yourself, okay?"

I procrastinated and waited until Sunday to go through The Black Binder again. As much as I needed it, I hated having it. I thought back to the hearing when Elaine said Todd was claiming I was stalking him, and wondered if there might be something in the court record I wasn't aware of. Since the district attorney's office decides whether you need a copy of a legal filing, the only document I had a copy of was the Motion to Revoke Bond that Gina had printed out for me. I needed more, so I decided to go to the courthouse and request to see the case file from the court clerk's office.

On Monday, I logged out at lunch and made my way to the courthouse. A few people were waiting in the clerk's office, so I took a number and joined them. Soon enough, my number appeared on the screen, and I approached the counter. I provided my case number, and the letter I'd received showing the hearing was scheduled for the next day, along with my driver's license.

She returned with what appeared to be a rather large case file. "I'm sorry. Because this is an active case, I can't hand this over to you. Is there something specific you're looking for?"

I gave her the date of the last hearing and asked for any available documents, as well as the Criminal Protective Order issued at Todd's arraignment. "I heard one was issued at the time he was released on bond, but I never saw it myself."

"Okay, take a seat, and I'll be back in a minute."

Sitting in the uncomfortable plastic chair, I received a call from what appeared to be my phone number. Confused as to how my phone could be calling itself, I answered. I said, "Hello," but there was silence. Then I heard Todd's distinctive southern drawl. "I know what you're doing, and you're not gonna win," he hissed into the receiver.

The call went dead. Chills ran down my spine, and the hair on the back of my neck stood up. I was in the courthouse and should have felt safe, but if he knew where I was, he could have been anywhere—by my car in the parking lot or nearby.

My breaths grew rapid and shallow, my mouth dry with each inhale and exhale. I stared at my phone in disbelief. I checked the recent call list, and there it was—my name, just as I'd seen it on the screen when the call was coming in.

How is this possible?

The clerk called out to the waiting room, and it took me a moment to realize she was calling my name. She repeated it louder. I wasn't hard of hearing, but I was in shock. I wandered over to her, and without a word, she handed me a small stack of papers. As I took the documents, she shouted, "Next!"

I sat back down in the waiting room, wondering what to do. The police would never believe me since the call registered as coming from my number. I looked at the elevator—it now looked like a metallic beast, threatening to swallow me whole and deliver me straight to Todd. After all, Todd's ankle monitor would only show he was at the courthouse, which he had every right to be at. It would be the perfect place.

Does he know something I don't about tomorrow's hearing?

My mind immediately went back to Raymond's words: *No cooperating victim, no conviction.* The walls of the room seemed to press closer, suffocating me as my thoughts spiraled into a dizzying sea of anxiety.

The woman's murder.

Todd.

A death I won't see coming.

I was helpless and alone—a pawn in this deadly game with no way out. I decided to take a chance on the police. I found the nearest officer and explained the situation. I expressed my fear that Todd might be waiting, ready to harm me. I made sure my tone was calm and clear.

"Listen, lady. I work courthouse security, so I don't take reports from the public. You need to go home, call dispatch, and file a police report."

I was stunned to be turned away and let down by law enforcement, once again. *I need to go home and file a report?* That was, of course, assuming I made it home alive.

My phone clutched tightly in my hand, I called Jacob, whose office was just upstairs. He invited me up and handed me a bottle of water as I explained everything.

"The officer is right. You need to go home and call it in. Once you have a report number, text it to me, and I will follow up on it. I'll walk you to your car."

We walked in silence, my heels clicking on the pavement. He watched as I approached my car, checked the back seat, got in, and drove off. At least I knew I was safe in my car. But if Todd was tracking me, I knew that as soon as I stopped, something might happen. Something coincidental, I was sure.

CHAPTER
FORTY-SIX

The moment I pulled into my garage, I closed the door. I waited in my car until I saw the garage door physically touch the pavement before turning off the car—the way I'd been doing it for a year now—then rushed inside and called the sheriff's department. I was told an officer would come to my house. I panicked that Todd would see the police at my house on camera, but I knew I had to take the chance.

While waiting for the officer, I wrote out my statement. By now, I knew the protocol, and it was helpful to get the incident documented as soon as possible. I printed screenshots of my phone and copies of my typed statement—one for the officer, one for The Black Binder, one for the prosecutor, and one for Gina. I was collating the copies when the doorbell rang. I hurried to the door, thankful to see a uniformed officer. I invited him into the kitchen, where I had everything organized on the table.

He glanced at the papers. "Why don't you explain what happened?"

Using the screenshots as a starting point, I explained everything, making sure to give him as much context as possible and to remain as calm as I could. When I finished, the deputy sifted through the documents on the table and lingered on the certified copy of my Civil Protective Order and the fresh copy of my Criminal Protective Order. He furrowed his brow, handed me the statement form, and gathered the documents I'd laid out. He offered a small nod and said he'd be right back. I watched him walk to his patrol car in my driveway, then completed the statement form.

He doesn't believe me, I told myself.

Moments later, the deputy returned and asked me to sit down. He remained standing and read my statement at least twice, as best I could tell. I'm not sure how many times he asked me if I was absolutely, without a shadow of a doubt, certain that it was Todd's voice on the phone, but each time, I answered truthfully. I never paused or wavered.

He went back outside to his patrol car for a short while, then returned without coming inside. He handed me a slip of paper with the report number. Like the theft report and the Google report, I assumed this would be sent to a detective for investigation. So I was surprised when he said a warrant was being issued for Todd's arrest.

I could hardly believe it. *Would this incite Todd even more?* If so, it was a risk I was willing to take. Todd had gotten away with far too much already. I texted Jacob and Gina the report number and a summary of what had happened. I felt disoriented, as if I didn't know which way was up. I sat at the kitchen table, my head in my hands, and Winston at my feet.

It startled me when my phone vibrated across the table with Sharon's name on the screen.

"I heard what happened," she started.

I breathed a sigh of relief—at least I wouldn't have to go through it all again.

"That must've been terrifying."

"Yes, it was. And it has me on edge because everyone keeps saying the most dangerous time is after a warrant has been issued and before the arrest," I said, trying to beat her to it.

"That's correct. The police went to his house to serve the warrant, but they didn't find him. So, make sure you keep your doors locked. Are you still doing check-ins with Lauren as part of your safety plan?"

I wasn't, but I lied and told her I was. I just wanted to get off the phone and have a moment to process everything.

"The most important thing now is that you don't go to the courthouse tomorrow for the pre-trial conference."

I was silent. *Has she finally realized what I've been saying all along—that I'm in danger?*

"Okay."

"Good. Do you have someone there with you now?"

"No," I replied.

"Can you stay at Lauren's tonight?"

"Yes."

As Sharon's voice faded from the call, I headed up to the office to make sure I kept all my documentation together. I put the screenshots from my phone, printed the photo I took of my statement, and the slip of paper with the report number into a folder.

My fingers trembled as I typed a quick text to Gina.

> ME
>
> Spoke to Sharon. She told me not to go to the pre-trial conference tomorrow. Are you going to be there?

Inhale. My back straightened, and my eyes closed.

Exhale. My hands clenched around my phone—the culprit of my unraveling day.

I know what you're doing, and you're not gonna win.

Breathe. The day had become a blur.

Finally, my phone chirped, alerting me to a new message. Then another.

> GINA
>
> I don't need to be there. The conference is going to be continued.
>
> GINA
>
> If Todd shows up, he'll be arrested. If he doesn't, he'll be held in contempt.

My heart pounded. Todd was backed into a corner—a desperate predator. I braced myself for the attack I was certain was coming. I couldn't think clearly, let alone explain the situation to Lauren. I just didn't have the strength. Exhausted and overwhelmed, I called it an early night and collapsed into bed. But even as I tried to rest, my thoughts circled around what might happen the next day.

When morning arrived, I debated taking the day off from work. But after already using so much leave for court dates, I couldn't afford to take any more time off. I tried to focus on my work, but my mind was elsewhere, fixated on what might be happening at the courthouse. My phone danced across my desk, vibrating against the solid oak. When I saw Sharon's name pop up on the screen, I snatched it up quickly.

She seemed distraught. "Are you sure there's a warrant for Todd's arrest?"

"I'm sure."

I reached for the information the officer had provided when she asked if I had a report or warrant number. I had both, and I rattled them off to her. She sighed, in what sounded like relief, and said she'd call me back. I waited.

About fifteen minutes later, another call from Sharon came in. She explained that she had received a call from the receptionist. "She was upset —apparently, there was a man standing outside the lobby, staring through the window, making her uncomfortable."

Sharon checked it out and recognized Todd, who was pacing and seemed to be talking to himself. She notified Jacob, who contacted courthouse security while Sharon kept an eye on Todd. Apparently, the warrant wasn't yet in the system, and since it couldn't be verified, courthouse security only offered to escort him away. As soon as I gave Sharon the warrant number, she texted it to Jacob, who called dispatch and confirmed the warrant.

Jacob then placed the handcuffs on Todd and detained him until police arrived. Something must have happened that nobody would tell me, because all they would said was that Todd was being placed on a psychiatric hold.

I was speechless. He had become so brazen—he actually had the nerve to taunt the district attorney's office. From one perspective, it was good for my case to have them witness Todd's antics. But from another perspective, it was dangerous.

He's coming unglued.

I went through my frantic "what if" scenarios again. The fact that he still had an ankle monitor meant little to me. I was convinced it would only matter if he murdered me.

What if he breaks into the house?
What if he attacks me?
What if he kills me?
What if he gets to one of the boys?

Winston was in boarding, so I moved back to Lauren's while Dylan stayed at his dad's. I realized I had to find some grounding in reality. One afternoon, when Lauren left to run errands, I took a dip in her pool. Relaxing in the water, I let the warm sunlight soothe me as I closed my eyes and floated. Scenes from the past year played over in my mind like a movie. I saw the significance of my friendship with Nathan and Lauren, along with the repeated affirmations of support from Gina, Elaine, and Jacob.

Todd bonded out and was released before the psychiatric hold expired, which skyrocketed my fear. Sharon called—not to explain how Todd was released early, but to discuss my safety plan. "Make sure you follow the plan—don't deviate from it. If you feel you need to stay in a shelter at any time, I can arrange that." She gave me her cell phone number and told me I could call day or night.

A few days later, I returned home—but I didn't let my guard down for a second. That's when Sharon called with some news. "I hate to tell you this, but I'm calling to let you know that a new prosecutor will be handling your case."

As her parting gift, she submitted a request to have the victim notification key fob ordered, and it was granted, further fueling my suspicion that there was more to Todd's arrest than they were telling me.

I was crestfallen. I'd hoped Elaine would be the one to bring my case to trial. From Sharon's vague comments, I surmised Elaine must be concerned about Todd's mental state and worried she might become a target herself. I couldn't blame her. The halls in the district attorney's office were haunted by another female prosecutor who'd been stabbed to death years ago.

I'd grown to trust Elaine, and now I had to start all over with someone new. Someone who didn't know me, or the twists and turns of the nightmare I was living. Someone who might think it's all a coincidence or misunderstanding.

Every time I thought I could catch my breath, a new obstacle emerged. It felt like I was trapped in some sadistic game, the rules constantly shifting.

CHAPTER
FORTY-SEVEN

Dylan was at Mark's house watching his younger half brother while his dad and stepmother worked a booth at a church fair. My emotions were running raw as the sun began to set, and I anxiously waited for Dylan to return home. Every hour, I would walk the same path through the house, checking windows and doors to help manage my anxiety. Suddenly, Dylan burst through the door, wide-eyed. His voice was raised—not at me—but as he told me about a blow-up he'd had.

A sinking feeling settled in my stomach, and I knew this wasn't going to be a pleasant conversation. Mark and his wife had told Dylan that after the fair, they headed to a local bar to unwind and were surprised when Todd pulled up an empty seat at their table without an invitation.

And he had a lot to say.

They shared every awful thing Todd said about me in great detail—things too intimate for any son to hear about his mother. Details that were completely untrue. Dylan stood, his fists clenched, as he recounted morsels of his conversation. "It's not worth repeating, Mom, but it's bad."

I could imagine the conversation—the allegations of promiscuity; the salacious details Todd had shared about my plaid panties. I watched as tears filled Dylan's eyes.

As he spoke, I stood with my hand on my chest. My heart shattered into a million pieces, and I was trying desperately to hold it together, for his sake. I couldn't believe the lengths Todd would go to. I held my son close and whispered, "I'm sorry."

The next day, Mark's name appeared on my phone, and I answered. I wish I hadn't.

"Kathryn, what the hell are you doing? You're going to ruin this man's life! Our kids are old enough to understand what you're doing. What kind of mother are you? What example are you setting?"

After telling me about the beer he shared with Todd and bits of their conversation, Mark explained that Todd had stopped by his booth at the fair several times. At first, they ignored him, but—like a boomerang—he kept returning.

"Mark, that alone should tell you he's a stalker. He stalked you. Can't you see it?" But I knew he couldn't.

Tears rolled down my cheeks. I was too emotionally drained to defend myself. Every breath was an effort as I struggled to hold myself together, my body trembling under the weight of a shattered heart.

Later, when asked what my lowest point was, seeing Dylan's relationship with his dad torn apart over this was it.

I sat at my desk, combing through a short list of mental health providers, but it was like reaching into a grab bag. I landed on three female names; it felt right to choose a woman. Most of the men I'd interacted with seemed to prefer dismissing my concerns as "drama." It's a female curse to be accused of drama and a man simply wouldn't understand my plight. I wasn't interested in finding a therapist who would make me justify myself.

I tried the female therapists, but none of them felt right. The first one kept steering the conversation to my childhood, insisting we needed to understand what had led me to this point. The second kept asking what stalking meant to me, refusing to accept the legal definition. The third seemed completely out of touch. She spoke slowly, and I imagined her comfort zone was traveling the country in a VW van with beaded curtains, not sitting in a room with me, trying to make sense of the chaos that had become my life.

I randomly picked one of the male names from the list and made an appointment—Dr. Saxton. When I sat down on a worn leather chair in his office, it didn't feel like the beginning of my sessions with the others. This man was different, comforting in a way. He was much older than me—his clothes might have been older than me, too. His hair was disheveled, and he wore round, tortoise shell glasses.

After some pleasantries, he laid out the agenda for our meeting. First, he would ask routine questions to gather personal information; second, he would invite me to tell him what was going on and why I was seeking therapy; third, he would outline a plan for future sessions. I appreciated this approach. It was the first time a therapist had set clear expectations.

We moved through the first, routine part, and quickly shifted to the second. By then, I had a solid, if brief, summary of my situation.

When I finished, Dr. Saxton asked, "In the coming days, weeks, or months, what do you look forward to?"

I shook my head. "To be honest, I don't think that far ahead anymore. I'm just trying to get through each day right now."

He allowed a silence to stretch between us.

I felt compelled to offer a better answer. "I guess, if I had to give an answer, it would be a project I have coming up at work. I'll be doing a statistical analysis, and I'm curious to see where the data points to an issue we're having."

He looked up at me with a slight grin. "I see you work in corporate finance. So, you like numbers?"

"Yes." I nodded.

"What is it that draws you to numbers? Why did you choose finance?"

Annoyed that we were getting off-topic, I responded casually. "Numbers tell a story. Even the subjective ones."

"We're veering a bit off track here, but I'm intrigued." He crossed one leg over the other. "Indulge me. Subjective numbers tell a story?"

"Yes. If we're both experiencing the same level of pain, and the doctor asks us to rate it independently, you might give yours a seven, and I might be experiencing the same pain but rate mine a three. Maybe I have a higher pain threshold. But those numbers are not entirely subjective—they carry meaning behind them."

Dr. Saxton nodded, jotting something in his notebook. "I think I know how to help you. I'll be right back."

As the door clicked behind him, I sank into his sofa, leaning back. His words were like music to my ears—solace. A feeling I'd long been deprived of.

Minutes later, he returned with an envelope and some forms. "This is a self-assessment tool. You should complete it when you're comfortable, not when you're at peak fear or anxiety. Once you're finished, drop it off at the office at least two days before your next appointment."

I hadn't committed to another session yet, but Dr. Saxton had already earned my trust. I was curious to see what his help would look like, and it certainly couldn't hurt to try. "Okay, I will."

He held up the envelope. "This is your homework. Inside are ten notecards. When you're feeling fear, use a notecard to write down what you're afraid of."

This will be easy, I thought.

"If you need more notecards, just use paper—please, only write one item per page. Bring them to your next visit."

I took the envelope. "Thank you."

"Now, let's schedule your next visit."

In the coming week, I completed the self-assessment form and dropped it off in advance. By the time our meeting arrived, I had filled out the ten notecards, plus two pieces of paper that were now in the envelope. Upon check-in, the receptionist smiled and said, "May I have the envelope, please?"

I handed it over and took a seat nearby. Soon, Dr. Saxton called me back. As our session started, he set the agenda. "I'll review your self-assessment with you. Then I'll open the floor so you can discuss anything you'd like. We'll finish with plans for the next session."

"What about the notecards?"

"We'll get to those."

I nodded, curious to see where this was headed.

Dr. Saxton shuffled the papers in his hands and leaned back. "Well, Kathryn, your ratings are nearly a perfect score for post-traumatic stress disorder, combined with a few other issues, including obsessive-compulsive disorder."

My stomach flipped.

"Are there things you believe you do obsessively or compulsively—like hand washing?"

I described the path I walked through the house, checking doors and windows. Tears pricked the backs of my eyes as I listened to myself. "I feel guilty that even when my children are over, I notice everything they touch so I can wipe it down, just in case Todd comes after me. I want there to be forensic evidence. Unless someone is with me, I sit in the chair at my kitchen table with the most available exits. From that spot, I could bolt through the garage, out the back door, sprint to the front door, or run down the hall to my bedroom."

Dr. Saxton nodded and took notes as I spoke.

"I know it sounds ridiculous," I added.

"It doesn't matter if it's ridiculous. If that's what you need to do to feel safe, it's perfectly fine. These are all normal reactions to a stressful situation for a rational person."

As we moved into the final part of the session, Dr. Saxton excused himself and returned with a clipboard. When he handed it to me, I saw all my fears—everything I'd written on the notecards—on a sheet of paper, each with a box next to it. "Tell me, what time of day do you feel most relaxed? Preferably in the afternoon?"

"About six o'clock, after I log off work and before it gets dark," I replied.

"Okay. Set a daily reminder on your phone at six p.m. to complete this exercise. It shouldn't take more than a few minutes. When the reminder goes off, reflect on your day and assign a number from one to ten to each fear listed. The number should represent how likely that fear is to come true, based on what the day has brought."

"I'm not sure I understand."

"Well, if you see Todd in your backyard, then you might rate the fear that he will kill or harm you at a ten. If you don't see him, but you've heard a noise, which turned out to be nothing, you might rate it a five. You should complete this daily and move the finished page to the back of the stack. Do not look at the previous days' ratings. Bring the completed pages on your next visit."

I set the reminder on my phone as instructed.

"I'd also like you to make a list of behaviors you believe are obsessive-compulsive. Then, as you go through your day, check off each behavior as you catch yourself doing it."

Dr. Saxton was clever—he was giving me numbers. I liked him. I was in a state where I couldn't even think for myself, and with him, I didn't have to. He had it under control. And he'd found a way to help that leveraged my natural way of thinking.

As I handed in my sheets each week, I saw the numbers shift. My fear ratings decreased, thanks in part to the anti-anxiety medication he prescribed. My compulsions lessened, and I realized that the exercises weren't about judging how often I behaved obsessively or compulsively; rather, they were about making me aware I was doing so at all. Over time, I started to settle into a new normal—one where I was still on high alert, but no longer sleeping fully clothed, in running shoes, ready to bolt like startled prey.

CHAPTER
FORTY-EIGHT

With a cup of coffee in one hand and my cell phone in the other, I trudged upstairs, ready to work. Halfway up, my phone rang.

"Hi, Kathryn. This is Aaron. I'm the new prosecutor assigned to your case. How are you?"

I sighed. I didn't want to do this right now. "I'm alright."

"Good. Well, I've examined the evidence in your case and reviewed everything associated with the other charges." His tone was gruff. His voice lacked the gentle touch I'd become used to with Elaine.

"Okay. Are the charges going to be treated as one case?"

"I have to be honest—that's not a good idea. By consolidating the cases, if there's one element of reasonable doubt, we lose on all charges. From a prosecutorial perspective, the Violation of the Protective Order when he called you is the weakest of them all. We can't prove that he was the one who called your cell phone."

I rubbed my eyes. "Okay."

"Listen, your stalking case is very strong. The private investigator's video, the photograph of the accident—all of that is irrefutable. That said,

Todd has offered to plead guilty to misdemeanor harassment, which is lower than the current charge."

"I don't understand. I thought stalking was a misdemeanor?"

"There are different classifications. When the ankle monitor was ordered, the stalking charges were bumped up to the highest-level misdemeanor. He won't be charged with a felony unless there is a second stalking charge."

My face flushed hot pink; anger rose from my gut, making its way up my throat. "That's unacceptable! The law says what he did to me is stalking. He needs to be convicted of stalking. I won't settle for anything less."

"Good. I'm glad we're on the same page. Can you give me a moment, please?"

"Of course." While I waited, I tried to focus on the fact that he had said my case was strong.

He clicked back on the line. "Kathryn, you there?"

I could tell I was on speaker. "Yes."

"Can you hear me okay?"

"Yes."

"I have Raymond in my office."

My stomach flipped. *What is Raymond doing there? Have I done something wrong by reaching out to him?*

"Hey, Kathryn. I'm Raymond. I'll be prosecuting your Violation of the Protective Order case." His voice was much different—younger—than the Raymond I knew.

"I'm sorry. I thought this was another Raymond."

He laughed. "I actually get that all the time. Funny enough, the Raymond you're probably thinking of is my dad. I'm a junior."

A wave of relief crashed over me. *Of course!* I'd forgotten his son was a prosecutor. I couldn't believe my luck of the draw. Surely, father and son talk.

"We have our work cut out for us to prove he made that call to you. Are you familiar with spoofing?" Raymond asked.

"I've heard the term before, but I wouldn't say I understand what it is."

"Okay, we'll get into all that later. I'll be in touch."

"Kathryn?"

"Yes, Aaron?" I could now distinguish between the voices.

"I want to introduce you to Matt. He'll be the prosecutor on the Bank Fraud case."

"Hello," a new voice said.

"Hi there. Thank you all for your work," I said meekly. I was impressed with the team assembled and the unity they presented. If the cases weren't going to be consolidated, it was important to have all three prosecutors working closely.

"Listen, the Bank Fraud charge isn't going to stick," Matt started.

My heart dropped. It was the only felony charge I had, and Todd needed to be a convicted felon.

"The reason is, we have the burden to prove Todd intentionally defrauded the bank. That would make your bank our victim rather than you. If we shift to Felony Theft, we only have to prove he stole from you, and you remain our victim. Does that make sense?"

"Yes. When the charges were filed, the detective explained he went with Bank Fraud because it carried a ten-year maximum sentence. And Felony Theft is five years, correct?"

"Yes," Matt answered.

"And what is the maximum sentence for Stalking?"

Aaron spoke up. "One year."

"And what is the maximum sentence for the Violation of the Protective Order?"

"Six months," Raymond said.

"But it's not his first offense. I'm sure you must be familiar with the previous case?" I asked gently, referring to the case his dad had handled.

"That case is too old to use. The judge will see his full criminal history, so even though we can't use it, I'm sure that will factor in at some point."

Hearing the punishments was disheartening—they felt so small compared to the enormity of my suffering. In the end, I reminded myself that it didn't matter how he was held accountable. The conviction was the most important element.

After speaking with the three prosecutors, I was filled with optimism. I trusted their expertise, and Gina reassured me they were the right team to take on Todd.

The optimism didn't last long.

Todd did all he could to rattle me. He proved the ankle monitor meant nothing. I stopped at a gas station one afternoon and was third in line to pay when Todd appeared. He made a scene, calling me names and making vile remarks. I just stood there, and so did the other customers, while Todd loudly proclaimed how bad my diseased vagina smelled, using words like "infested" and "cheese" along the way. It was mortifying. It was horrifying. And nobody was looking at him. They were all looking at ME. Worse, the guy who owned the gas station had contributed to my nonprofit in the past, and I dared not ask him for help.

Even with three pending trials—Stalking, Violation of the Protective Order, and Bank Fraud—and two protective orders, Criminal and Civil, the police were still telling me the same thing: "It's a small town; you're bound to be at the same place every so often."

What law enforcement failed to recognize was the message Todd was sending. He had found ways to make me feel his presence, to remind me that I was being watched, and that he could get to me. The charges and ankle monitor were nothing more than an inconvenience to him, and it only reinforced his point that I could not—would not—escape him. It was a message I received loud and clear, but to untrained law enforcement, it was just a coincidence, if anything at all.

Shortly after a meeting with Dr. Saxton, I received a call from Matt and Jacob. They said Todd had agreed to pay back the funds he used from my account if I would agree to drop the charges.

"No. Absolutely not," I responded emphatically.

"Todd's attorney anticipated that would be your response, so they prepared a second offer," Matt said with a detectable huff. "Todd will pay back the funds he stole in exchange for reducing the charge to a misdemeanor."

"No," I replied firmly.

"Why are you so adamant that the charge remains felony theft, Kathryn?" Jacob asked. "If it's about the money, you'll get it back."

"The law says the crime he committed is felony theft. That's the crime he should be prosecuted for. Jacob, someone needs to hold Todd accountable for these crimes. He worked for the police department and violated not just my trust, but the public's. If he keeps getting away with these antics—and, by looking at his criminal history, he has—then he is going to do things like this again and again and again."

"Kathryn, look, here's the bottom line. Todd says you're the one stalking him. That you have pursued a continued relationship that he doesn't want, and you are abusing the system to make him pay."

Silence.

Dead silence.

I was livid.

I steadied myself, knowing I needed to maintain an even tone.

"Then he needs to prove that in court. I'm confident he can't because it's an absolute lie. I have done everything I can possibly do to hand you a bulletproof case. Have you even been through The Black Binder?"

"It's just that they've offered what I consider pretty good plea deals, and you are unwavering in your position, which gives credibility that you are seeking revenge of some sort," Jacob said.

"I am unwavering in my position because he broke the law and needs to be held accountable for the laws he broke." I remained as controlled as I could.

"Okay, Kathryn," Jacob said, patronizingly.

"One more thing, Kathryn," Matt said. "You have video cameras at your house, correct?"

"Yes, the ones Todd installed."

"The equipment he purchased with your card was delivered by FedEx to your address. If I give you the tracking information, can you pull video footage from that time?"

"I can try. Todd disabled the cameras a long time ago, and I replaced the DVR when I had a technician bring them back online for me. Send me the details, and I'll see what I can do."

Later that day, I received the date and time that FedEx showed the equipment was delivered to my house. Afraid I would mess something up if I tinkered with the DVR, I called the technician who had helped me with the cameras a few months prior. He was the same technician who found the two hidden cameras.

"Yes, I remember you," he said. "Unfortunately, my schedule is full at the moment."

"What's your first available opportunity to help me find the footage? It shouldn't take long. I have the exact date and time."

He let out a long sigh. "Look, lady. I feel for your situation, but I run a small, one-man business, and I can't be involved with this. I'm sorry. I wish I could help."

"I understand. I'm sorry if I put you in a difficult position. Believe me, I'd rather not be asking." I gently put my phone down.

My fists clenched. My muscles tensed. I trembled with rage as I felt an uncontrollable urge building inside me. I wanted to scream, to lash out, tear down the walls, knock down trees, and tear a hole in the sky.

Inhale.

Exhale.

This is the reaction Todd wants.

I will not give it to him.

I took a few moments to breathe deeply, my eyes closed as I rested in my chair. If the prosecutor wanted the footage, I would give him the DVR; he could sort it out himself. I was exhausted from doing all the work only to find myself on the wrong side of Todd's accusations again and again.

CHAPTER
FORTY-NINE

The sessions with Dr. Saxton were going well, and I felt a sliver of myself returning. It was Wednesday, and I thought about going to happy hour, but wasn't sure I was ready for that. Instead, I texted Nathan. He was at Oskar's and urged me to meet him.

> **NATHAN**
> The coast is clear. I've already put in an order for your favorite tomato basil soup.

When I arrived, he was seated at the bar. He pulled out the barstool as I approached and opened his arms for a hug. As I relaxed into his arms, I realized how much I needed to get out of the house.

"You doin' okay, hon?" Chuck asked. He'd texted me off and on for months, keeping me posted on Todd and the rumors he was spreading. Like all the others, he didn't want to get involved with the court case. I didn't mention that I'd included his text messages in the documentation turned over to the prosecutor.

"I'm okay."

"Whiskey or wine tonight?" Chuck asked.

"How about you decide for me?"

"Great," he said, placing my soup in front of me.

For the next ten or fifteen minutes, I filled Nathan in on my conversations about the DVR footage. As I took a long sip of wine, Chuck suddenly appeared in front of us, a wild look in his eyes. He leaned over the bar. "You need to leave. Right now!" The urgency in his whisper startled me.

"What's going on?"

"Todd just walked in. He's wearing a body cam to prove you're stalking him. Don't give him any ammunition. Come this way." He tilted his chin toward the end of the bar closest to the kitchen.

"Go. I'll take care of the bill," Nathan offered. The urgency in his voice was palpable.

My jaw dropped. My mind spun. I was paralyzed by the sudden shock, unable to think or speak. Nathan tugged at my arm and Chuck stood at the end of the bar waiting for me.

My heart raced as I followed Chuck toward the kitchen; my purse tightly knotted in my hand. The kitchen employees stared at me as I quickly navigated around their stations. Chuck threw open the back door and I raced out of the restaurant, the metal door slamming ominously behind me.

I stumbled into the alley, engulfed by a wave of putrid smells emanating from discarded, rotting food and empty bottles that had sat outside far too long. My stomach churned, as if I had been thrown out with scraps like a piece of unwanted trash. My lungs heaved in desperation as I staggered to my car, searching for answers amid the chaos. Two minutes ago, I was dining at the bar. Now I was among the trash. Alone.

That sliver of myself that had returned? Gone.

This setback landed me back in Dr. Saxton's office. I recounted the restaurant experience in detail. "I just can't figure out how Todd manages to show up in all these places where I am. It's like he doesn't have a life outside of targeting me."

"If you found out how he is getting information about where you are or who you're talking to, how would that change what you're doing today?"

I shrugged. "I'd be able to tell the prosecutors, and they could use the information to convict him."

"But the police are aware of your incident log, the number of times he's followed you, etcetera, correct?"

"Yes."

"These incidents you're logging and providing to the appropriate people handling your case have the ability to cross-reference it against his ankle monitor, I presume."

"I'm sure they have that ability, but I don't know if they're actually doing it."

"And they haven't searched any of his media—cell phone, computer, etcetera—correct?"

"Correct." I saw where he was going with this. "I've had to do all the legwork myself."

"Yes, you did. In the beginning. Are you afraid your stalking case is weak?"

"No, not at all. I have private investigators, videos, and photos. I guess I just have a need to know for myself."

"Um hum. So let me go back to my original question. How would that change anything today?"

"It wouldn't change anything I'm doing."

"Think about it. Each time an intrusive thought about Todd's methods comes to your mind, write it down. If you can identify a trigger for that thought, include it. Then I want you to imagine that you figured it out. Write down what change that would bring about for you. Let's review it next session."

On my way home, I thought about the spyware found on my phone that the police couldn't use. I thought about the wires to the hidden cameras that were cut and couldn't be used. It seemed like, aside from the private investigator and the social messages, nothing I did helped my case. It only served to drive me to the brink of insanity.

I never made the list because I realized it didn't matter what tactics he was using to surveil me. Each incident only strengthened my case. My fixation on *how* Todd was surveilling me waned, which was liberating. Dr. Saxton was right—the incidents I continued to document could be matched to Todd's ankle monitor. If the prosecutor wanted to know, they had the means to do it.

The reality that I was trying to control my own case to have the best chance at conviction set in. But that wasn't my job. Staying safe and taking care of myself was.

The summer sped into fall, with my visits to Dr. Saxton's office occurring every two weeks. One by one, the shattered fragments of my former self were pieced back together. Like a broken vase glued back into place, I remained fragile and would never be the same again.

Although I remained hypervigilant, I discovered a new normal. My concentration at work returned. Nathan and I were now meeting for breakfast on Sundays. I would spontaneously show up at happy hour—smiling. Two or three times a week, I'd go to Lauren's house and hang out with her. I continued to record run ins with Todd and attended every court hearing I was notified of. With Dr. Saxton's help, I began to do something I didn't think was possible: trust the system.

One Sunday morning, Nathan and I were leaving breakfast. Sheets of rain were coming down, and I didn't have an umbrella. I was sprinting to the car to pick Nathan up at the door when my ruby red flats slipped out from under me, and I ended up with a fractured foot. I'd had a metal plate in my foot for the past twenty-three years, which had weakened the surrounding bones. I was in a boot and couldn't put weight on my foot for the next four weeks.

Another hearing was scheduled, but it would be difficult for me to manage on crutches at the courthouse. The Black Binder was overflowing. I had another binder for the theft charge and another for the spoofed call —one binder for each of the three charges awaiting trial. I took a rolling bag with me to court each time, just in case I needed my documentation. Dylan was around, so he offered to go with me and help.

I texted Jacob once we arrived to let him know I was there. Minutes later, he entered the courtroom and signaled to me to join him in the atrium. Dylan and I walked out, and Jacob motioned for me to sit on a nearby bench.

"Listen, it's highly unusual for a victim to be so involved in a case. Most victims don't want to be anywhere near their perpetrators," Jacob said, accusingly. "But you come to every court date, and it's almost like you want to see him. I know you said you weren't stalking him, but your behavior is hard to understand." I could see him studying me, waiting for a reaction.

I remained composed. "Why have I not received clear instructions from you about the court dates? This is my first time dealing with the criminal justice system. I want to be sure I'm in the right place at the right time. I don't want to risk charges being dismissed in my absence."

Jacob pressed on, restating Todd's claims that I was the one stalking him. My growing anger was now boiling over, and I searched for something to say other than what was really on my mind.

"Jacob," I said as calmly as I could, "I know you don't believe that. I remember you were the one who picked up the woman from social media a year ago to testify at the Motion to Revoke Bond—the one who didn't want to pursue charges against Todd. I remember our conversation about how hard it is for you when victims don't pursue charges."

I shifted my tone to firmer, more aggressive. "I am a victim. And I am pursuing charges."

"I know," Jacob relented. "Just don't put yourself in a position where you're anywhere near him. I'll make sure the office touches base with you next time there's a court date so you know if you're needed."

As Dylan and I left the courthouse, I couldn't help but wonder what kind of impression this made on him. *Will this cause him to doubt me?* I wondered.

On the ride home, I could tell he wanted to say something but was hesitant. After several minutes, I finally worked up the courage to ask, "What's on your mind?"

"I still firmly believe you, Momma" he said, clenching the steering wheel, "but I feel like the prosecution team isn't taking this case seriously."

"Sometimes you have to be your own advocate. Even though this is a massive, life-altering thing for me, my case is just another file on their desks."

Hearing myself say this, I realized I was becoming jaded. It no longer surprised me that victims hesitated to take legal action. I understood how Todd was arrested in three states, involving four victims, without a single conviction. The system didn't feel built to support victims—it felt like it was designed to protect the criminal.

As our small town streaked past, I started to feel something I hadn't anticipated: regret. I had judged the women I'd read about in Todd's criminal history. I'd judged Gina's friend, who had filed charges but maintained a distant relationship with Todd for ten years. I'd labeled their behavior as weak.

Now I saw the truth—the judicial system is not for the faint of heart. It's not about strength or weakness. It's not about winning or losing. It's not about what is right or wrong. My fight was about exposing Todd for the predatory criminal he is, receiving the validation I'd been deprived of, and getting up no matter how many times the system tore me down.

Veterans Day was approaching. I typically celebrated by taking Nathan to dinner and a movie, but this year, Nathan invited me to dinner with him, and his friend—a fellow veteran that was now a retired physician. I happily agreed, telling Nathan the evening would be my treat. My smile quickly faded when he told me they were meeting at Oskar's.

"Nathan, you know I can't go there," I said.

"You need to pick yourself up and get back on the horse."

He was right—I couldn't let Todd control my entire life.

On the night of the dinner, I ran late, rushing around my house applying lipstick and trying to find the right purse to match my shoes. My phone pinged.

> **NATHAN**
> Todd is here.

> **ME**
> Then I won't come. Please give my best to your friend.

> **NATHAN**
> I talked to Chuck. He can bring u in through the kitchen and put us in the private dining room since nobody's using it. Todd will never know you're here.

> **ME**
> Can't. I'd be in violation of the PO. It's not worth it.

> **NATHAN**
> Please? U missed last year.

> **ME**
> Let's just meet at Café Calais.

> **NATHAN**
> Okay. Todd is making an ass out of himself. He is crazy!

A short time later, we were seated at a table far from the cameras Todd had installed at the bar. Nathan sipped his beer and said, "So, we were waiting for you at the bar when Todd came in. Instead of spewing hatred about you, he targeted me."

I was horrified and disgusted. How could Todd do that to an eighty-something-year-old man? "I can't believe that. What did you do?" I rubbed my temple.

"Ignored him. I think that set him off even more."

Nathan's wife chimed in. "He was standing ten feet away from us, shouting that Nathan was a piece of shit." She glared at me as if it were all my fault—and it was.

My heart shattered.

My head pounded.

I was a toxic presence; a plague that poisoned anyone associated with me. I couldn't leave the restaurant fast enough.

The next day, Nathan called to check on me.

"You'd been gone just a few minutes, maybe ten, when Brandi came by the table. She said Todd had just come in and asked, 'Where is she?' Brandi said she shrugged her shoulders like she didn't know who he was talking about. He looked at something on his phone, then left."

This was the same restaurant employee who let us know Todd had installed the cameras—the same one who witnessed that crazy dinner the night of the attempted kidnapping. The one who didn't want to get involved because she might lose her job at the restaurant.

Todd was there looking for me. Hunting me in the open.

CHAPTER
FIFTY

Once again, the calendar welcomed the new year. Three years ago, Todd was on my roof, taking down my wreaths and slurping my soup afterward. The Google police report was still pending, and there would be nothing new to add to my log.

But there was a good reason for that.

For weeks, the news ran continuous coverage about Coronavirus. Considering the abuse my body had taken from extended stress, panic attacks, and the use of nicotine and alcohol, it wasn't surprising that I fell ill with the virus. My symptoms worsened before they got better, and I started to recover before I received my test results. The labs were so overwhelmed that it took eighteen days for me to find out I was infected.

The pandemic was in full swing, and daily news reports broadcasted the number of people who'd succumbed. For two months, our nation had been on lockdown. Lauren was distraught, believing it would never lift, but I welcomed it. *Let other people see how I've been living as a recluse*, I thought.

A few days had passed since I received an email from Winston's doggy daycare that they had reopened. The owners had been vaccinated and shared that they were reopening because they were at risk of losing their small business. From my initial tour of the facility, I knew the couple had invested their retirement savings into the place, hoping it would be enough to carry them through their years and serve as something to leave behind for their kids.

I decided a little socialization would be good for Winston, so I planned to take him in.

"Alexa, what's the weather today?" I called out.

Today's forecast calls for sun—

I breathed a sigh of relief. I always checked the weather because if it was raining, the outdoor play area at Winston's daycare would be closed. Not today, though—this would be a full day of fun for him.

I raised the garage door and called out to Winston, who happily made a giant leap into the backseat of the car. I'd been taking different routes, but I decided to stick to the shorter, usual roads. I was waiting to turn left when I noticed a truck at the exit of a fast-food parking lot. It wasn't the make, model, or even the color of Todd's truck. I didn't pay attention to it, but I did take notice. No cars were coming or going on the road where the truck was waiting to turn, yet it sat there, waiting. I shrugged it off, assuming the driver was digging through a bag of food.

When traffic cleared and I turned left off the main road, the unfamiliar truck raced out of the parking lot and cut me off. I slammed on the brakes and swerved to avoid hitting it. I assumed the driver was more interested in their food than paying attention to oncoming traffic. The truck rolled slowly forward, as if the driver had just let off the brakes.

I grew frustrated with the snail's pace of the vehicle and started getting a bad feeling in the pit of my stomach. As I approached doggy daycare, I put my blinker on to turn left into the parking lot. The truck in front of me did the same. It pulled into a parking spot on the right, and I pulled into one on the left. I watched intently in my rearview mirror. Todd stepped out of the vehicle, stood at the rear of my car, and yelled continuously. Panicked, I backed out slowly so as not to hit him, even though I wanted to roll right over him.

My mind raced. I called Gina's office, but she was in court. I threw my phone into the passenger seat, resting my arm against the door as I wiped my brow. I glanced in my rearview mirror to check if Todd was following me. He wasn't but I turned down a different road that would take me home another way. I tried to figure out how Todd could possibly have known to wait for me—it was obvious he was waiting.

Todd knew I always asked Alexa about the weather when I was taking Winston there. He'd given me the devices, and they were set up on his account. *Could Todd be monitoring my Alexa devices?*

When I arrived home, I yanked the plug for both Alexa devices, nearly breaking the sockets. I wanted to smash them into tiny pieces, but controlled myself, hoping they could somehow be used as evidence. The detective handling the Google police report had given me her card and told me I could call her anytime. So I did. I left her a voicemail explaining that I'd had an encounter I wished to discuss. I waited impatiently for her or Gina to call me back.

It was a Tuesday, and I should have been logged into work, but I wasn't in the right headspace. Everyone was working from home now, and suddenly wanted video calls or meetings. I'd been working remotely for two years, and nobody had ever asked for a video call before. But this was the world we now lived in.

It was good for me to get dressed, fluff my hair, and even dab on a little makeup—just in case a colleague decided to video call me. It brought a sense of normalcy I'd been missing. It made me wonder if the stalking would've taken such a devastating, isolating toll had I been working in an office all along. But none of that mattered now.

My thoughts drifted to the car—who was to say he wasn't tracking it through the app *he* had set up? Even though I'd long since changed the password, it would have been easy for Todd to set up a new account. He only needed my VIN number, which was etched on my windshield. I knew I had to come to terms with letting it go. It had only twelve miles on it the day I drove it home. It was five years old, but it was still brand new to me. I didn't just own the car outright—I *earned* it. Letting it go felt like like Todd was taking something else from me.

The alternative, however, terrified me.

I was searching for a new car, but had to be discreet so Todd wouldn't find out. Fortunately, I had a friend who lived out of state and was willing to help. Edmund lived up north and found a car nearby that fit my budget. After negotiating the purchase, I made an unusual request.

"Can you ask them to install front and rear dash cams that upload to an online storage account?" Edmund said the salesman had never been asked this before, but was happy to arrange it for an additional cost. It would take about a month for my vehicle to arrive, but it was worth the wait.

Dylan's truck was having transmission problems, so when he found out I had bought a new vehicle, he asked to use mine. I hesitated.

"Mom, it could help your case if I am able to report that Todd followed me as soon as I started using the car."

Dylan wasn't afraid of Todd and made a good point. I nodded in agreement, wishing I wasn't in a situation where my son would have to use himself as bait.

Gina called the next day, and I unloaded everything. She urged me to file a police report, but I was certain it wouldn't make a difference. I wasn't going to let the police tell me again that nothing criminal had taken place.

Restless, I ended the call with Gina, got into my VW Bug convertible, and drove to the doggy daycare facility. I parked across the street and took a picture of the parking lot to show where my car was and where Todd's truck was. I looked around the building for any signs of a video camera system. Preferably, one that Todd hadn't installed, but there were no cameras to be seen.

As I headed home, the detective from the Google report called me back. I explained what had happened, and she agreed with my instinct—on the surface, nothing criminal had taken place. Todd and I both frequented the daycare, and we both "happened" to arrive at the same time.

I pressed her. "The thing is, he was sitting at the exit of the parking lot, waiting for me. I don't go there all the time, so how did he know? What excuse could he possibly have for sitting at the exit like that? Can't someone pull his location from the ankle monitor?"

"Those are good questions," she said. "And ones that can't be answered without an investigation." She knew the fast-food restaurant had video cameras and could potentially have footage showing how long he waited at the exit and if he went through the drive-thru. "But I'd need a report to be filed to initiate an investigation."

Like so many other times, I went to the sheriff's department. Armed with The Black Binder, I explained I needed to file a report after speaking with a detective. The deputy handed me the statement form—no surprise there.

As he read my handwritten statement, I couldn't shake the feeling of frustration that always seemed to linger in the sheriffs department's air. I glanced over at The Black Binder resting on the corner of the table, a constant reminder of the tangled web that had brought me here once again.

After what felt like an eternity, the deputy handed me the familiar slip of paper with the police report number. He offered a small nod of acknowledgment. "Thank you for coming in, Miss," he said in a tired tone.

CHAPTER
FIFTY-ONE

Amid the unnerving silence of the following days, my mind wandered to the two protective orders I had, prohibiting Todd from coming within a hundred yards of me or attempting to communicate with me. I had those pieces of paper; those supposed guarantees. Yet, here I was, dealing with another incident. It seemed they didn't matter. Paper was paper; the ankle monitor was just something for him to work around.

My stress climbed like a rollercoaster car. I started drinking regularly again, but I was cognizant of the mistakes I'd made in the past. I was careful only to drink when others were around to corroborate anything that might happen. Which meant I was going to Lauren's house a lot. Gina had said my strategy of documenting others' involvement in incidents by sending them a text message afterward was better than nothing, so I did just that.

First, it was mimosas at breakfast with Nathan, which turned into glasses of wine and a few whiskies at Lauren's. Soon, however, I yearned to let my body relax in the warmth of booze coursing through my veins—to fall asleep, to dream, to breathe.

I figured Todd wasn't dumb enough to pull another backyard stunt and reasoned that one drink would be fine. But one drink never stayed at one, and the anxiety never stayed at bay. It wasn't long before I resumed drinking late into the evening, hoping to be so exhausted that I would fall asleep without bolting upright at every creak of the floor or rattle of a pipe. It worked. Alcohol came back into my life, joining me as an unwavering support system.

It felt like I had been waiting forever to hear back from a detective about the doggy daycare incident, so I eventually called the non-emergency line to ask about the status of my report. The dispatcher said they would get a message to the responding officer on my case. When the officer called me back, he sighed and said, "I'm sorry to tell you this, but your case has been closed. Unfortunately, your Civil Protective Order expired before this incident occurred."

The air seemed to freeze as his words slowly seeped in, leaving a trail of numbness in their wake. The metallic taste of fear and anxiety filled my mouth. I felt as if I had just been stabbed repeatedly with a knife carved from ice.

I steadied myself. "But a Criminal Protective Order was issued at the time of arraignment—that should provide *more* protection, right?"

The officer refused to provide any explanation and suggested I reach out to the prosecutor regarding the Criminal Protective Order, then clicked off the line.

My shoulders dropped. Arguing was futile; it seemed he was viewing this incident in a silo, without considering all the other police reports and arrests. I walked to my bottle of whiskey, sloshed some into a glass, and took a sip.

I was crushed that Gina missed this expiration date. I had placed so much trust in her, simply because the private investigator had referred her. But what did I really know about her? And why, after all this time, was I still an island—alone in this battle?

I raced into my bedroom and ripped my copy of the Civil Protective Order out from underneath the pillow on my bed. I needed to see it for myself, in black and white. It had, in fact, expired fifty-four days before the incident. *How did I not see this?* I asked myself repeatedly. While my inclination was to direct my anger at Gina, I couldn't help but turn it inward. Blame rained down on my shoulders—a suffocating avalanche of guilt and self-loathing. Everything started to feel like a steep decline into an abyss of failure and despair, and I couldn't allow myself to go there.

Not yet.

There was more work to be done.

I called the district attorney's office and asked to speak to Aaron. He wasn't available, so I asked for Jacob instead. He wasn't available, so I asked to speak to Sharon. The receptionist transferred me, but Sharon's voicemail picked up, and I didn't leave a message.

I felt like that crazy person everyone in the office wanted to avoid.

I texted Gina that I needed to speak with her as soon as possible about the new police report. She responded that she'd call in thirty minutes.

When my phone rang, I answered. "Listen, the police report has been closed. The Civil Protective Order expired!"

"What?! Oh, my God, Kathryn!" Gina yelled into the phone. "How did this happen?"

"I don't know. You tell me," I said sarcastically. But I needed Gina, so I quickly added, "I should have set a reminder in my phone to alert me. I honestly don't know how this slipped by us both." I told her what the officer said about the Criminal Protective Order, which seemed to mean nothing.

"The courthouse has been closed because of the pandemic, and the online filing system has been having some problems," Gina weakly offered. "I'll need to file a Motion to Renew the Protective Order. Let me get on this. Keep me posted about what the D.A.'s office says."

We hung up, and I felt beaten—another point of failure in my never-ending journey to justice.

The phone rang with the main number to the D.A.'s office. It was Raymond, the prosecutor handling the Violation of the Protective Order case stemming from the creepy courthouse phone call Todd made. I gave him all the details of the latest incident and provided him with the police report number. He said he'd need to discuss it with Aaron and get back to me.

Twenty minutes later, he called me back.

"I spoke with Aaron and relayed everything you told me. I hate to tell you this—because I know how frustrating this process has been for you—but we won't be filing charges under the Criminal Protective Order."

"Then what good is the Criminal Protective Order? He was waiting for me. He knew I was going to doggy daycare," I pleaded, knowing it was futile.

"I understand your frustration. The problem is, there's no evidence he was waiting for you in that parking lot. I know you said he was there when you pulled into the turn lane, but he could have been making sure they got his order right or something."

My heart raced in anger. "But, Raymond, I can't get evidence. The detective said there are cameras at that fast food restaurant. Can't somebody get the footage?"

"Usually, we can't get it without a subpoena or a search warrant, which would require probable cause, and we don't have that."

"What about his ankle monitor? Wouldn't that show he was sitting there for a period of time?"

"The ankle monitor is through a third-party, so, again, we need probable cause." He let out an audible sigh, and his tone softened as he offered some comforting words. "I'm sorry, Kathryn. I hate to see you so wound up over this one report. Look at the three charges you have on him and keep your focus there."

He was right. But what Todd did was wrong, and I was convinced he had been sitting there, waiting for me. Logically, I knew I should let it go. But emotionally, I couldn't. I was living as his mental hostage—under his coercive control—believing that he could kill me, and I wouldn't see it coming.

I obtained a copy of the police report and, unable to grasp why my legal team didn't think it broke the Criminal Protective Order, I called the sergeant at the sheriff's department to explain it. He said he'd look into it, with no promises.

I knew this waiting game, but I was no good at it.

I mulled over the ankle monitor record that Raymond couldn't access. The tracker should have sent me an alert when Todd was nearby. *Had Todd managed to disable the tracking device?* It wouldn't surprise me if he found a way.

Panic-stricken, I dialed the number for the ankle monitoring company's technical support and gave a brief explanation.

"I should've gotten alerts. That's the whole point of the victim-fob, right? To let me know if he gets too close?"

"Are you sure he was close enough to set off the alert?"

"I mean, I was . . . we were . . . he was driving right in front of me. How much closer does he need to be for the alert to go off?"

There was a pause on the other end of the line. I could hear the clacking of computer keys.

My fingers drummed against the phone as seconds stretched into minutes. "And there was this other time. I was at a restaurant, sitting at a bar, when he came in. I didn't receive an alert then, either. The bartender told me he was close."

"Ma'am, I show an alert was sent. The victim-fob wasn't deactivated, so we notified the police."

I let out an exasperated sigh. "Well, I didn't get anything."

The technician asked to verify my cell phone number.

"Was that a five you said?"

"Yes, five."

"I see the problem. We had six in the system. I'll correct it now."

Just one incorrect digit separated me from disaster—my life hanging by a thread between a six and a five.

CHAPTER
FIFTY-TWO

A Temporary Restraining Order had been granted and would last until a hearing to determine if the judge would issue another Civil Protective Order. As soon as I received a copy, I clutched it to my chest before returning it to its rightful place—on top of my gun in my nightstand. I settled into bed with a sense of relief, unaware of the consequences this piece of paper was about to unleash.

The upcoming Civil Protective Order hearing was a month away, so my radar was up. Gina's paralegal called and set up a meeting later that afternoon. I'd been texting and speaking directly with Gina, so the call from her office made me feel like something was off.

I rolled my bag of documentation across the parking lot of Gina's office, the cool breeze rustling my hair. A cheerful receptionist greeted me, and instead of offering a drink, she handed me a bottle. I think it's because she knew I'd need it. Gina came in with her paralegal in tow, and neither made eye contact with me. As she dropped her own black binder on the table, she asked, "How are you doing?"

"I'm sorry, let's just get to the point—what's going on?"

"I received Todd's response to our request to renew the protective order. It's not good," Gina started slowly. She shuffled some papers around and rubbed her brow. "We're going to go through this together, but I'll warn you, this will be difficult."

"I'd rather read it myself, if that's okay."

She handed it to me, and I scanned the first few pages, which contained standard language denying that I needed protection. I expected that. But it kept going:

> *Petitioner has contrived to create situations whereby Defendant would be compromised and subject to the continual harassment of responding to allegations, restraining order requests and criminal charges for violations; Defendant should be entitled to reciprocate with requests for Restraining Orders and be granted protection from repeated harassment from Petitioner.*

I paused to absorb what I had just read. I grabbed the bottle of water, took a sip, and read on:

> *Defendant has been the subject of repeated harassment at the hands of the Petitioner, through her use and overuse of the legal system, which level of harassment has continued despite Defendant having initiated no contact with Petitioner.*

My throat tightened as Todd told a much different version of what happened that day at the doggy daycare. He claimed he arrived well before I did, entered the premises, interacted with the owner, dropped off his dog, and was coming out of the lobby when he saw me pull in. It further stated that no communication had taken place; therefore, the incident that prompted the request to renew the protective order would not apply to the terms and conditions of the expired order.

Todd claimed that on Veteran's Day—the night I met Nathan at Café Calais instead of Oskar's—he was advised by the restaurant manager that I was covertly attempting to enter through the kitchen—an outright lie. I never even went to Oskar's that evening. He also forgot to include how he accosted Nathan that night.

The response asserted that I filed a police report claiming Todd called me while I was at the courthouse, but no such call was made. It also included his version of events at the dog park, claiming he left once he saw I was there and moved to the nature trail.

> *Despite the overreaction and harassment of notifying authorities, Defendant alleges that Petitioner could not have known the location of where Defendant had relocated without following or otherwise tracking him.*

My eyes burned with fierce intensity as I forced myself to read what I desperately wanted to turn away from. My fists clenched as I swallowed the bile rising in my throat, pushing through the rage threatening to consume me with every word I read.

I pushed through the seething anger to read how he had received emails from Google indicating that an unknown device had logged into his email. Since he was a subject matter expert, having testified on these types of cases before in a wide variety of courtrooms, he investigated this potential security breach. The investigation revealed that the logins were coming from my phone. The wave of anger that washed over me was dizzying.

I had been so consumed by reading each blatant lie that I was unaware that Gina and the paralegal had been watching my reactions. When I looked up from the page at their faces, they seemed like they were waiting to see if I would explode. I clenched my teeth and sipped the water.

"Can I please have a copy of this?"

The paralegal scrambled to pull one from her stack of papers and slid it over to me.

"Kathryn, I can't imagine how you must feel right now," Gina said kindly, but it sounded patronizing. She was the reason I was in this situation—she let the order expire. "Let's not do anything today. Take some time. When you're ready, type up a response and email it to me. I'll also be working on a reply based on the documentation you've provided."

"When do you need it?" I curtly asked.

"We have ten days to file a response. Ten days from the date they filed." She pointed to the court's stamp on my copy.

All I saw was red. I narrowed my eyes. "I assume since this has been filed, it's in the public record?"

"Yes."

I nodded to show I understood. "Obviously, what has been written is completely, utterly, and disgustingly false—"

"I know," Gina said, reassuring me.

"And I intend to disprove and discredit each allegation. I need you to believe in me and my case, Gina."

"I promise you, Kathryn. I believe you. I believe *in* you. I believe in your case. You have my word. Now, whether you believe it or not, there's good news," Gina smiled.

I tilted my head. "What good news could there possibly be?"

"I believe your response will disprove and discredit each allegation, which the prosecutor can also use to refute his testimony in the criminal trials."

As if the burden of responding wasn't enough, Gina had tied my next move to the criminal trials. My stomach knotted.

"And if I don't manage to disprove and discredit his statement?"

"You will."

Returning home, I left my rolling bag—and Todd's answer—sitting in the car. I headed to my bedroom and collapsed onto the bed. In the soft glow of lamplight, the emotions of the day hit me. Winston sidled up to me. I cried into his soft fur, and ran my hand along his spine.

"It'll all be okay. When this is over, we're going on vacation."

I took Winston out for a quick bathroom break and we trotted upstairs to the office, stopping at the car for me to collect everything. I had to get my response for Gina drafted—right then. I couldn't let this linger.

Hot tea was my drink of choice as I spread dozens of files across the floor. I grabbed a stack of sticky notes, writing numbers that matched Todd's allegations, and stuck them on the relevant documents. I assembled neat piles by their corresponding numbers. I eventually switched to soda after hours of poring over the paperwork.

I was determined. I was on a mission.

I seemed to leave my body as I reviewed the events that had caused me so much pain. I looked at them as if they happened to someone else. It was as if I were the paralegal assembling a case for an attorney.

Determined to finish a first draft before bed, I didn't realize how late it had gotten. By four a.m., I had drafted my response and scanned all the attachments into separate PDFs, each named to match the corresponding allegation. I attached it to an email and sent to Gina without re-reading it.

When morning came, I checked my phone to see if Gina had responded.

> **GINA**
>
> OMG! You're a beast. Will look through everything and get back to you. Wish all my clients were as organized as you.

I allowed myself a moment of pride before words like "contrived" and "overuse of the legal system" flooded my mind. I believed in my case. I believed in the evidence I worked so hard to gather. I believed in the fairness of the judicial system. Anyone examining the evidence should see through Todd's malicious attempt to paint me as the stalker . . . right?

CHAPTER
FIFTY-THREE

Several days passed, and I was nervous about ensuring the response was filed on time, so I reached out to Gina. She was finishing her review and asked me to come by the office so we could go over it.

Going into the meeting, I felt confident that I had everything carefully prepared. I brought Binder No. 4 containing the original motion to renew, his answer, the draft of my responses, and the documents I had so meticulously organized. The sticky notes had been replaced with tabs in the binder to keep everything neat and accessible.

"The responses you prepared were magnificent and I appreciate the effort that must have taken. I didn't expect to hear back from you so soon."

"Were you able to use everything I pulled together?"

"Not exactly. I'll try to explain, but stop me if you have questions."

The paralegal quietly sat next to Gina with a notepad and a stack of papers. I'd met her before, but she'd only sat in on the previous meeting and hadn't uttered a word the entire time. When we made eye contact, she looked at me sympathetically.

Gina started with my draft and the accompanying documents. I learned there wasn't enough "meat on the bone," as she put it—that is, I had documented the incidents, but there wasn't much we could do to substantiate them. Starting with the first allegation, she explained how she would attack my response if she were the opposing counsel. I knew Gina was firmly on my side, but it was still heartbreaking.

"He's clever," Gina said with a sigh. "He knows how to manipulate the system. The log shows a pattern of stalking behavior, but without proof or actual threats or violence, it's not enough on its own."

My heart sank. Once again, what I had wasn't enough. Todd's time working for the police had equipped him with an intimate knowledge of the legal system, allowing him to expertly navigate the gray areas and push the boundaries without leaving a clear trail of wrongdoing.

"We have to balance what we submit for this hearing with what could impact the pending criminal charges. We can, of course, submit anything we want."

I nodded my head, but I knew this wasn't going in the direction I'd hoped. *Were my efforts all for nothing?* I wondered. I pushed away those thoughts, wanting to hear Gina out fully before reacting—or overreacting—or just losing it entirely.

"There's something I need to show you." Gina slid a piece of paper across the table.

The paralegal leaned forward. She tucked her blonde hair behind her ear and began. "What you're looking at is the list you sent over of the incidents you've experienced since his initial arrest nearly two years ago. I noticed a pattern here, and on a hunch, I searched for scheduled court dates. I found six incidents where he essentially taunted you, on average, about a week before a court date."

I stared at the list. Beneath each bullet point describing the incident I had with Todd was a court date in bright red. My lips curled into a small smile—someone had finally confirmed my intuition. I was sure, from Todd's behavior after he was arrested, that he was trying to scare me into not testifying, hoping the charges would be dropped, like the other women who'd dropped charges against him before me. This was undeniable proof. I felt a flicker of hope, but I couldn't trust it. I'd felt hope before, only to have it ripped away.

"We've got him!" Gina declared confidently. She planned to introduce these correlated events at the hearing to demonstrate not only that he had been charged with stalking but that he continued to stalk me with the intent to intimidate. After the hearing, Gina planned to share this information with the prosecutor, hoping they could charge Todd with witness intimidation.

I nodded at the paralegal. I wanted to thank her, but I couldn't remember her name. Was it Stacie? Emily, maybe?

Gina moved on. "Now, let me walk you through what I put together."

Her confidence was infectious, but I was still guarded. I watched as she pulled out a copy of her draft response and walked me through how she framed it—why she framed it that way, what the potential implications in court might be, and, finally, she asked how I felt about it. We went through each of Todd's allegations this way, and I appreciated it. It felt good to have someone holding my hand.

When it came to the doggy daycare incident, I had already resigned myself to the report being closed—that the police wouldn't investigate further. But Gina had something to show me.

"Now, this wasn't part of what the defense filed with the court, but Todd's attorney emailed me something." She opened her tablet and turned it toward me. It was supposedly a dashcam video from Todd's truck from the day of the incident.

"His attorney and I ran into each other at the courthouse on other cases. He pulled me aside and urged me to reconsider representing you. He claimed Todd has a lot of video footage he's saving for the stalking trial, which proves you're lying and that you're, in fact, the stalker." Gina couldn't contain herself as she repeated this, bursting into laughter, before she even got the word "stalker" out. The paralegal's glossy peach lips had also spread into a smile, her perfectly white teeth gleaming as she laughed.

I wasn't laughing.

"So why wasn't this submitted as evidence? If they're saving it for the criminal charges, why would they send it to you?"

"It's a bluff. And not a good one. It doesn't take an IT expert," she used air quotes, "to know how to change the date and time on a camera before recording bogus footage. It won't hold up in any court—civil or criminal—given his profession."

"That's insane. Gina, that absolutely can't be from the day it happened."

"What makes you say that?"

"Because I was there. I know. It didn't happen the way the video shows. You never even see my car in the video. How could this prove I'm stalking him?"

"As I said, it's a bluff. Take another look at the video. Is there anything else you see that we can use to refute it? I'm not worried about it, but I want to make sure our bases are covered if there's anything we can leverage."

"Actually . . . there is one thing. The day after it happened, I went to the facility to see if there were cameras in the parking lot. I took pictures." I fumbled for my phone. "He claims he went inside and spoke with the owner . . ." I said, voice rising.

The paralegal was already flipping through the response Todd filed to find the part I referenced. I bolted out of my seat when I found the picture I'd been looking for. I turned my phone around, and Gina and her paralegal huddled over it.

"See? There's a big sign outside that says the lobby is closed—just like everything else—because of the pandemic. Dogs are clipped on a fixed lead on this pole out front, and they're only taken inside once the owner is back in their car."

"That's perfect. We can definitely add this to our response as an exhibit. Email me the photo. Good job!"

I did just that. The paralegal left the room, and when she returned, she handed me a color photo, still warm, fresh off the printer.

After we finished the exhausting two-hour review of the response, Gina shifted gears.

"I know we've reviewed a lot of information, but we need to talk about your pending police reports."

"Okay." I brushed a loose strand of hair that had fallen from my ponytail.

"The Google police report has gone nowhere—"

"I know. I met with the detective, and she had me turn over my phone for analysis. She said she's keeping the report open in case anything else surfaces. I don't understand why they aren't looking through *his* phone or computer."

"They must not feel there's enough hard evidence to get a warrant to search his electronics. I followed up on both the dog park incident and the doggy daycare report, and I learned they are both closed."

"It figures."

"This will hurt us at the hearing. He'll use it to support his claim that you're gaming the system. I know that's not true, but I'll need to come up with an argument."

"What am I supposed to do? Not go to the police?"

"No, that's not what I'm saying. Maybe you and I should discuss it first. Unless, of course, there's an imminent threat. Use your judgment."

"All the resources on the Internet advise victims to maintain an incident log and contact the police. I've done both. And now you're telling me *I* need to justify why I contacted the police on these occasions?"

Fury doesn't even begin to describe the tsunami of rage swelling inside me. My fists clenched, my heartbeat thundered in my ears, and yet my anger wasn't directed at Gina. It was aimed squarely at the system that consistently fails to protect victims like me. The injustice gnawed at my insides—how could he fling such a baseless accusation my way, and in an instant, I'm the one scrambling to defend myself?

Gina sighed, looking down at the table. "Let me worry about that." Gina turned to the paralegal, "Emily, I want a printout of every stalking resource website that advises victims to go to the police. Let's start there."

That's right—the paralegal's name is Emily. I made a mental note.

Now all I could do was wait. The hearing was a week away, and I had never been the patient type. Todd's lies echoed endlessly in my mind, like the relentless ticking of a grandfather clock—every second, every minute.

My new car was scheduled for delivery two days before court, and it couldn't come fast enough. On the morning of its arrival, butterflies fluttered in my stomach as the flatbed truck beeped and backed into my driveway. Once I signed the paperwork, I pulled it into my garage, out of view of the cameras Todd might still access. The smell of new leather washed over me as I ran my hand along the luxe steering wheel and sank into the buttery-soft seat.

As the hearing approached, the knot in my stomach tightened. His lies whipped through my mind like hurricane winds. I thought about taking the stand, seeing Todd, and being cross-examined. I sighed and closed my eyes. *No matter what happens, I have a new car that Todd can't track.*

I smiled.

CHAPTER
FIFTY-FOUR

The benefit of the pandemic was that finding a parking space close to the courthouse was a breeze. The downside was that nobody could be in court with me. I'd have to go alone. I texted Gina to let her know I'd arrived. I waited in the car, twisting my pearl necklace, until she pulled in next to me so we could mask up, sweat in the sweltering summer heat, and walk in together.

A cool blast of air hit us as we pushed through the courthouse doors and made our way to the security checkpoint to have our temperatures checked. We looked like twins in our black sheath dresses, mine slightly longer. The officer waved us inside, then through the metal detector. I was then handed a sticker that read:

KATHRYN CARAWAY
WITNESS

We approached the towering wooden doors of the courtroom. My pulse quickened, each thud echoing in my ears. The distant murmur of others faded as I followed Gina inside. The cold sweat on my hands nearly caused the handle of the case I was wheeling to slip—The Black Binder tucked safely inside. It felt like my whole life was in that binder. Gina slid into a bench and patted a seat marked with a sign confirming it was six feet apart.

Unaccustomed to wearing a mask, I felt confined, fiddling with the elastic bands when my phone vibrated with a notification that Todd was nearby. It was the first time the tracking device had worked. Even though I had mentally prepared for this, I felt my breath catch and my heart hammer against my ribcage when I saw the message on the screen:

> THE SUBJECT HAS BREACHED THE RULE 'VICTIM PROXIMITY.'

Gina caught my eye. "You should do your breathing exercises."
Inhale.
Exhale.
Repeat.
The back of my neck tingled as I rummaged through my purse and deactivated the fob.

Gina leaned over. "Todd and his attorney are here. They're seated over your right shoulder on the opposite side of the room, in the last row."

I stared forward.

The clerk called case after case. Gina leaned over and whispered, "Our judge is out today. We have a visiting judge." My stomach sank. We were supposed to have the judge who had decided the gun prohibition last time, based on my photograph. I liked his decisiveness. I liked *him*.

After what felt like hours, our case was called. As with all the other cases, the judge instructed Gina and Todd's attorney to confer and see if they could reach an agreement. Gina stood. "I promise, you will not be out of my sight unless it's absolutely necessary."

"Okay," I said, fiddling with my mask once more. I needed the reassurance. My back was to Todd—I wouldn't see him coming. Even though I was in a courtroom, the bailiff in plain sight, I'd already calculated that he couldn't get to me faster than Todd.

I allowed myself a glance over my shoulder. Gina had moved to the back of the courtroom to speak with Todd's attorney. The room was quiet, whispers barely audible, as they talked. I stared ahead, my eyes following the swirls in the grain of the wooden bench in front of me. I felt the heat of Todd's stare, his eyes drilling into my back. My skin crawled with fear and apprehension as I imagined his beady gaze hardening like lumps of coal, stoking a hot rage inside him that threatened to spill over. The tension in the room was palpable, thick enough to slice through with a knife.

Moments later, Gina slid onto the bench next to me. "Okay. They've offered a mutual order of protection. According to Todd's attorney, it's all or nothing. I'm required to inform you of this, but I strongly suggest that you do not accept their offer."

I shook my head. "I'm not accepting that."

Gina walked back to Todd's attorney and delivered the news, then headed to the front of the courtroom to notify the clerk that we were at an impasse.

The clerk whispered to the judge, and our case was called. The judge looked irritated; her brows furrowed. "Just so we're all aware, this matter *has* to be about compromise because the evidence submitted is not entirely clear."

Gina responded, "Your Honor, clarity will be provided through testimony."

The judge shook her head. "I'd like both attorneys to confer once more. And I'd like you to do so in the spirit of *compromise*."

We went through the same exercise as before; it was only moments before we reached the same result.

As Gina watched the judge process other cases, her confidence waned. The judge handled everyone as if they were squabbling children rather than people with major disputes to settle. As Gina shifted in her seat, I felt a weight on my chest. My heart pounding, I reached for my purse to see if the anti-anxiety medication Dr. Saxton prescribed was with me. I fumbled with the bottle, discreetly shook a pill into my hand, slipped it beneath my mask, and swallowed it without water.

While we waited, another case was called, and the judge only had to sign an order mutually agreed upon. Two young women stepped forward—they looked like they were in college.

The judge narrowed her eyes and asked, "Would either of you wear your current outfits to church and sit next to your grandmother?"

"No, ma'am," the girls replied in unison.

I felt sad for them. I sensed what was coming.

"I can't believe you'd come into my court like this—how dare you disrespect the legal system this way?"

My face flushed as the judge finished with them, essentially saying that what these girls really needed was a good, old-fashioned ass-whooping. I shrank into my seat. I knew I couldn't take such harsh words—I'd already been through too much.

Gina motioned for me to follow her. As soon as we stepped through the doors, she leaned in. "I'm going to file a Motion to Continue, extending the Temporary Restraining Order, and reschedule the hearing."

I nodded. "We're on the same page."

We walked back into the courtroom, and I returned to my seat while Gina approached Todd's attorney. She spoke with him briefly and then quickly returned to my side. "They won't agree to the continuance."

I felt sick.

The clerk was notified of our third impasse, and our respective attorneys were called into the judge's chambers. I was left in my seat, with a monster behind me, chewing my lip beneath my mask.

Gina re-emerged and motioned for me to follow her. I sat with her on a bench outside the courtroom, my eyes cast downward as she recounted that the judge was sympathetic to Todd, whose attorney had portrayed him as a victim in this process. I was cast as the vengeful ex-girlfriend wanting to punish Todd for the breakup he allegedly initiated, as evidenced by the handwritten note he'd left in my mailbox.

"What guy tells a woman that a relationship with her isn't healthy?" Gina scoffed.

Todd's attorney also claimed the justice system always sided with women, but in our case, the woman was actually the perpetrator.

Gina told me the judge deemed the police reports too biased to be considered. Nobody saw what happened, so my allegations couldn't be confirmed or denied independently. When Gina asked the judge to review the reports more closely, Todd's lawyer surprisingly agreed. He said that my Google police report supported his claim that I was stalking Todd.

In a desperate attempt to salvage the motion, Gina presented the document showing the relationship between the incident dates and the court dates, but it didn't sway the judge. The judge said she viewed this as a he-said-she-said case and wasn't inclined to rule in favor of either side.

"Bottom line is," Gina explained, "the judge is not going to renew your Civil Protective Order. Unfortunately, it won't be beneficial to have a hearing. Besides, Aaron has previously expressed concern that testimony at the hearing could jeopardize the stalking case."

Fat tears welled in the corners of my eyes. "I can't believe this is happening," I whispered. "I need that Order." My head dropped into my hands.

"I'm so sorry, Kathryn. The only way for you to get this protective order is to agree to a mutual order of protection."

The consequences of agreeing to a mutual protective order were too great. First, it would restrict me from owning and possessing firearms, just as it would Todd. I couldn't let that happen; I needed my guns for my peace of mind. Second, Todd would pin the order to his shirt next to his body cam and wave it around town. It would be part of the public record, even after it expired, with long term implications for my career and relationships.

"There's no way I'm doing that."

Gina had no choice but to file a Motion to Dismiss. After all, insisting on a hearing could risk angering the judge, which might result in her granting Todd a protective order.

As I burst through the courthouse doors into the sweltering, humid heat, I ripped off my mask and gulped the muggy air. After all our preparations, I left the courthouse feeling defeated, scared, and unmoored. I didn't have a Civil Protective Order. The Criminal Protective Order was essentially worthless. And with this small win, I was certain Todd would be emboldened. I began to unravel before I reached my car.

With victory on his side, I was afraid of what Todd would do next.

CHAPTER
FIFTY-FIVE

The memory of the hearing wouldn't leave me. Nearly a week had passed, and it still played in my mind like a loop with no escape. Todd's arrogance, the judge's decision—it all felt like a betrayal. Fuel for my paranoia, for my gnawing fear. I was exposed, raw, and alone. Even with a room full of people I believed would protect me, I was fighting this battle alone.

I knew I was spiraling, but I didn't want to admit it. It seemed I'd managed to put two fragments of myself back together, but three would fall off. Because of the pandemic, Dr. Saxton had offered video sessions, but I declined. In truth, I blamed our sessions for this rollercoaster effect instead of Todd or the judicial system—the real culprits. I had to blame Dr. Saxton because my sessions with him were the only thing I had within my control.

The grapevine was an unstoppable force. It was the pandemic, and everyone had been confined to their homes for months, with seemingly nothing to do but gossip. Even Lauren was video calling me now. She sat on the edge of her couch. The mid-week happy hour had moved to virtual drinking nights at home.

"It's not drinking alone if everyone's on video," she said, her eyes gleaming with the thrill of fresh gossip. "He's telling people you're the stalker, and that the court agreed. You couldn't get a protective order against him because he has evidence you're the stalker."

Todd omitted details that didn't serve his narrative to make people see his side of the story. And in his version, he was always the victim. I can't blame anyone—I fell for it, too. Like that night after the charity event when he was telling me about the mother of his children and how she's kept his kids from him.

Lauren dropped her voice, feigning seriousness. "People love the drama. They're eating it up."

I felt the gossip seep into my skin, infecting even the safe spaces. How long until it reached the people I relied on for donations to the nonprofit? Or Pastor Nick? How long until it grew bigger and uglier, stripping me of any remaining shred of credibility?

Lauren shrugged off my anxiety, trying to buoy my spirits with humor and hollow reassurances. "I say you embrace it," she said. "Let Todd have his moment. You'll have yours when he's convicted."

I appreciated her optimism, but her nonchalance was infuriating. "You don't understand. It's people perpetuating his lies and *helping* him destroy me in the community."

"Let him," she said, leaning back. "You can't stop it anyway. I just thought you should know."

That was easy for her to say. She wasn't the one on the receiving end. My fear seemed like paranoia to everyone but me. Lauren was sweet, but she didn't get it. Nobody did. They didn't see how insidious it was—how Todd's version of events was becoming the truth, erasing mine. I wondered if the truth even mattered anymore. If the court cared about it. If anyone besides me cared about it.

"You need to chill. Seriously. It's going to be fine."

Fine. Like the hearing went fine. Like it's fine for him to hurl accusations with no evidence. If that's what Lauren meant by fine, then, yeah, it's fine.

After the video call, I lingered on the couch. I missed the days before

Todd. Before Jason. Before the chaos and uncertainty. When I had control of my life and the only voices in my head were my own.

The next day, I sat in my office, steeped in fear but pushing through, trying to be normal—trying to pretend I was a functioning human being. The aftershock of the hearing left me raw.

Todd would be emboldened, I knew it. I feared it. And the fact that he was spreading the news around town confirmed it. I wondered what he would do next as the unsettling silence of the office deepened into chilling uncertainty. Work emails flooded in—physical reminders that life was moving on. I was still here, still Kathryn, still supposed to be a professional. But it felt like a lie. I was a shell of myself, going through the motions.

I tried to block out the imagined whispers, the conversations behind my back. I could feel their judgment: *Is this who Kathryn is? Is it true? Oh, poor Todd.* The tension was unbearable, a string wound too tight, threatening to snap. I forced my hands to move, typing—becoming a ghost at work, present but not truly there. I went through the motions, but nothing felt real. Every second was surreal—as if I was watching from a distance, detached and powerless. I couldn't shake the feeling that Todd was lurking just out of sight, waiting for the right moment to strike. All I could think about was how to survive this, how to come out the other side with any part of myself still intact.

The clock ticked like a bomb counting down. The day dragged on. I was a fraud, pretending I was capable of anything more than basic survival. Todd's story was erasing me, leaving me powerless to fight back. The pressure was relentless. It squeezed the air from my lungs, leaving me breathless. I couldn't keep living like this.

I stared at the screen, the words a blur as tears filled my eyes. It wasn't long before my phone rang. Pastor Nick's disappointment spilled through the line.

"What's going on, Kathryn?" His voice was laced with frustration.

"Pastor Nick, I . . ." The phone trembled against my ear. I wasn't sure what to say.

"I've heard things I'm not happy about. We can't have a stalker on the board of a children's nonprofit. I think you should consider resigning." He paused, waiting for my response. "At least until this blows over."

Whatever "this" was. His words stung—they echoed my worst fears, confirming what everyone else must be thinking. I tried to explain about the hearing, but Pastor Nick cut me off. His tone suggested it was best I resign, given the unfavorable attention I was drawing to the entire board. He even suggested I consider counseling and focus on myself. The words felt like a death sentence—as if Todd had already won without even trying.

I felt betrayed by Pastor Nick's reaction. I'd turned to him at a low point when the kids were young. His suggestion to resign felt like a rejection of everything I'd worked for in our community.

"You think I'm the problem?" I said, my voice cracking under the weight of it all.

"Kathryn," Pastor Nick said, a sigh in his tone. "Maybe you need to take some time away. A leave. To focus on a . . . reset, of sorts."

The words were meant to be caring, but they sliced through me like a knife. I could hardly breathe, the injustice choking me. How did it all get so twisted? How was Todd's narrative so much louder than mine?

"He's spreading lies. He's trying to ruin me," I said, desperation bleeding into my voice.

Pastor Nick kept talking about the group, about how my personal issues were casting a shadow over everything. I tried to defend myself, to make him understand how serious my situation was, but he didn't get it.

"You have no idea what I'm going through," I said, the words more bitter than I intended.

"You're right," Pastor Nick said. "But I know it's not healthy."

I wanted to scream, *What is it with people? When did I become not "healthy" enough for Todd, for this nonprofit?* The suggestion that I was the problem was more than I could bear. I wondered if Todd would be satisfied once I lost everything. Or would that still not be enough?

I hung up feeling defeated, the weight of it all crushing me. My heart pounded, my hands shook, and the room seemed to close in around me. I wanted to shout—to make them all hear the truth. But Todd's version of the story was louder. It was taking over my life, and I had no control over it.

Gina was right: the fact that the police closed the doggy daycare report probably contributed to Todd's claim that I was overusing the legal system. It was so obvious to me that he'd been waiting at the fast-food restaurant—I couldn't let it go. I called the main number the sheriff's department and was eventually routed to a public information officer. I explained my plight calmly and straightforwardly—no drama, as if I were explaining how to use the system at work.

"Maybe the officer who took my report was having an off day or drowning in paperwork? Whatever it is, I'm just asking for a second look. Stalking is a pattern. It's not about this isolated incident."

"I understand, ma'am. We're stretched thin, and sometimes things slip through the cracks. I'll see what I can do, but I can't make any promises."

"That's all I'm asking. Just give it another once-over. Thanks so much for your help—I really appreciate your kindness."

After I hung up, I gave myself a mental high-five for not sounding like a crazy woman.

CHAPTER
FIFTY-SIX

Two weeks after the hearing, a new detective reached out to follow up on my police report regarding the doggy daycare incident.

"I'm sorry, Ms. Caraway. Your request for my team to take another look at the report came from a higher-up. It must have fallen through the cracks amid shifting personnel. Please know this is not what you should expect from my team."

"And what team is that?"

"Special Crimes. Very few reports of stalking ever make it into the system. They are referred to the Special Crimes team for investigation if charges cannot immediately be filed. Your original report went to the Domestic Violence team before it landed on my desk."

I didn't know what to say—*how is this the first time I'm hearing of Special Crimes?*

"It looks like an interview with the owner of the doggy daycare did take place, but she didn't witness anything."

"Right, but Todd does have access to my home video cameras despite my best efforts and a judge's order. I'm certain he saw me load my dog into the car. That would have given him enough time to put his dog in the truck and wait for me at the fast-food restaurant."

"I see." She took a breath. "Okay, I'll reach out to the fast-food restaurant and see if I can get that footage. I'll be back in touch," she promised, then clicked off the line.

I wanted to feel hope in her words, but couldn't allow myself that luxury. I wanted justice, but all I could feel was frustration—frustration that distracted me from my failure to renew the protective order. A failure I took *very* personally.

I'd just made my way up to the office with my first cup of coffee when my phone rang at full volume. I jumped, splashing scalding hot coffee into my lap. Dabbing at it with my sleeve, I set my mug on the desk and checked the screen.

Aaron.

I stared at his name for several seconds, nauseous with the crushing weight of dread.

"Hi, Kathryn. I'm concerned about Todd's claims at the hearing that you are the one doing the stalking . . ." He paused, presumably for dramatic effect.

I was silent but screamed internally, *How can this be happening? After everything I'd done to prove he was stalking me, Todd's words alone are enough to put my entire case at risk.* A raging fire of fury erupted inside me. Yes, the hearing had been a disaster, but that was the fault of the visiting judge with a poor attitude, *not* because Todd had any evidence to support his claims.

Evidence I was required to have just to be believed.

Evidence obtained by the private investigators I paid for.

Even evidence they said I couldn't use—like the spyware on my cell phone or the wires cut to the hidden cameras.

Are you fucking kidding me right now?!

". . . they've offered a plea deal."

I fiercely fought my instinct to scream at Aaron until his ears bled.

"Todd will plead guilty to harassment in exchange for time served."

"Correct me if I'm wrong, but he was in jail less than twenty-four hours when he bailed out. Is there other time served that I'm not remembering?" I was being sarcastic, but I didn't care. Bile bubbled in the back of my throat. We'd been through this before, so I waited to see if there was something new he'd share—some other way this deal would make sense.

Finally, Aaron resumed, "Look, Kathryn, I know you don't want to take it, but this could drag on for quite some time. Frankly, the incidents you recorded could be coincidences, like Todd says. With the pandemic, juries aren't being seated. Todd is determined to prolong the trial. For your sake, consider the deal so this can be closed, and you can move on with your life."

"*Closed*?" I said, trying not to let my anger bleed into my voice. "Sure, we could settle this case, but there are two others. Are you recommending I roll over on those as well?"

He sighed. "If you're okay prolonging this process and enduring Todd's behavior, we can hold out for trial."

"I'm not okay with Todd's behavior, and I'm not okay that nobody sees his antics as witness intimidation. Just look at Todd's criminal history," I said, voice rising. I grabbed the paper Gina's paralegal had prepared, showing the correlation between the incident dates, police reports, and scheduled court dates. I rattled them off quickly before he could stop me.

"Kathryn, he's claiming that you're gaming the system to seek revenge because he doesn't want a relationship with you. His attorney said that it's time you both move on. Todd wants nothing more to do with you, and I know you feel the same way."

Red.

All I could see was red.

My eyes burned as their red veins burst forth like tiny tributaries. I felt the metallic warmth of blood as I clamped my teeth on my tongue. To avoid erupting, I remained silent.

"He's been wearing the ankle monitor for over a year now, and it hasn't registered any evidence supporting your early claims of seeing him in your backyard."

I detected a faint hum coming through the phone and sensed Aaron was lingering, awaiting my reply. But I had nothing to say. I cleared my throat.

"So, no plea deal?" Aaron finally asked.

"Right."

"Okay," he said, sounding defeated. "I know you're scared of Todd, but I don't think you have anything to worry about. He doesn't have a violent record, so I think he's just toying with you."

He may as well have told me that Todd wasn't really a stalker because he'd never been convicted of stalking.

"Yeah, well, nobody's a murderer until they kill their first victim, either." And I was determined it wouldn't be me.

The news hit me like a freight train: my nephew had attempted to take his own life and was now on life support. In a heartbeat, I was behind the wheel, barreling down the highway, my mind a storm of worry and urgency. Yet, the cruel reality was that it would still be hours before I could reach my family. We held vigil, doing what little we could to support my sister. Three days inched by, his life in limbo.

My sister made the difficult decision to remove him from life support. One by one, we filed in to say our goodbyes. It was a Friday. Later that day, I received a call. I recognized the number as the prosecutor's office. My grief had numbed me, but I answered.

"Kathryn, it's Raymond. How are you doing?"

"Okay," I responded hesitantly, unsure of what to make of the call.

"Did you get the notice that we're scheduled for trial on Monday? It's for the Violation of the Protective Order."

"I don't remember. Maybe. Jacob told me to disregard those notices."

"Will you be able to make it to trial on Monday?"

I explained my situation and asked if it could be postponed.

"I'm sorry for your loss, Kathryn. I understand, and we *could* postpone the trial. Right now, we have a good judge—one who's fair but stern. We can't prove that Todd spoofed that call to you. You'll testify it was his voice, and he'll testify it wasn't. But I feel good about trying this case in front of this particular judge," Raymond said with a confidence I hadn't heard from him before.

I settled back on the couch, rubbing my eyes with my palms. I stared blankly ahead. Raymond explained that once we had this first trial, the others would likely follow. He said he felt confident with this judge, and after the fiasco of renewing the protective order, I knew how important this was.

"I'll be there."

The next morning, I told my family I was returning home to gather clothes for the funeral and to prepare the boys. Dylan would wear his military uniform in solidarity with my nephew, who was a Marine. Caleb would need a suit.

Instead of driving, I decided it would be best to fly home and Uber from the airport back to my house. I don't remember the flight—only that I stood in my closet that night, contemplating what to wear to the trial, then to my nephew's funeral. I collapsed onto the closet floor, sobbing and shaking uncontrollably. There, on the floor, I learned that the depth of despair is infinite. You can spiral and spiral and never hit bottom.

PART THREE
THE CONVICTIONS

CHAPTER
FIFTY-SEVEN

The trial was looming, just ten hours away, casting a long shadow over my thoughts. Time seemed to crawl, each minute stretching endlessly. Sleep felt impossible. Anxiety had wrapped its icy fingers around my chest, squeezing tight. The nausea was unrelenting; my stomach twisted painfully as I doubled over.

I thought of Todd's face—his icy eyes, his flared nostrils.

You are mine. And I don't share.

His hands clenched into fists.

If I wanted to hurt you, I would do it right now.

I raced to the bathroom, my hand clasped tightly over my mouth. The boys had been over for dinner, and the food I'd managed to eat threatened to come back up. I clenched the toilet seat with one hand as I held my hair back with the other. With my stomach now empty, I curled up on the bathroom floor, dry heaving. I stumbled over to the sink and splashed cold water on my face. Looking into the mirror, I saw haggard, puffy eyes staring back at me. My face was pale, my lips tinged with a blue hue, and my hair was disheveled.

I threw on pajamas and crawled into bed, where I tossed and turned all night. Anxiety had banished any hope of sleep. As the light from the TV danced across the room, I began to drift. Just as my body relaxed, my stomach churned with acidic panic, sending me rushing to the bathroom again. After heaving up whatever was left in my stomach, I crawled back into bed and pulled the covers over me, cradling my childhood teddy bear in my arms.

I don't know if I managed to sleep at all—if I did, it was the kind of sleep where your brain is so busy that you swear you were awake the entire time. I sat up in bed, staring straight ahead as the sun greeted the sky with streaks of orange and pink.

The pandemic was still in full swing, so I'd have to face this trial alone. No friends. No family. Just me. I wanted—no, I needed—to feel powerful. I clasped a costume pearl necklace onto my neck, letting it rest above the conservative neckline of my navy-blue sheath dress.

A pair of patent leather navy blue heels caught my eye from the shelf. These were treasures I had found at a consignment shop years ago. The pointed-toes boasted a delicate bow with a pearl accent in the middle. I slipped my feet into them and was now standing two inches taller. I rolled my shoulders back and lifted my chin. I had been slouching for far too long, but today I vowed to walk into the courthouse with confidence.

I sloshed coffee into a travel mug and headed to the car in my carefully curated outfit, a wheeled bag at my side with The Black Binder. I had to drive my old car—the one Dylan now drove—since mine was still at my parents' house. My hands gripped the steering wheel tightly, the leather cool against my palms. The hum of the engine was the only sound in the car as I stared down the road, eyes fixed on the dotted lines that zipped by. Trees and asphalt merged in my peripheral vision. I drove as though I were on auto pilot. No radio. No thoughts.

Arriving at the courthouse, I waited in my car and reviewed the police report about the spoofing call that ultimately led to this day in court. A line had formed on the courthouse steps, even though it had not yet opened. I carefully scanned the crowd. There was no sign of Todd.

I watched as more people gathered. Everyone in face masks, standing six feet apart while I cowered in my car. I knew Todd was nearby, and I knew he was angry. *The world would be a better place if you just weren't in it*, reverberated in my head on a continuous loop, echoing like the toll of a funeral bell.

When the courthouse finally opened, the line of people began to shrink. Temperatures were checked by an officer at a folding table and waved inside. There was still no sign of Todd. The line was small enough that I felt safe to leave my car. My car was parked in a space where I could see officers at a folding table checking temperatures, which meant they could see me if I screamed for help. Just beyond the table, people formed tiny clusters at the top of the steps. If I had to guess, they were clients with their attorneys discussing the proceedings ahead. Confident that I had assessed the crowd adequately, I stepped out of my car and made my way to the steps, my mask over my mouth and nose, pulling my bag full of binders.

When my turn came for the temperature check, the officer scanned my forehead and asked the nature of my business at the courthouse. I explained that I was a witness for the prosecution and showed him my subpoena and license. The officer clicked his radio and provided my name, with a "10-4" crackling back.

"Step aside, ma'am. Someone from the prosecutor's office will be out soon to escort you in."

I moved slightly to the left to stay as close as possible to the officers.

Beep! Beep! Beep!

I scrambled as a dramatic emergency alert screamed from the phone in my hand. I stared at the screen and scanned the alert:

> THE SUBJECT HAS BREACHED THE RULE
> 'VICTIM PROXIMITY.'

The noise caught the attention of the officer who had checked my temperature.

"No cell phones allowed in the courthouse," he commanded, before I showed him my phone screen. He looked at me sympathetically, nodding his approval.

I swallowed hard against the lump forming in my throat.

My breath caught.

My stomach lurched.

I rummaged through my purse and found the victim-fob. I had just deactivated the alert when I heard a voice that sucked the oxygen from my lungs. I gasped as I spun around, my meticulously curled hair fanning out. There he was, Todd, with his attorney. Our eyes locked. They say eyes are the window to the soul, but his eyes seemed more like the window to hell: cold, dark, and full of hate. I stared at him, chewing the inside of my cheeks until I tasted copper.

The officer took note of my reaction and quickly cleared Todd from the queue. His attorney grabbed him by the arm and led him inside the courthouse, but not before Todd flashed an ominous grin my way—a grin that seemed to hold a secret, a dark promise he was intent on keeping. I held my breath, keeping my eyes trained on Todd as he and his attorney disappeared inside the building.

I had been waiting outside for what felt like an eternity when a familiar face appeared. It was Sharon, the victim advocate from the district attorney's office, and she beckoned me to follow her inside. I was relieved to see her—her kindness and warmth were comforting.

After we passed through the metal detector, I was ushered into a cold room with stark white, bare walls that seemed to whisper warnings about the trial ahead. A single table with plastic chairs was all that greeted me. It looked institutional, as if an orderly was about to appear and fasten me in a straitjacket. I took a seat and placed the array of binders on the table in front of me.

Sharon sat down next to me and said, "There will be no jury today. The judge is hearing the case and will be the sole decision-maker on the verdict."

My heart sank, flashing back to the previous judge we'd dealt with, but I knew it wouldn't be *her* this time. Today, we'd be in front of someone I already knew—the judge who had issued the original Protective Order and added the gun prohibition clause.

"Okay." I nodded. If anyone was going to be the sole decision-maker, I was glad it was him.

"As a witness, you can't be in the courtroom, so you'll need to be patient."

"I will." I smiled, knowing full well I'd be pulling my hair out waiting.

Once Sharon left, I sat alone in the windowless witness room as the docket of the day was called. The sounds were muffled, but I could tell there were people outside. And I knew Todd was among them.

I wasn't alone long before Gina entered. She hugged me before we sat down and started talking. Shortly after, Sharon came through the door like a breath of fresh air.

"Hi, you two." She made her way over to me and placed her hands on my shoulders. "How are you feeling?" she asked kindly.

I took a deep breath, trying to steady my shaking hands. "I'm okay."

Sharon gave me a reassuring smile. She knew how scared I was about testifying against Todd and asked if I had any questions about the process. Gina had already explained everything, and I was familiar with the courtroom layout, so I shook my head.

"No, I think I'm good."

"Okay." Sharon knelt beside me. "Just remember, listen to each question carefully. If you don't understand, ask for it to be rephrased. If you don't know the answer, it's okay to say you don't know. Answer only the question that's asked—no more, no less. Keep it short and simple—you know the acronym, KISS. You've got this!" Sharon pursed her lips into a kiss, breaking the tension in the room, and Gina and I laughed.

The door creaked open, and Raymond entered, looking exhausted. I needed him fresh for the trial ahead, but he was clearly juggling many cases. He rubbed his eyes. "They're running a criminal background check on you now—standard procedure. Is there anything we should know about?"

"Nothing!" I responded, offended by the very idea. My father always said he understood why some animals eat their young, and I surmised as a small child that if I stepped out of line, he'd have eaten me. If I'd had a criminal history, I'm sure he wouldn't have let me live this long. Nonetheless, the report was run, and nothing was found.

The wait felt endless. Eventually, as the clock's hands inched toward noon, Gina stepped out and returned with salads. She sat across from me and slid one my way, with a dressing packet and a plastic fork. I managed a few bites but mostly pushed the lettuce around the container. Gina asked questions about my childhood and family life, weaving stories of her own in between.

I knew she was trying to distract me, but in the back of my mind, all I could think about was the fact that she charged hourly. We'd been there nearly four hours, and the trial hadn't even started.

CHAPTER
FIFTY-EIGHT

After lunch, Raymond once again rushed into the room and announced that the trial would be starting shortly. I felt the little salad I had eaten for lunch rising in my throat, but I managed to keep it down. Everything I had been through had led up to this moment. I would finally be able to tell my side of the story.

Raymond cleared his throat. "After your testimony, you'll need to come back here—you can't stay in the courtroom."

I nodded.

Sharon opened the door and leaned inside. "Raymond, can I see you out here for a moment?"

Raymond walked outside, closing the door behind him.

Gina stepped away to answer her cell phone, which gave me an opportunity to look at the file Raymond left behind. I squinted my eyes and noticed that it was my entire case folder. My stomach flipped. Unable to contain my curiosity, I began to look through it. Among the dog-eared, rumpled papers were other police reports featuring Todd in each incident with different victims. I flipped through them until one caught my attention. It bore the name of the woman Todd claimed was stalking him the night of the police department's charity event. I wiggled it free from its place between the others—it turned out the detective who had submitted the bank fraud charges was the investigator on her case, which brought into focus his comment that he was familiar with Todd. He was a street cop at the time, responding to a call she'd made that Todd was outside her house and had keyed her car.

Gina finished her call and turned back toward me before I could finish reading. "What are you doing, Kathryn? Put that away!"

"Todd said this woman was stalking him. I saw her an event he took me to. This is a police report she filed."

"It doesn't matter. Trust Raymond. He knows what he's doing."

I begrudgingly tucked the report back into the file, closed my eyes, and took a deep breath. My face was red, my foot was tapping, and I chewed the inside of my cheek to keep from saying anything more.

Gina sat down beside me and placed her hand on my arm. "What can I do?"

"Since I can't be in the courtroom, I need you to be my eyes and ears."

"I will, I promise."

The door swung open, and Raymond hurried in, collecting the case file. "See you on the stand," he called casually as he walked out.

Sharon walked in, cocking her head. "Do you have any last-minute questions?"

"I don't, I—" My breath hitched as tears filled my eyes. Reality was crashing down on me. I'd be in the courtroom with *him*. I would have to describe everything in detail in front of *him*.

Sharon came around the table, knelt beside me, and took hold of my hands. I didn't even realize they were trembling.

"Breathe," she said softly, her voice calm. "Take your time. I'll be in the courtroom—you can look at me the whole time. When you answer a question, just speak to me as if we were talking right now. Keep it short and simple—KISS." Sharon pursed her lips again, and I cracked a smile.

She rose, patted me on the back, then looked at Gina. "Now, let's go flush that piece of shit down the toilet," she exclaimed, then burst into wild laughter. I was surprised to see such a professional woman make such an offhand comment, but it broke the tension in my body. I joined in with my own nervous laugh.

"You've got this," Sharon said before closing the door behind Gina, leaving me alone. All I could hear was the steady thump of my heart pounding in my ears. Although anxiety flooded my veins and threatened to drown me, I reminded myself why I was there—I had to take the chance that I might lose because I deserved to win.

I paced the floor, trying to focus instead of thinking about my grieving family. For the first time since I arrived at the courthouse, I pulled my phone from my purse and saw a text from my sister. They had taken my nephew into the operating room for organ donation. In that moment, I felt an intense wave of emotion. Fear and anxiety were temporarily replaced by grief and loss, followed by pride and admiration. Even in death, my nephew was giving life to others—a true testament to his beautiful character.

After about thirty minutes, the bailiff walked into the room. "Follow me. Leave all of your personal effects here," he said. "You'll return to this room after your testimony."

Walking into the courtroom, I focused on putting one foot in front of the other. I tried to keep my eyes trained on the floor. I couldn't help myself—I looked at *him*. For a moment suspended in time, I studied him, stared at his sallow skin and knitted brows. I clenched my teeth. The man sitting at the table was far from the charismatic, charming man I had been introduced to at Oskar's four years earlier. His jaw, receding into his thick neck, was tight and rigid. His lifeless eyes stared straight ahead. The fury and hatred he emanated were palpable—at least to me. The mere sight of him evoked a fear so primal that I had to suppress my physiological 'fight, flight, or freeze' response to appear collected and credible.

I was told to raise my right hand and place my left hand on the Bible. I swore to tell the truth, the whole truth, and nothing but the truth before taking my seat. My eyes wide, I folded my clammy hands neatly in my lap while gripping my nephew's military dog tags, which my sister had asked me to look after. He was a Marine who had served in Afghanistan, and I drew strength from his tags in my hands.

The first few questions from Raymond were easy and required no thought, but then he asked for details of the phone call I received while at the courthouse. I became nervous. As hard as I tried to stay focused, I was scared I would forget an important detail. I swallowed hard and began.

"I was preparing for an upcoming hearing in the stalking case and compiling everything I needed, but I was missing some documents. I went to the courthouse and was waiting in the clerk's office for copies of my case that I had requested. My phone vibrated, and I looked down at it. It was lying on the top of my purse in the seat next to me. My name was on the screen, which confused me. I answered out of curiosity. It was Todd. He said, 'I know what you're doing and you're not gonna win.' I was stunned, panicked. I may have stayed on the line a few seconds before I hung up." I went on to recount even the smallest details of speaking to courthouse security, calling Jacob and his escort to my car, and finally calling the sheriff's department once I arrived home to file a report, as I had been instructed.

While I was speaking, it was nearly impossible to ignore Todd. He made a spectacle of himself, reacting dramatically every time I spoke. He shook his head in disagreement or nodded yes anytime I said no. He rolled his eyes, and at one point, he threw up his hands as if to say, "I have to listen to this?" The judge stopped Raymond to ask the defense attorney to have his client respect the court, which worked.

Raymond played the audio recording of my call to the sheriff's department. I heard my voice on the recording—hoarse and scared, like a small child's. Todd's attorney sat back in his chair, his eyes fixed on me as the recording played.

I looked around and saw Sharon sitting nearby with her lips pursed into a kiss—a reminder for me to keep it short and simple, for reassurance. She raised her right arm, giving a thumbs-up. In one swift motion, she lowered her thumb and swiped her index finger, mimicking flushing a toilet—our private joke.

After the recording finished, Raymond asked, "Can you confirm that was your voice on the recording?"

"Yes," I responded.

"Okay. Now, describe to me what happened when the officer arrived at your house to take the report."

My throat suddenly felt dry. I cleared it and recounted the events in a steady voice. Raymond seemed satisfied with my answer and asked if I wanted to add anything else. I paused, in a panic, thinking maybe I left out a key detail that Raymond was looking for, but nothing came to mind. I simply responded, "No."

He looked over to the judge. "No further questions."

As Raymond sat, Todd's attorney stood. I felt the heat of his gaze. My hand clenched the dog tags, nails digging crescents into my flesh. I took a deep breath, reminding myself why I was there—to tell the truth and seek justice.

Todd's attorney paced as he asked several questions carefully crafted to make it sound like I was seeking revenge because Todd didn't want to be with me. I remained calm, answering his questions methodically, never showing the nerves that jolted my body like bolts of electricity. He then began to ask about my previous failed relationships, peppering in what I felt were invasive questions about my personal life that had nothing to do with the case. Raymond didn't object, so I steeled myself and answered every question honestly. I reminded myself that my past shouldn't matter. The facts are the facts.

The defense attorney grew aggressive, raising his voice and speaking quickly. I took this as a sign that I was doing well. He asked technical questions about my cell phone—questions I didn't know the answer to because I'm not very technical. He then brandished his cell phone, which was the same brand as mine, and showed me how he could do certain things I claimed mine couldn't do.

"How do you explain that?" he asked, narrowing his eyes.

"Even though we have the same phone, your software has probably been updated since the incident last year. My phone might do those things today but didn't at the time of the incident." I felt this was a brilliant response and was proud to point out something that should have been obvious.

"You said that when your phone rang, you knew it was Todd. Correct?"

Listen carefully to each question.

"No, sir. My phone didn't ring. It was on vibrate," I corrected, consistent with my earlier testimony.

"Okay, but you said you knew it was Todd."

"No, sir. I said I was confused when I saw my name on the phone. It was as if my phone were calling itself."

"But you said that before you answered, you knew it was Todd."

"No, sir. I didn't know it was Todd before I answered. Only after I heard his voice." I tried to recall the exact words I used when testifying for Raymond, but my mind was spinning. A wave of anxiety surged through me, pushing an acrid, metallic taste to the back of my throat. I licked my dry lips, swallowing hard. I rubbed my thumb over the raised name of my nephew, then clasped the dog tags so tightly that my knuckles turned white.

"Wasn't that your testimony just a few minutes ago? That you knew it was Todd?"

I squeezed the dog tags tighter. *God, please help me.*

Raymond stood and asked the judge to have the defense attorney identify which part of my testimony he was referring to and to have the court clerk read it back.

Before the judge could respond, Todd's attorney threw up a hand. "Disregard." He moved to the outside of the table where Todd was seated. One hand in his pocket. "What color shirt was Todd wearing that day?"

An odd question. I hadn't seen Todd that day. "I don't know. I never saw him."

"But you testified earlier that you had to get a police escort because Todd was in the parking lot, so you must have seen him. Correct?"

"No, sir. I was afraid he was waiting by my car in the parking lot and might harm me before I could leave safely, so Jacob walked me to my car."

"So, you *assumed* Todd was waiting for you in the parking lot, like you *assumed* it was Todd on the phone?" He emphasized "assumed."

"That's incorrect. I didn't assume Todd was in the parking lot. I was *afraid* he was in the parking lot." I matched his emphasis on the word "afraid."

"When's the last time you spoke on the phone with my client?"

"Two years ago." I looked at Sharon as if we were back in the witness room.

"Uh-huh. And when was the call in question?"

"Last year."

His arms flung out, palms up. "And after over a year of not speaking with Todd on the phone, you claim to have recognized his voice in a call that lasted just thirteen seconds with less than ten words spoken? Is that your testimony under oath?"

Todd let out an audible chuckle.

I was the victim, yet I felt like the one on trial. I felt myself losing control, but I stayed stone-faced.

"Absolutely." My conviction was unwavering.

"Amazing."

Todd's attorney returned to the table and rifled through papers. I glanced at Raymond, but his face was like granite. I couldn't tell how the trial was going.

The attorney waived a piece of paper in the air. "Isn't it true that Todd broke up with you, even going so far as to explain," he propped reading glass onto his nose, "and I quote from my client's own words 'a relationship with you isn't healthy'?"

My heart dropped. He was reading directly from the handwritten letter Todd left in my mailbox. He'd already asked a similar question, so I waited to see if Raymond was going to stand and object, like I'd seen on television. He didn't.

"Yes, he—"

He threw his hands in the air. "Well, hell hath no fury like a woman scorned!" He swiped his reading glasses from his face. "I have no further questions, Your Honor."

I looked at Raymond, my eyes pleading to let me speak. To tell the court that letter came after the first no-contact letter. Instead, Raymond informed the judge he reserved the right to call me to the stand for rebuttal testimony. The judge acknowledged and dismissed me.

The bailiff escorted me through the now-silent courtroom back to the dull room where I had nothing to do but wait.

And wait.

And wait.

My innards felt like a twisted mess, as if I'd thrown myself on a hand grenade. I carefully placed the dog tags on the table, rubbing my hand where their indentations had left a crease. I thought about checking my phone to see if my sister had texted that my nephew's surgery was over. But I couldn't let myself go there—not yet. I could be called as a rebuttal witness.

The questions. My testimony. They kept turning over and over in my mind as I waited. I questioned whether the judge, too, would find it absurd that I recognized Todd's voice on the phone that day. But when someone terrorizes you the way Todd has me, you don't forget that voice.

I'll never forget that voice.

CHAPTER
FIFTY-NINE

The door opened, and the bailiff instructed me to return to the courtroom. I had no idea what I was walking into. Was I being put back on the witness stand? I just wanted this to be over. I grabbed the dog tags, quickly jumped to my feet, and followed the bailiff. I had already convinced myself that the judge wouldn't believe I recognized Todd's voice on the phone, so my expectations walking back in were low. This case would likely meet the same fate as the renewal of the protective order.

When I entered the courtroom, it was dead silent. Raymond, Todd, and Todd's attorney were all standing. Sharon and Gina were sitting on a bench. My eyes quickly darted between them all, but they gave nothing away.

The bailiff motioned for me to stand near a wall. I backed up until I found the smooth surface—*I might need it to hold me up*, I thought, realizing how absolutely drained I was. The judge was stoic and expressionless. Todd stared straight ahead, and I was thankful not to meet his cold, dark eyes. His stance was rigid, his hands clasped in front of him. He didn't seem nervous. He didn't seem uncomfortable. He just looked like he could leap over the table and strangle me with his bare hands at any moment. I was thankful to have the bailiff next to me.

The judge read the case number and Todd's full name aloud. He looked directly at Todd. "Guilty on the charge of Violation of a Protective Order."

As soon as the judge uttered those words, I gasped as if I had been miles underwater and just broke the surface. I focused on remaining vertical, hiding the relief that rippled through my body—the relief that threatened to crumple me to the floor.

Todd's attorney asked to immediately move to sentencing. I understood the sequence of events, but it seemed to be moving so fast.

"Your Honor," Raymond began. "We'd like to provide a victim impact statement." He looked over at me, and we locked eyes. I had not been prepared for this—not by Raymond, not by Sharon, not by Gina.

I gulped air. This was a big opportunity, but it came with major conflict. I wanted the judge to understand how traumatic and creepy that phone call was. Doing so was counterintuitive with Todd being present. I never wanted Todd to know how much his actions affected me and disrupted my life. I never wanted to give him that sick satisfaction.

The bailiff escorted me back to the witness stand to speak into the microphone. I glanced at Sharon, who was beaming as if her child was sitting at the piano on recital day. I couldn't smile back at her—I was afraid to look too overjoyed.

Instead of looking at Todd, I turned and faced the judge. He put his pen down, sat back, and rested his elbow on the arm of the chair, propping his right hand against his temple. His eyes were fixed on me. I felt his undivided attention, gathered myself, and found my voice.

"Your Honor, first and foremost, I want to thank you. This day has been a long time coming, and I feel so grateful that the court has recognized the defendant's actions as criminal. Sir, *you* ordered Todd not to contact me, but he did. *You* ordered Todd to remove his access from the cameras at my house, but he continued to watch me. *You* ordered him off the GPS in my car, but he continued to track me. It was the only way he could have known I was at the courthouse that day and gauge his timing to call me and say such a creepy thing. After that call, I was paralyzed with fear and wracked with anxiety. I took it as threatening, even if the legal system does not. I beg you to impose the harshest sentence available in the hopes that Todd will finally learn to respect the Orders of this court."

The judge thanked me, and I stepped down. After reclaiming my spot against the wall, the bailiff at my side, the judge announced that Todd was sentenced to six months in jail, with five months suspended, and would be on probation for two years. It was a small price to pay for the three years of hell I'd endured—yet, it was a victory nonetheless. He explained that Todd would serve one month in jail and be under house arrest for the five months suspended. I was certain this had something to do with the pandemic, but house arrest was of little comfort. Todd would be allowed to leave his house for work, medical/dental/legal appointments, and meetings with probation. I had no idea if he still worked for the police department, but with his freelance IT work, he could have countless reasons to leave the house.

Todd's attorney loudly proclaimed they would file an appeal, as if to stomp out any feelings of victory I might have had. He didn't realize that my body was completely numb—I felt nothing.

The judge announced he would issue a Civil Protective Order that would last for the next six years—the one thing I coveted but had been denied. Even better, he included a prohibition on firearms, which I took as a sign he remembered my case.

Todd's attorney cleared his throat. "Your Honor, my client is a small business owner with obligations to his clients. We'd like to request a week so that he can get his affairs in order before reporting to jail."

I watched as the judge turned his attention to Raymond. "No objection, Your Honor."

No objection?! My heart sank. My safety would have to wait a week.

"The defendant is ordered to report to jail to commence sentencing on . . ." The judge shuffled some papers. It was Monday, and he ordered Todd to report on Wednesday, allowing only two days instead of a week.

Gratitude swelled in my chest. Still, I knew better than anyone that with Todd, anything could happen in two days.

The bailiff escorted me back to the witness room, leaving the others behind in the courtroom. My whole body was numb as I sat in silence. There was no cause for celebration, even though I'd just won. Todd would be free for the next two days. Sure, he was still wearing an ankle monitor, and pandemic restrictions were still in effect. But it was Todd. If his high was winning the protective order renewal hearing, I wasn't sure what to expect from his low after this loss.

A crowd flooded into the witness room. Gina, Raymond, and Sharon all took seats around me. Raymond explained that six months in jail with five months suspended meant Todd would have to spend a month behind bars; however, the jail was giving two days' credit for each day served, which reduced his time to fifteen days. But the judge also credited him for time already served between his arrest and bond hearing, so the one night he spent in jail (which wasn't even a full twenty-four hours) deducted another two days from his sentence, thanks to the two-for-one credit. Ultimately, Todd was to serve thirteen days in jail for violating the protective order, then be on house arrest for five months. Fortunately, the two-for-one credit only applied to jail time, so he would serve the full five months on house arrest and two years of probation.

Raymond also informed me that, since the ankle monitor was ordered in the stalking case, it would stay on until the stalking trial took place. He slid several papers my way and handed me a pen, pointing to the places I needed to sign.

I read through each document carefully.

"Hey, Raymond," I said. "On the protective order, the judge said it was being issued for six years. But the expiration box shows this year."

"It's okay. The six-year period is on record."

With my experience, I wasn't about to accept that answer. I pushed the paper back to Raymond. "Please ask the judge to correct the expiration year. Then I'll sign it."

With a huff, Raymond headed out the door.

"Good catch," Gina said, patting me on the back.

When Raymond returned, he showed me the correction. Satisfied, I signed the document and handed it back. He leaned forward, his eyes serious. "Listen, do not post anything on social media. Given Todd's accusations that you are gaming the system, anything that could be construed as bragging might be used by the defense as validation in your next case."

"I won't," I agreed with a nod. Inside, anger bubbled like a boiling pot. Todd had plastered his victory from the protective order hearing renewal all over social media and paraded around town claiming he was the victim of a stalker. Meanwhile, I was told to stay silent, to keep my head down. I felt the sharp sting of restraint. My side of the story would have to remain untold.

As the door clicked shut behind Raymond and Sharon, Gina grinned. "You did it!"

"I can't believe it." My body was still tense. "I was almost certain that the judge would side with Todd. What happened in the courtroom?"

Gina erupted into a delighted laugh, her eyes sparkling like glitter. She sprang to her feet, clasping her hands together in pure, unbridled joy. "I'll tell you as soon as we leave this place!"

The bailiff reappeared with a certified copy of my protective order in his hands, and offered to escort me to my car. He looked at his watch. "The defendant left about ten minutes ago."

Once I was safely in the driver's seat, I called Gina. I could hear the excitement in her voice and imagined how animated she was behind the steering wheel.

"First of all, your testimony was perfect. You were so calm, cool, and collected up there. I know how much strength that took. You are incredible!"

"Thanks."

"Here's what happened. Todd claimed he was with a friend at a restaurant when the call to your phone was placed. His friend even took the stand to testify and corroborate his story, but neither of them had a receipt or any documentation of the time they were together."

When Gina mentioned the witness's name, I immediately recognized it. It was a man I'd met several times through Todd, but didn't realize they were so close that he would agree to testify. Besides Lauren and Nathan, I couldn't seem to find a single person willing to testify.

"Okay, but how was he found guilty if he had someone vouching for him?"

"I have to be honest—I was afraid Todd might win with his claim that he was at a restaurant. Even though your testimony was great, in was still a he-said-she-said case. We've learned from the protective order hearing that those cases are hard to win, so I was nervous. But Raymond was brilliant. He could see that Todd thought he was the smartest person in the room. He knew that Todd didn't like to be challenged."

"He nailed that one," I said.

"He did, and you won't believe what happened next. Todd repeatedly and emphatically said he did not call you. Raymond then asked him, 'As a technical person, can you tell me what spoofing is?' Todd launched into an explanation that spoofing is when you intentionally alter the caller ID display to make it appear as though the call is from a different number. As Raymond kept asking questions, Todd acknowledged that to make an incoming call look like it's coming from another phone, the caller doesn't need physical possession of the phone. Raymond then asked Todd if he were going to spoof a call, how would he do it? Todd launched into his expert explanation again. That was the moment I knew the verdict would go in your favor."

I laughed for the first time in a long time—my case wasn't won purely on evidence, but on Todd's narcissism. It wasn't that I found the situation funny; it was more about my body releasing the stream of emotions I'd suppressed all day. Barely a minute later, the laughter turned to tears as I thought about my family, my nephew, our collective pain. I gripped the steering wheel.

"Just remember, today was a win. Congratulations!" We hung up, and my watery eyes stayed fixed on the road ahead.

Gina also explained this was a test run for the prosecution team. They needed to see how each of us performed on the witness stand to plan for the larger cases of stalking and theft. I had three cases and three different prosecutors working together to achieve the outcome I deserved. This was the weakest case, yet we'd won it.

With the psychological war raging, round one was over. I was still in the arena with a narcissistic monster who felt entitled to win but had just lost. I wondered how this would manifest in Todd's unpredictable behavior, and I knew I'd have stay vigilant for my own safety. The bear had been poked, and I couldn't stop thinking about the consequences.

CHAPTER SIXTY

Immediately after the trial, Dylan and I set out for the long drive back to my hometown. The Black Binder, along with its sister binders, was in the trunk. Among them was my freshly signed Civil Protective Order that covered me for the next six years. But I couldn't think about the trial. I was a mother, and I couldn't let Dylan see how affected I was at a time when we were mourning a member of our family. I needed to be strong.

Dylan and I talked for several hours as we drove. It was the first time in his life that he would be a pallbearer, and he wanted to do a good job. I could tell he was nervous. I was no longer a victim on this drive; I was a grief-stricken mother who had to nurture her twenty-year old son facing the realities of death.

Since we got such a late start, we decided to stay overnight at a hotel and finish the drive in the morning. Once Dylan and I settled in, sleep eluded me. He never had a problem sleeping, but it had become my new normal to toss and turn, listening intently to the sounds around me. I watched Dylan sleep the way I did when he was a child. I could hear his breath and see the rise and fall of his chest under the covers in the bed opposite mine. Only a mother knows how comforting it is to see her child breathe. I couldn't imagine how my sister felt knowing she'd never be able to see her child breathe again. There was nothing I could say or do to take that pain away from her, no matter how much I wanted to. All I could do was lie there in the dark, grateful for every breath Dylan took.

The next morning, we arrived at my parents' house, and I jumped in to help with planning my nephew's funeral. The last thing I wanted to do was talk about a trial I still hadn't fully processed, so I kept this detail from my family.

On Wednesday, Todd was scheduled to report to jail, but he didn't. Sharon called to make sure I was somewhere safe and asked for an emergency contact where I was staying. I was at my parents' house, so I provided their contact information.

Dylan was out with my father while my mom was grocery shopping.

I was alone.

I peered out the window into the driveway where Dylan's car—the car that Todd could track—was parked, and I scanned the front yard for any sign of Todd. I double-checked all the doors before taking a seat at the breakfast table, my head melting into my hands.

It wasn't long before my mom called because she had received an alarming text message from Sharon. I told her about the conviction on Monday and explained that Todd did not report to jail. Before my mom could respond, my father was calling on the other line. Mom told me to answer it. Once again, I explained the situation, and Dad instructed me where his firearms were in the house. He insisted on staying on the phone with me until I had a gun in my hand.

"I'm on my way. Be there as soon as I can."

My heart raced as I stared at the gun lying cold on the breakfast table. Beside it sat the black steel magazine, packed full of bullets that could take away my pain and misery in an instant. My mind flashed back to the murdered woman whose case has remained unsolved for three years now. I stared at the bullets and thought about the one that violently entered her skull. My hands shook uncontrollably as I contemplated the same fate for myself.

Or Todd.

I sat in silence. The dull ache in my chest became a full-blown roar of terror as I waited for something—anything—to happen.

My dad was careful not to walk in unannounced when he and Dylan arrived, aware that I had a loaded weapon. Seeing his face, I felt a surge of relief. He was there to protect me.

We were all in fear. The details of the funeral had been published in the paper and online, complete with the date, time, and location of the service, and my name was listed as a relative. We feared Todd would show up at the funeral. I knew my father would look after me, even as we mourned his grandson, my nephew.

Caleb and Annie arrived the next day and checked into a hotel near the funeral home. Dylan followed me as we drove over to meet them. I was eager to see Caleb. Feeling his arms around me was what I needed most, and he did not disappoint. He hugged me tighter than he normally did, and I was thankful for that. I lingered in his arms longer than Caleb seemed to want, but he did not let me go until I lifted my head from his chest.

While spending time with Caleb at the hotel, I received a text from Sharon asking if I could take a call shortly after five o'clock that afternoon. I hurried outside and called her, anxious for an update on Todd.

"He's in custody," Sharon said.

I let out a sigh of relief. Hot tears streamed down my face.

"He turned himself in at the jail, and I wanted to call you as soon as I found out. I don't have any more details than that. I just wanted you to know that you're safe."

Safe.

He's in jail.

I am safe.

I repeated this in my head long after the call with Sharon ended, trying to release the fear and anxiety that had gripped my body. I was exhausted—

drained beyond what I'd ever imagined my body could withstand—but I was okay. I was safe.

The next day, I pulled on a black dress and slipped my feet into heels before running a brush through my hair. The hot, sticky air outside felt like a weighted blanket being draped over our shoulders as we made our way to the funeral. As we entered, my primal brain overtook my thinking mind. Instead of focusing on my family, I was distracted by my surroundings. As if operating against my will, my eyes kept scanning the crowd, looking for signs of Todd. While my fears were unjustified since Todd was in jail, they robbed me of fully participating in the funeral. I couldn't help but doubt whether the concrete walls could hold him. After all, he was charismatic, and there was always the possibility that he could have persuaded someone to do it for him. *No witness, no stalking conviction*—those thoughts kept running through my mind.

After the funeral service, my family hosted a gathering. I drove in my new car while Dylan followed me and behind him, Caleb and Annie. I had a few minutes alone, so I quickly dialed Sharon.

"Hi, Kathryn," she chirped. "Are you okay?"

"To be honest, I'm not. I was just wondering if you had any more information about Todd. Will the judge order additional jail time since he didn't turn himself in when he was supposed to?"

"This was all a big misunderstanding," she said, her voice calm and soothing.

A misunderstanding?! I wanted to explode.

"When Todd failed to report, the judge agreed to give him twenty-four hours to report to jail, or a warrant would be issued for his arrest. His attorney explained that Todd got the date he was supposed to report wrong. Todd turned himself in before the twenty-four hours expired. And since he turned himself in late in the day, his sentence didn't start until the next morning."

"So, he got *one* extra night?"

"Yes, just one."

I sighed and told Sharon I had to go before clicking off the line. I clenched the steering wheel until my knuckles were white. I clenched my jaw. My breath hastened. I wanted to scream. I knew the truth—this was just another attempt by Todd to control the situation. After what he had just put me and my family through as we mourned, he wouldn't be held accountable.

It was not a misunderstanding.

CHAPTER
SIXTY-ONE

After returning home from my nephew's funeral, everything felt strange. I knew I'd have to return to work soon; I didn't want to take advantage of the kindness my boss extended when she found out about my nephew's death. However, I admit I wished for more time off. The trial had taken place only a week earlier. I had always believed that the law was the law—period. But I was discovering that the application of the law and its sentencing depended on the individual judge. The system was nowhere near as black and white as I had believed.

On Monday morning, Todd's fourth day in jail, I went up to my home office with coffee in hand and a big stack of mail that had collected while I was gone. I sat down at my desk and began to sort through the pile. Somewhere in the middle was a notice from the district attorney's office.

For two years now, it seemed I was receiving notices of hearings, pre-trial conferences, and trial dates for all three cases every other week. Each time, the proceedings were postponed for one reason or another. I had grown accustomed to this rhythm of the court system, so each time I received a notice, I filed it away. Jacob had made it clear that I shouldn't come to court unless the prosecution team invited me, so I could avoid any inference that Todd's claims might be substantiated. So, when I received a notice that the trial in the stalking case had been scheduled, I didn't pay attention to it.

Until my phone rang a week later, on Monday.

"Hi, Kathryn," Aaron said. "I wanted to update you. It looks like Todd's newest attorney—his *fifth*—has withdrawn the motion his previous attorney filed that's been holding things up."

"That's great news," I responded.

"Yes, and more importantly, we're going to trial in one week."

"One week?"

"Todd gets released this Thursday, and we'll be going to trial on Monday."

"Who's the judge?" I'd learned the hard way how important the judge presiding over the case was.

"Judge Chambers. He's good. He's fair."

Even though I had waited for this day to come, I was neither happy nor sad that it was quickly approaching. I'd never heard of this judge, so I had no idea what to expect. I felt utterly drained; my mind, body, and soul had been hollowed out. I had been living in an abyss of physical exhaustion. Every morsel of food was a struggle to keep down. The thought of being in the same room as Todd again, forced to breathe the same air, made me nauseous.

The week crawled by. I thought about how his attorney had asked questions on the stand that made me uncomfortable to answer—questions about my past relationships, questions that seemed to imply I was a scorned ex seeking revenge. I knew it was a tactic to introduce doubt about my character and credibility. But it still stung. I'd been a single mother for eleven years before I married Jason and had dated plenty. But I wasn't the town jezebel Todd's attorney was trying to make me out to be.

I pondered how Todd's attorney would spin his accusations of *me* being the stalker. Those words—the very idea—churned in my mind like a whirlpool, eating away at my soul.

My fortitude was crumbling. I wasn't sure I could put myself through another trial. I thought about the women in Todd's other police reports who didn't go through with it. How I'd blamed them for being weak, but now I was the weak one.

This was a big decision, and one I couldn't make on my own. I emailed Dr. Saxton, and he made himself available for a video session. After catching him up on the last trial and the tragic death of my nephew, he started asking me questions.

"Kathryn, what are you most afraid of about facing Todd in court again?" Dr. Saxton asked gently through the monitor, his brow furrowed with concern.

I let out a shaky breath. "I'm afraid of . . . of him twisting everything around, making me out to be the crazy one. Of having to relive everything he put me through. I don't know if I have it in me anymore."

"Have what, exactly?"

"The fight." There. I said out loud what I didn't want to acknowledge.

Dr. Saxton nodded thoughtfully. "Those fears are completely valid and understandable, given the trauma you've endured. But I want you to remember how far you've come, Kathryn. You've already faced him in court once before at a time when others might have crumbled under the weight of grief."

Tears pricked at my eyes. "I don't feel strong right now. I feel like I'm barely holding it together."

"And yet, here you are, reaching out for support and guidance. That takes immense strength and courage. Don't discount that." He leaned forward, his gaze intent. "Kathryn, only you can decide if you're ready to face him again. Forget how you feel today. How will you feel a year from now if you choose not to participate in the trial?"

I knew where he was going with this. Yes, I probably would regret it if I didn't go through with it. But I couldn't see past today. I couldn't think past today. My life had been reduced to simply one breath after another.

Dr. Saxton's eyes were filled with compassion. "I know that you have a deep sense of justice. You've fought so hard for the truth to come out. Why stop now?"

I let his words sink in. He was right. As much as I wanted to run away from all of this, I knew I couldn't live with myself if I didn't see it through.

"What if I can't handle it?" I whispered, voicing my deepest fear. "What if I fall apart on the stand?"

"You are stronger than you give yourself credit for." Dr. Saxton suggested I keep a notepad with me. "Make a list of reasons why you should follow through with the trial—and only focus on those reasons. The morning of the trial, read this list and let it guide you."

After we ended our session, my body moved with purpose. I didn't need to make a list. Dr. Saxton had given me the reassurance I needed to find my strength. Despite my depleted state, I was determined to seek justice. The judgment I had privately passed on myself, I was certain, was far harsher than what I was about to experience at the hands of the justice system.

I focused on what I could do to prepare. I remembered that after Todd's first conviction, I was unprepared to deliver a victim impact statement. I sat down at my computer to prepare one and stared at the blinking cursor. I had no idea how to put into words what I had experienced due to Todd's stalking. What do you say when your life has been ravaged, torn apart, and irrevocably changed in front of the very person responsible?

Words were a luxury I did not have; instead, images of Todd's actions flashed through my mind. His narrow eyes trained on the road the night he drove me to his house. My bleeding feet as I hid, paralyzed, in the bushes waiting for Lauren to find me. Seeing him in my backyard, masturbating. Watching in horror as he climbed into my car at the grocery store. The grainy video of him in the bushes, peering into the window of Oskar's. His disdain for the murdered woman and how he asked if I would want to see death coming.

The world would be a better place if you just weren't in it.
You are mine. And I don't share.

I thought about the hearing to renew the protective order and Todd's accusations that I was the stalker. I knew that would be a lynchpin in the defense's case. I felt sick imagining his twisted face as he recounted lies that sounded like the truth. I knew I'd also have to prepare for attacks unlike anything I'd ever faced before—this time, from people acting as witnesses for Todd. I had been hearing rumblings in my small community, mostly from Nathan, about different people who'd received subpoenas to testify for the defense. My stomach knotted thinking about the awful lies people would spew about me and somehow do it without falling apart.

While others were receiving subpoenas to testify for Todd, I wasn't aware of anyone that had received one from the prosecution. I wasn't sure of what to make of this. It was all I could do to muster the strength to get myself to court that I never questioned it. I just kept reading the list Dr. Saxton asked me to make and following his advice to keep my focus there.

As these thoughts raced through my mind, my fingers flew. Sentences formed on their own until, before I knew it, my victim impact statement was complete. It was gut-wrenching and visceral; honest and heartfelt; but measured rather than melodramatic. Writing this statement gave me a small semblance of comfort, even though no words could ever truly describe my experience. I just hoped Todd would be convicted, and I would get to read it in court. I wanted the judge to know the depths of despair Todd was responsible for so that the maximum sentence—one year—would be imposed. After all, even though I was still breathing, Todd had taken my life long ago.

At war with this thought was the notion that Todd would hear my words, too. How do you give that level of satisfaction to the person responsible for decimating your life? I was convinced he would take pleasure in it. Despite my fears, an unwavering strength remained within me to carry on, even if it meant sacrificing parts of myself along the way.

By Thursday—the day of Todd's release—I had found a way to keep myself focused: I practiced reading aloud my victim impact statement. Red ink littered the page in my hand as I paced the floor reciting it.

Even though I knew it was coming, my stomach tied itself in knots when I received the call from the jail, letting me know that Todd was being processed for release. His thirteen days, plus one for not reporting to jail on time, were completed. I confirmed that he would be leaving with the ankle monitor affixed to his leg. The stalking trial was four days away, on Monday. I prayed that, at the very least, I could make it until then.

The ankle monitor provided some reassurance, but deep down I knew it wouldn't stop him. Dread knotted in my stomach. He had slithered through the gray areas of the law too many times for me to delude myself into thinking he'd tread a straight path in the coming days.

CHAPTER
SIXTY-TWO

Less than twenty-four hours after Todd was released from jail, I received a call. It was the monitoring company. I quickly answered the phone.

"This is Kathryn."

"Ms. Caraway? This is Greg with the monitoring company assigned to your case. We've received a ping from Todd's ankle monitor. It seems he's near your home. I see your key fob, and it shows you are at home as well. Are you inside?"

My stomach flipped.

My breath caught.

I froze.

"Yes. Where is he?"

"It looks like he's just beyond the perimeter of your property, but he's close to breaching the boundary set by the court. Stay on the line with me."

Close. That means he's just outside the one-hundred-yard perimeter.

My body responded as if I'd been punched. My heart pounded. My eyes burned. He was taunting me—letting me know the conviction meant nothing, the jail time meant nothing. He was likely just far enough away that he could claim it was an accident—that he was just driving somewhere to handle a work matter since he was supposed to be on house arrest. But I knew better; he was on the hunt. I could feel him, lurking like a hungry lynx, ready to tear me to shreds.

I was paralyzed by the gravity of the words he had uttered the day he drove me to his house against my will—*The world would be a better place if you just weren't in it.* Those words sank into my bones again. That stare from his icy eyes. The spit flying from his mouth as he hurled insults at me.

I stayed on the line with the monitoring company. I became dizzy with panic as I waited with bated breath for them to track his movements away from my home. Finally, Greg told me he'd moved out of range. Even then, I was still on high alert, waiting for him to make contact. Every nerve in my body was charged, ready to call 911 at a moment's notice.

As soon as I clicked off the line with the monitoring company, I dialed Gina and told her what happened. I tried to be as calm as possible, asking her to add it to our existing list of times he'd used this method to intimidate me before a court date.

"Please," she begged, "don't stay at your house this weekend. Find somewhere else to go. He's acting out; it isn't safe."

"I'll be okay," I responded. I refused to be scared away. I was determined to stand my ground despite my overwhelming fear of danger. To put my mind at ease, I steeled myself and texted the tech at the ankle monitoring company, hoping to get some clarification but also to document what had happened.

ME

> Thank you for letting me know Todd was nearby. I know he is under house arrest, but do you know if there is a "curfew"? Given his job, leaving for work seems to be subjective.

TECH

> I agree. His terms are very loose.

I thought maybe the ankle monitoring company could provide clarification, but instead, they validated my concern that there was no real "safe" window when I would know he had to be home. I wondered how I could weave this into my victim impact statement in a way that would urge the judge to better define home incarceration.

The weekend was a nightmare. I barricaded myself inside the house, too scared to venture out. Every time I heard a noise outside, my heart raced, and my body trembled violently. I especially didn't feel safe going to bed at night, even fully dressed in running shoes. I was terrified that Todd would come through the window and kill me while I was sleeping. Instead of resting, I read through every piece of evidence again and mentally prepared for the enormity of the trial on the horizon. This wasn't like the violation of the protective order, where my testimony was focused on a single event. The stalking case was based on a number of incidents that formed a pattern.

When Monday morning finally came, my cheeks were sunken, eyes hollow with dark bags beneath them. I managed to get into a presentable outfit, fix my hair, and apply makeup, but nothing could conceal my misery. My heart rate quickened as I got into my car and raised the garage door—the sunlight a reminder that I was now outside, in the open—an easy target. The pandemic rules still dictated that only witnesses, attorneys, and people named in a case were allowed in court, so I drove by myself. Aaron had not subpoenaed Nathan or Lauren, for reasons he never shared. The private investigator was not subpoenaed either. Only me.

This time, I didn't arrive early to find a nearby parking spot; I wanted to spend as little time at the courthouse as possible. When I pulled in, the parking lot directly in front of the courthouse was full, so I parked in an adjacent parking garage. I hopped out of my car and strode toward the courthouse—in the open parking garage, completely exposed. As my heels clicked on the cement, I braced myself to be physically taken down by Todd at any moment. I imagined the headlines:

*WOMAN GETS MURDERED
BY STALKER MOMENTS BEFORE TRIAL*

It wasn't that I didn't care. It was that I needed to portray that level of confidence, in case he was watching.

And Todd was always watching.

I gazed up at the sprawling courthouse steps, which seemed infinitely tall, my stomach turning at the thought of what awaited me. Every step felt like I was pushing against a wall of resistance. I went through the same pandemic protocol as the previous trial and waited to the side of the building's entrance for Sharon to escort me in. Thankfully, she rescued me from this unsecured area before Todd arrived.

Or maybe he was already inside.

We walked in silence to the prosecutor's office, where she asked me to wait in the lobby. As I waited, the familiar alert screamed on my phone:

> THE SUBJECT HAS BREACHED THE RULE
> 'VICTIM PROXIMITY.'

I deactivated the alert on the victim-fob, then pulled out my victim impact statement while I waited. I read it repeatedly, partly to commit as much of it as possible to memory, but also to find strength.

At the last trial, I was taken directly to the witness room, so I assumed this instruction meant that Aaron wanted to meet in his office to go over the case details. While waiting, I pulled out my victim impact statement. I read it repeatedly, committing as much of it as possible to memory.

Gina and Aaron walked into the lobby from a side door. Neither made eye contact. They sat on either side of me. Aaron's brows furrowed as he ran his eyes over me—I knew I looked awful. Sharon walked in and took a seat next to Aaron. A knot formed in my throat—I thought he was going to tell me the trial had been delayed. As much as I wanted it to be over, I was in no state to testify.

Instead, he said, "Kathryn, I have some great news. Todd agreed to plead guilty to stalking instead of going to trial."

My shoulders dropped, and tears pricked the backs of my eyes. Todd would now and forever be a convicted stalker. I closed my eyes and swallowed hard. "Thank you, Aaron." I looked at Gina, then at Sharon, their faces somber. If this was a win, what was I missing?

"So, what happens now?"

"The judge will sentence Todd to the same punishment he received for violating the protective order. But there's a catch. He'll be credited with time served."

"What does that mean?" I already knew, but I wanted to hear him say it.

"It means that rather than serving two sentences for the two different charges, Todd will only serve one. And since he has completed that sentence, he will not serve any more time in jail after pleading guilty to the stalking charge."

I wanted to scream.

I wanted to fall on the floor in a heap and never get up.

This meant that because Todd served fourteen days in jail—after putting my family through hell while we navigated the immediate aftermath of my nephew's death—he wouldn't serve any additional time.

"I don't understand," I pleaded with Aaron. "How can he plead guilty to a crime but not have a punishment for it? Do you know he came by my house after being released from jail?"

"Kathryn, you said Todd needed to be held accountable for the crime he committed, which was stalking. He is agreeing to plead guilty to stalking, so take the win," Aaron counseled.

"Let me ask it another way. How can he be convicted of stalking, but face no jail time? I don't understand."

Aaron exchanged glances with Gina. She piped up, "This is a win, Kathryn. He will forever be a convicted stalker now, and if he continues to stalk you, a second offense will be considered a felony."

"So, the judge has already made up his mind?"

"Yes," Aaron explained. "Todd's attorney and I had a conference with the judge in chambers, and this is the agreement reached."

Unbelievable. What is it with these judges who want everyone to agree so they don't have to decide for themselves? I know courts are busy, but this is ridiculous. This isn't some frivolous lawsuit—this is a criminal matter that deserves to be heard.

"So, even if I read my victim impact statement, it wouldn't matter. He won't get any additional jail time," I said, dejected.

Gina placed her hand on my back. "I know it's hard to process, but I promise, this is a good thing. Remember, to win at trial, Aaron would need to prove beyond a *reasonable doubt* that your fear was caused by Todd's actions—which is a pretty high threshold."

I felt a sense of dread—Todd would never stand in judgment for what he had done. The details, the video of him hiding in the bushes at the restaurant, none of it would see the light of day. I'd never get to go on record with all that I'd endured. Todd's lies in the protective order renewal hearing would forever remain in the court record. This wasn't a win. It was a slap in the face disguised as one.

I stared blankly ahead. My mind was blown that Todd could wield an inordinate amount of power over my life—be convicted of stalking—and then go home that evening, sit on his couch, eat pizza, and watch a movie.

Todd had already been caught close to breaking the perimeter when he got out of jail. He'd already shown me what he was capable of. The image in my mind of him splayed out on his couch, plotting his next move, was almost too much to bear. Yet, I had no choice in the matter. No say whatsoever.

This was the bitter pill of justice I had to swallow.

CHAPTER
SIXTY-THREE

Aaron led me to the courtroom, with Gina and Sharon flanking my sides. I felt like I was a lamb being led to slaughter. Once inside, I noticed Todd was already seated at the front, next to his attorney. Aaron motioned for me to sit on a bench, then walked to the front and sat at the table. Gina and Sharon sat with me.

A few minutes later, the judge entered through a door at the back of the room. The proceedings felt very procedural, as though my life hadn't hung in the balance over the past few years. The judge allowed the defense attorney to change Todd's plea from "not guilty" to "guilty." Todd had to verbally acknowledge that the plea was made of his own free will, to which he responded with a very curt, "Yes." He didn't seem any happier with the outcome than I was.

I was so deflated by what had transpired that, when I was called to deliver my victim impact statement, I didn't move. I didn't have the energy to read it aloud. It simply didn't feel like it would make a difference. Todd would be home eating pizza in a few hours.

The judge called me a second time to the stand. Sharon leaned over and said, "If you don't want to do this for yourself, do it for his next victim. Get your statement into the court record."

I thought of my nephew and how he soldiered on in Afghanistan as a Marine, even after some of his best friends died. With his dog tags once again embedded in my hand, I took the stand. My voice quivered; my hands shook but I was determined not to let Todd see me cry. With the judge's eyes fixed on me, I began to read.

"When the court granted me a protective order against the defendant, I believed I was safe from the threat of stalking and harassment. I could not have been more wrong. After violating the conditions of the law, he was sentenced to thirty days in jail and five months on house arrest, which briefly gave me a sense of freedom I hadn't experienced in years. Though I was technically free during this time, it was tainted with fear over news of his release. I spent that time wondering how soon I would have to return to my life as a recluse for safety, so I tried to confirm his release date with the jail. My queries were met with silence. Apparently, Todd's privacy matters more than my safety.

"My fear was realized when, the day after his release, I received an alert warning me of his proximity to my house—my safe place. I took the advice of professionals and locked my doors. How many times will I have to face the reality that he can harm me if he wants to? How long will I have to live in fear and paranoia? Will he ever stop?

"The night that I caught sight of him from my window sent my panic into overdrive. My migraine headaches returned, more aggressive than ever, affecting my ability to work. Todd's actions made my life so difficult that I questioned whether it was worth living.

"Over the past three years, he has crossed more lines than I can count, contacting almost everyone in my life, humiliating me in front of people I care about so that I felt ashamed and withdrew into myself. It became harder and harder to know who to trust, to the point where I had to cut contact with people I'd known for years. I had to upend my entire life to avoid him: replacing all technology, changing my phone number, installing an alarm system, and even using cameras on my vehicle so that, should something terrible happen to me, I can be confident there will be evidence.

Not only have these taken time and energy to set up, but they've drained my bank accounts. I've made all this effort, and I still feel unsafe.

"I can tell you with certainty that he is capable of far worse than you imagine. His actions will lead to greater acts of violence if you don't do something about them. He will keep coming after me. He will never stop. Please, give him the maximum sentence permitted and provide me with a permanent protective order so that I can leave my house without triple-checking every window and door. So that I can drive without constantly gazing into my car mirrors to see if he's on my tail. Order a three-hundred-yard perimeter so that I can sleep at night without holding my breath every time I hear a noise. I want to live my life in its entirety, but I can't under the current conditions. You have the opportunity to change that. Will you?"

As I walked back to my seat, I passed Todd. His icy eyes narrowed on me. "You're going to regret this," he hissed.

The hairs on the back of my neck stood up; my heart hammered against my ribs. Aaron immediately barked, "Please instruct your client to refrain from making remarks."

I leaned over to Sharon and asked, "Did you hear that?"

"I did. Aaron shut him down. There's nothing we can do about it."

I was appalled that a threat would be tolerated in the courtroom, but then again, this was the same court that didn't believe a stalking conviction was worth any additional jail time either. Apparently, my expectations of the judicial system were too high.

The judge announced the sentence Aaron had prepared me for, but added a stipulation that Todd undergo a full psychiatric evaluation and counseling while on probation.

My heart sank.

My head throbbed.

He was, in fact, going home. I couldn't get out of the courthouse fast enough.

Instead of feeling victorious, I felt the crushing weight of defeat constricting my stomach. Two of the three charges had been decided, but the sentencing seemed insignificant compared to the offenses. The more I thought about it, the more frustrated I became. The sentence for the stalking conviction was essentially no sentence at all.

You're going to regret this.

When the day finally ended, Todd's words wouldn't leave my mind. I texted Gina, asking why his menacing remark hadn't been taken more seriously. Seconds later, my phone rang.

"Kathryn," Gina began. "I don't want you to worry about what Todd said. Sharon was right. There's nothing we can do because it wasn't a direct threat. You can only pursue legal action if it's a direct threat."

"That doesn't make any sense."

"Well, he might have meant that you'd regret your victim impact statement after some reflection. Or that he meant you'd feel sorry you got him convicted at all. He never actually said he would hurt you."

I understood where Gina was coming from, but I couldn't agree. I knew what Todd meant by his words. Arguing with her felt pointless. The law always seemed to twist in his favor.

"And Kathryn?"

"Yes?"

"Don't forget—you can't post anything about this on social media. There's still the theft charge pending."

It sickened me to be reminded. I hadn't posted anything on social media for nearly two years. Once again, I was powerless to defend myself in the court of public opinion.

The theft case was my only hope now—and it was a felony. I believed Todd needed to be a convicted felon, so I wasn't about to jeopardize that.

Once again, Todd's conviction should have been a moment of triumph. A way to reclaim myself after years of feeling unheard, helpless, and robbed. I wanted to move on, but I felt something deep inside me had been stolen—my voice. I desperately wanted to tell my story, exercise my right to set the record straight, and receive validation from the authorities, the community, and those who had remained silent while passing judgment on me thanks to Todd's manipulation and lies.

I could already picture how he would spin these convictions. Blame a lack of money, happenstance, or whatever else suited his narrative. And he'd make sure this spread through the community, invalidating everything while I had to remain silent.

All I could do now was wait—and prepare to regret it.

CHAPTER SIXTY-FOUR

Less than twenty-four hours after the trial, my phone screamed.

> THE SUBJECT HAS BREACHED THE RULE 'VICTIM PROXIMITY.'

In seconds, the panic spread, seizing new regions of my mind, consuming me, devouring me. Rage and fear coursed through my veins simultaneously. My mind reeled with the implications of Todd's presence.

His threats, his menacing glances in the courtroom. His ominous promise to me: *You're going to regret this.*

Could he have finally come to kill me?

With trembling hands, my earbud firmly in place, I dialed 911. Before the call connected, I had a gun in my hand. Fortunately, I had brought it up to the office with me that morning. I tried coherently explaining the situation while battling my racing, incoherent thoughts. My voice quivered as I rapidly fired off details—name, address, phone number—along with his history of violating protective orders.

"He was convicted of stalking me yesterday, and now he's at my house!

Hurry!" I pleaded to the operator. I shoved my phone in my pocket and faced the door. My dominant hand firmly wrapped around the pistol, my other supporting it. Arms out in front of me, knees slightly bent and shoulder-width apart.

"I have officers on the way. Stay on the phone with me."

"Please hurry!" I pleaded desperately.

"Where are you in the house?"

"I'm upstairs, in a room over the garage."

"Is the door locked?"

"No."

"Can you reach the door to lock it?"

"No." To lock the entry to the home office, I would have to walk down the stairs, and my feet felt like they were encased in concrete. I couldn't move.

"Okay. Is there another room you can lock yourself in?"

"Yes. There is a bathroom." I slowly walked backwards, not taking my eyes off the top of the stairs. The knee wall was solid drywall instead of the more common spindles found protecting staircases—a cost-saving measure when I was finishing construction. I could only see when someone was on the top three steps. Todd knew the layout of my office. I was convinced he could be on the stairs already; if he were down a few steps, I wouldn't know it.

"I have a gun! It's loaded and I will shoot!" I continued back-walking, never taking my eyes off the stairs until I reached the bathroom.

"What type of gun do you have?" the operator asked. Speaking loudly, I described the .40-caliber Glock, including the hollow-point bullets loaded to inflict the maximum damage on its intended recipient.

Finally in the bathroom, I locked the door and crouched in the shower —my feeble attempt to protect myself. I kept my eyes on the door and the barrel of my gun pointed at it. My finger was a shaky hairline above the trigger.

"Please hurry!" I begged.

"The officers are getting close. Just stay on the phone with me."

Time slowed as my adrenaline spiraled further out of control. The operator asked me questions to keep me talking but now, crouched, I whispered short answers.

"I'm home alone."

"I have a dog."

"I only received the alert and have not actually seen Todd."

"Ma'am, I have confirmed officers have arrived. I need you to put the weapon down and let the officers in."

The cold steel seeped into my skin from the iron-clad grip.

A bullet in the chamber.

My finger was ready to curl in a split second and pull.

The gun had become an extension of me, fused into my hand like an extra limb.

I heard the 911 operator's harsh tone demanding again that I put the weapon down. But I couldn't. Officers were at my house but refused to come in unless I was disarmed, she explained.

But they can't save me from the front lawn if Todd is inside my house. In Todd's twisted game of life and death, the gun was my only hope.

I was frozen. Paralyzed by fear. It was as if my body were glued to the floor of the shower.

The operator repeated her request, more forcefully this time. I screamed into the abyss, "I will shoot!"

"Ma'am, the officers cannot come in while you have a loaded weapon. You need to put your gun down." She sounded angry.

How did I become the problem?

I stood at the bathroom door and held my breath as I rotated the lock on the handle. With my left hand, I flung open the bathroom door before quickly resetting my grip on the gun. I craned my neck around the door jamb, the barrel following my eyes.

I looked beyond my desk at the video cameras on the TV monitor and saw a uniformed officer at my front door. I was relieved, but not out of danger. I had to get to the front door, which meant I had to walk through the garage. I slow-walked with my gun fixed in the direction of the stairs.

My spine tingled. My eyes darted around, searching for any signs of movement. Each step felt like an eternity, but I eventually reached the top of the stairs and peered down into the darkness below.

"I don't see him on the stairs. I'm going to walk through the garage into the house now," I whispered to the operator.

"Do you still have the gun?"

"Yes!" I could feel myself growing annoyed with her insistence about the gun. What about "Todd could be in my house," didn't she understand? An officer at my front door would not protect me as I walked through the garage.

Every move I made felt like it could be my last.

I stood at the door to the garage and considered where Todd could be. The once compassionate 911 operator demanded a third time that I put down the gun and allow officers inside. I raced through the garage and flung open the door to the house, once again with my left hand, quickly returning it to the iron grip on my pistol, my arms outstretched to allow the gun to cross the threshold before I stepped into the house.

Adrenaline coursed through my veins. Every second was a battle of wits between me and death as I ventured through the kitchen toward the front door. I narrated my actions to the operator. I knew she needed this information. I discharged the magazine from my pistol and ejected the bullet from the chamber. I locked the slide before placing the gun on the table, so the officer could see the pistol was not armed.

Now unarmed, I raced to the front door and hurled it open. An officer had his gun drawn but down by his side. I stood at the door, frozen and unsure of what to do. He reached out with his free hand, grabbed me by the arm, yanking me out of the house. I was on the porch when he raised his gun, and walked past me inside.

Another officer came from the side of my house with his gun gripped firmly out in front of him, pointing toward the garage. "Walk to me!"

I put one foot in front of the other, my hands raised, making my way toward the officer.

As I got close, he roughly grabbed me by the arm. He rushed me into a police SUV with its lights on parked perpendicular to my driveway. His body was stiff. His back to me. His pistol pointed at my house. Once I climbed in, he ordered me not to leave the vehicle and slammed the door shut.

My eyes strained against the heavily tinted windows, past the smudges from those who had sat in this same seat, clawing at their freedom. Officers scurried across my lawn, guns drawn, and the door to my house wide open. I couldn't tell what was going on. My mind raced, each thought colliding with the next in a vortex of disorientation.

Where is he? Have they found him? My hands trembled uncontrollably, sweat slicking my palms.

Why am I in the police car and not him? My heart thumped against my ribs like a caged animal trying to escape this nightmare.

Is he being arrested, or am I? The taste of copper filled my mouth as I bit down hard on my lip, drawing blood in my desperation to make sense of what was happening.

I thought about all the times I went to the police, only to be turned away. I closed my eyes, hoping the stalking conviction meant something to them. Then I remembered that I was the one holding the gun when they arrived.

I shifted uncomfortably in the backseat at the thought of being arrested for not putting my gun down when I was ordered to. I wanted to scream from inside the police vehicle. *Why don't you believe me?* I should have expected this; I'd become accustomed to the police not siding with me. Still, I wondered what was going to happen to me. *Were they going to arrest me?* Would they release me and blow the whole thing off, leaving Todd free to come back and finish whatever he started?

I rubbed my forearm where the officer had grabbed me and put me in his car. As I tried to comfort myself, I thought about the murdered woman with the fatal bullet lodged in her skull, and I began to spiral. I caught a glimpse of my reflection in the rearview mirror and was horrified by what I saw—face twisted with fear, tears running down my cheeks, eyes wild and disbelieving. My trembling hand slowly rose to my face as though I needed confirmation it was actually me in the reflection. I touched my wet cheek and realized this was not a nightmare I would be waking up from.

The officer had been so forceful with me, I was certain I was about to be placed under arrest. I pulled my phone out and texted Gina in case I needed her to get me out of jail.

ME

Todd came to my house. Police are here. I'm in trouble because I didn't put down my gun.

My phone instantly rang. Seeing Gina's name on the screen, I quickly answered. "Hello."

"Are you safe?" Those words broke through my numbness like a sledgehammer, and I started gasping for air as uncontrollable sobs overwhelmed me.

"I . . . I . . . I'm in a police car." I did my best to explain what happened, but spent more time telling her about refusing to put down my gun. I should've complied when the operator first asked, but I didn't. I physically couldn't.

"Kathryn, it's okay. You are not in trouble. Did they find Todd?"

"I don't know."

"Okay. Listen. You have a right to protect yourself, Kathryn. You haven't done anything wrong. I'm going to call Aaron, and you need to follow directions from the officers. Call me back if you need anything."

I don't remember hanging up the phone. I don't remember putting it in my lap. I had never been in trouble with the law before, and I definitely had never been put into the back of a police car. Experiencing what it was like to sit in a cruiser for the first time was overwhelming. My arms were wrapped tightly around my body, as if to keep myself from falling apart.

I looked out the window. Officers were gathered on my front lawn. One was talking into a radio attached to his shoulder. No guns were drawn. No Todd in handcuffs.

I remained in the police car. One of four surrounding my house. Waiting for what? To be arrested? To be told the alert had been in error? I grabbed my cell phone and took a screenshot of the alert. I couldn't risk it disappearing in case I had to defend myself for not putting the gun down. I sat there, watching the officers confer on my front lawn.

Todd's seething anger had burned into my skin from the courtroom, taunting me. Every moment since I left the courthouse felt like a ticking time bomb, waiting for him to strike. And now, his message had been received: a conviction meant nothing, and, if he wanted to, he could get to me.

CHAPTER
SIXTY-FIVE

The officer who placed me in the car opened the door and asked me to step out. He explained they had searched my house and property, but hadn't located Todd. He asked to see the notification I received, and I pulled it up on my phone. As I held it out with trembling hands, he took a photograph of the text message displayed and then asked me to return to the vehicle. My chest was heaving, my voice was broken, and I was shaking. I lowered my head to avoid eye contact as I lifted one leg, then the other, into the car.

The officer extended a bottle of water. "You're very brave," he said gently. "Is there someone I can call for you?"

I accepted the water and politely thanked him before declining his offer to call anyone.

This is where I must pause my story. I know I'm not supposed to, but I have to give the officer the credit he deserves. He told me I was brave. Those words, his voice—they still stick with me today. I've never forgotten that simple act of compassion.

My senses were beginning to return. I relaxed, feeling foolish for calling Gina. Of course, I had the legal right to own a registered gun. Of course, I had the right to protect myself. Of course, I wasn't about to be arrested.

I watched as the officer joined the group of uniformed men on my front lawn, the front door of my house still wide open. I heard muffled voices but couldn't make out what they were saying. At times, one or the other would speak into the radio on their shoulder, and something would crackle back.

Finally, the officer who called me brave walked back to me and opened the door. He said he needed my driver's license.

"It's in my purse, inside the house. Is it okay for me to go get it?"

"I'll get it for you, ma'am. Where in the house?"

"In the kitchen, next to the fridge. It's under a wine rack."

He returned with my purse, and I pulled out my license.

"We're attempting to locate Todd now," he said, taking my license. "We're in communication with the ankle monitoring company. I hope it won't be much longer. I need you to just sit tight."

He walked away, leaving the door open so I could get some fresh air. While I waited, Raymond called. He said Aaron was in court but that he'd spoken with Gina. He asked me to explain the situation. I gave a rapid, broken description in short sentences. He asked me to put one of the officers on the line, so I walked over to where they were gathered on the lawn. I told him the prosecutor was on the phone and had asked to speak with someone. One of the officers took my phone and walked out of earshot, so I returned to the police vehicle.

I wasn't sitting there long when the officer came back with my phone. I was surprised Raymond was still on the line.

"Kathryn, I have Sharon here—you're on speakerphone. Listen, we made arrangements at a shelter where you'll be safe until the police locate Todd."

"I appreciate it, but I'd rather go to a hotel." I needed time to myself, and the thought of taking a bed from someone else felt selfish.

After ending the call with Raymond, the officer said he would drive me to the hotel. Since I had a new car that Todd couldn't track, I declined. I wanted my own vehicle in case Todd tracked me there and I needed to make a quick escape.

The officer walked me from the police car to my vehicle and said he'd follow me to the hotel. Arriving there, he parked next to the double sliding front doors in the unloading area, while I pulled into a spot across from it. Sharon had already arranged a room under a different name, and once I had the key, I stepped outside, thanked him for his help, and headed inside.

Entering the cold hotel room alone, I took a seat at the sad excuse for a desk and looked around. A faint smell lingered—evidence of the use of some kind of cleaner, though it seemed like little effort had been made. The dull gray walls carried an odor; a sign that cleaning had been attempted, but not thoroughly. The fading daylight filtered through the window, a reminder of life as I knew it being snuffed out.

The bed let out a creak as I climbed onto it, clutching a bottle of pills Dr. Saxton prescribed. I grabbed the water from the nightstand and stared at the pills, realizing that this nightmare would never truly end. The only permanent solution is death—either his or mine.

Shaking my head, I pushed those dark thoughts away. I took a Xanax and sank into bed, the soles of my shoes catching on the crusty comforter. I shut my eyes and let the medication work its magic.

The next morning, I contacted the non-emergency police line and learned there was no warrant in the system, but I knew that didn't mean one hadn't been issued. I remembered the day Sharon called, asking for the warrant number because it wasn't in the system then, either. I called the probation office to see if they had any updates. My call was shuffled between several people before I spoke to Tammy, Todd's probation officer. She was unaware of the situation and asked for the report number, which I fortunately had from the officer before we left my house. There was nothing to do now but wait for news of Todd's arrest.

I felt sluggish and needed coffee to shake off the Xanax hangover. The thought of leaving my room was tempting, but I knew it could put me in harm's way. Even though the hotel was booked under a different name, I paid with my credit card. I couldn't shake the paranoia. If Todd suspected I was here, I was certain he could hack their system—or maybe he already had. The decision to get a cup of coffee spiraled into paralyzing fear.

To hell with it. Come and get me, you son of a bitch. It seemed people would only help if Todd hurt me first. I trudged downstairs and made myself two steaming cups of coffee. A continental breakfast was available, so I helped myself to a blueberry muffin.

Back in the room, I lay on the bed and reached for the remote. It was sticky, but it still worked. There weren't many channels, and I dared not log into any TV apps out of fear that Todd could track me. I clicked through the channels until I settled on a mindless nature program that segued into a fishing show, then to something about ancient Mayan ruins.

I was flipping channels when my phone rang. I stared at the screen but didn't recognize the number. It could have been the jail calling to inform me Todd had been arrested, so I answered, trying to sound coherent.

"This is Kathryn," I rasped.

"Ms. Caraway, this is Officer Johnson, the one from your house the other day. How are you?"

As I listened, I recognized him as the officer who'd called me brave. I was shocked he would call to check on me. "I'm holding up okay."

"Listen, we've cleared things up with the monitoring company. They said the victim notification alarm went off in error. Your protective order states Todd can't come within one hundred yards of you or your residence, but the monitoring company had increased the perimeter to five hundred yards. Apparently, there was a recent issue, before this incident, where he was close?"

"Yes, the day after he was released from jail for his conviction on the Violation of a Protective Order."

"That makes sense. Their representative explained they had done this to give you more time to get to a safe place, because one hundred yards to a determined criminal is nothing. I know this scared you, and I hate that this happened, but despite the alarm, there was no actual breach of the one-hundred-yard rule. Therefore, no charges will be filed."

Classic Todd move, I thought. "Thanks for your call." I clicked off the line.

I wish I could say I was surprised, but I wasn't. Todd had been able to get away with so much, this was just another example. Instead, I channeled my frustration into gratitude. It was a pathetic effort, I admit. I thought about returning home, but checkout time had passed, and I'd already paid for another night. I decided I needed to update Gina. I reached for my phone but checked email instead. There was a message from the probation officer, so I opened it. Todd's ankle monitor indicated he was three states away, but it hadn't been confirmed.

Hopefully, the GPS is accurate for your safety, her message read. She explained that the police were still looking for Todd. If he was out of state, it would be a probation violation.

I didn't trust that Todd was far away. I called Gina back. As we talked on the phone, I heard her gasp. She rattled off some names and asked me if I recognized them.

"Yeah, they're Todd's family members. I recognize his parents."

"I just texted you a screenshot of an obituary for someone Todd is related to. The visitation is this evening, and funeral services are tomorrow."

I stared at it in disbelief. He'd skipped town while out on probation to attend his relative's funeral. I forwarded the screenshot to Tammy. I was eager to confirm that Todd was out of state and that he'd be arrested. Instead of waiting for a response, I called Tammy as soon as I finished talking with Gina.

"Thanks for the link you provided, Kathryn. It's enough to issue a warrant for probation violations in both cases."

"Will officers be sent to the funeral to arrest him?" I asked desperately.

"I'm sorry, Kathryn. We won't be coordinating with the out-of-state authorities because extraditing him would be too costly. We'll wait until he returns to the state."

They'll wait.

Sure, they'll wait.

They'll wait until Todd shows up at their door and says, "Here I am."

As the call ended, a red-hot wave of rage engulfed me. They knew where Todd was. They knew I was hiding at a hotel at my own expense. My vision narrowed to a tiny point on the dirt-streaked wall in front of me. There, a minuscule bug crawled. With a swift, furious motion, I crushed that bug, leaving nothing but a smear of my wrath behind.

Gina called back. "There's more. Todd's attorney filed a motion in the stalking case, requesting permission for him to leave the state for his relative's funeral and requested an expedited response."

I gnashed my teeth in disbelief that the judge granted him permission to leave the state. If so, there would be no probation violation.

"The judge expedited the decision and *denied* the request!" I could hear the excitement in her voice—Todd had finally pushed the limits of the judicial system too far.

"But I talked to Tammy," I said. "She said it would be too costly to extradite him, and they're just going to wait until he comes back."

"What?!"

"That's what I was told."

"I'm going to call Raymond. The motion to leave was only filed in the Stalking case. He never requested permission from the other judge—the one who presided over the Violation of the Protective Order case."

"What is that going to do?"

"The two cases are completely separate, which is why there were two different judges. Todd only asked permission in one case, which the judge denied, and he defied a direct court order. In the second case, the one we went to trial on, the judge will be blindsided by this. And judges do not like being blindsided. Are you going back home?"

"I don't know. The website shows the funeral is tomorrow morning, so assuming he comes back after, I don't feel safe at home. After talking to Tammy, I don't trust the police to pick him up."

"I agree. It's probably best that you stay put."

I wanted to do something—scream, cry, punch the wall. I knew where Todd was, but I felt powerless. My mind drifted to methods of tracking him down on my own, ways to take justice into my own hands. But I knew I wasn't that person, and I refused to let Todd turn me into a monster.

CHAPTER SIXTY-SIX

Two days.
    That's how long it took after the probation violation warrants in both cases were issued before Todd was in custody. But it didn't go smoothly—not for me. When my phone rang, it wasn't the jail calling. It was the monitoring company. They informed me that Todd was at their office, and they had removed the ankle monitor because he was going to turn himself in.

I was flummoxed. "Hold on. You knew there was a warrant for Todd's arrest, and you didn't call the police? You just removed the ankle monitor?"

"Ma'am, I—"

"No. If he doesn't report to jail and something happens to me, it's on you," I replied angrily.

My breath quickened.

My throat began to close.

My limbs started to shake.

My mind raced with scenarios of how he might try to hurt me, and primal fear kicked in. I raced to my car, jumped in, and sped toward a local department store—the only public place I could think to go. Fear flooded my veins, and my stomach churned like a washing machine. I barely made it to the store's restroom before I wretched, my dry and pained stomach heaving and spewing out bile. Each retch sent a sharp, stabbing pain through my abdomen and a wave of dread through my soul.

I sat on the floor in the public bathroom, my knees drawn to my chest and my head in my hands. *I can't keep doing this.* I stayed there for over an hour until I confirmed with the jail that Todd was in custody. He was scheduled for arraignment in a few hours.

After four days in a shitty, sticky hotel room under a crusty comforter, I returned home. Driving to my house, I rolled down the windows, allowing my oily, disheveled hair to swirl into a nest suitable for birds. I was hypnotized by a song on the radio, singing along loudly. I let myself breathe, taking in the beauty that surrounded me. The white and yellow lines on the road became like giant paintbrush strokes, painting vibrant streaks beneath my car.

Darkness seeped into the edges of dusk when I called the jail to ask if Todd was going to be released. I learned the judge had denied the request for bail. He'd have to stay locked up.

I curled into a ball and wept. I could breathe.

Todd sat in a jail cell as Thanksgiving, Christmas, and New Year's ticked by on the calendar. The winter months passed in a haze of cautious optimism. With Todd behind bars, I began to rebuild the life I'd lost under his dark shadow. I started to rediscover the simple joys that I had been robbed of during those dark months. I had very few people I still called friends, but I treasured each of them deeply. I reconnected with them in the new way the pandemic had forced upon us—tentatively at first. Conversations about Todd and stalking soon gave way to the familiar rhythms of normal chit-chat.

The weight I'd been carrying began to lift, bit by bit. I savored long walks with Winston, the feel of sunshine on my face, and the sound of my own laughter.

While walking Winston around my neighborhood, a stemless glass of wine in my hand, I came across a familiar face. He stopped mowing his lawn as we passed, holding out his hand for Winston to sniff.

"Officer Johnson? I didn't know you lived in this subdivision."

"Hi, Ms. Caraway," he said politely. "I do. We moved in about a year ago. How is everything going?"

"Todd's in jail on probation violations, so I'm enjoying a tiny taste of freedom."

"He's definitely where he belongs. When my wife fell in love with this house, I pulled all the police reports to check the crime in the neighborhood. I became familiar with your case and have been keeping an eye out. I've seen him circling your house like a shark. I even ran him out of the neighborhood once."

"Really?"

"Yeah. That last call you had," he shook his head, "as soon as I heard it over the radio, I came over. I called my wife on the way and told her to stay inside and lock the doors."

I was stunned and didn't know what to say. I had no idea I had this kind of support.

"You don't know how much I appreciate it. I feel better knowing you're here already."

"I'm around if you need anything."

My steps felt lighter as I left his house and continued my walk around the neighborhood. Well, until Winston saw a squirrel. He jerked the leash so hard I face-planted, and my wineglass went flying. At least it was plastic.

I found solace in the simple routines of daily life. The hiss of the coffeepot in the morning, the soft rustle of book pages, the click of my bike gears as I pedaled—these ordinary moments took on new significance, becoming small victories. The freedom was so delicious I wished I could eat it with a spoon.

The pandemic was settling down as scientists learned more about the coronavirus. More and more people were getting vaccinated and pharmaceutical companies were making breakthroughs with treatment. But we still had a long way to go.

It didn't surprise me to receive a notice that a revocation hearing had been scheduled and would be held online. Todd had spent eighty-four days in jail waiting for this hearing. I confirmed with Aaron that I could attend, but he was adamant that I keep my camera off. He said the same judge who presided over the stalking trial would be hearing it. *Great—can't wait to see how the judge handles the probation violations*, especially since he didn't think stalking was worth additional jail time.

On the morning of the hearing, I poured myself a mug of coffee and logged in from my office. The warm tendrils of steam danced above my desk, providing a brief distraction from the task ahead. As the virtual proceedings began, I kept my camera off, as promised, so I could observe without being seen. Todd was wearing a black and white striped V-neck top that hung on him like a pillowcase—the stripes were thick, unmistakable jailhouse attire.

Todd pled guilty to the probation violations, and the judge revoked his five-month suspended sentence. With credit for time served while waiting, Todd would spend another twelve days in jail—since the two-for-one credit didn't apply. Once he was released, there would be no more ankle monitoring, no more probation.

Nothing.

Bile rose in my throat. There was no mention of my 911 call or the four days I hid at the hotel while Todd evaded arrest. *How could this atone for the Violation of a Protective Order conviction, the Stalking conviction and the two probation violations?* I dropped my head in my hands, gutted by the utter injustice.

Half an hour after the hearing, I was still sitting in stunned silence when my cell phone danced across the table. It was Sharon calling, so I answered.

"Hi, Kathryn. I wanted to check in and see if you had any questions about today's hearing."

"I don't understand. Both judges ordered six months in jail and two years of probation and now one judge has just decided that spending the holidays in jail fulfills both sentences. He didn't give him any additional time for the probation violations? It doesn't make sense."

"I know, but that's how the system works. Remember that in the stalking case, Todd gets credit for time served. So, yes, the one sentence he served fulfills the sentencing for both convictions. The penalty for the probation violations in both cases was serving time in jail rather than on house arrest."

"After his release, will he still have the ankle monitor?"

"No. Once he is released, both cases are over. If he tries anything, you still have the protective order."

I muttered a goodbye and hung up. It was almost too much to bear. I moved through the next few days on autopilot, fighting the urge to stay in bed. On the twelfth day after the hearing, I received the dreaded call: Todd was being released.

Freedom, as I knew it, was over.

Now that Todd wasn't wearing an ankle monitor, I couldn't shake the feeling that he was lurking nearby. But I wasn't going to leave my home, either.

A couple of days after his release, I called Tammy from probation.

"Hi, Tammy. It's Kathryn. I'm calling about my case against Todd."

"Hi, Kathryn. Is everything okay?"

"Yes, everything's fine. I understand Todd has been released from jail."

"Correct."

I cleared my throat, knowing I was about to tell a white lie, but I was really struggling to understand the judicial system. "I was unclear after the recent hearing as to whether Todd would still be on probation for the next two years—can you clarify that for me?"

"Yes, he is. I'm still his probation officer, so if something happens call 911 first, then let me know."

"Okay, thank you."

I was more confused than ever. Sharon seemed to think Todd wasn't on probation, but Tammy said he was. No wonder I couldn't make sense of the judicial system—those who worked in it didn't even seem to know what was happening.

A month later, I received a call from the special crimes detective who had promised to review the footage from the doggy daycare incident, nearly eight months earlier. "I'm sorry for the delay," she said. "My caseload has been out of control."

"I understand," I responded, my expectations low.

"After reviewing the footage from the restaurant, I can confirm that Todd's vehicle was in the parking lot. He didn't purchase anything, so the evidence suggests he entered and waited for you, but it's not very strong."

"Just so you're aware, Todd's attorney sent dashcam footage to my attorney."

"Alright. Can you email that to me so I can compare it to the restaurant footage?"

"Of course. But you should know, he likely altered the date and time stamp. I can tell you that it doesn't show what happened that day."

"I'm aware of his technical abilities," she scoffed. "I've never worked with him, but I have a pretty good idea of his skillset."

Thirty minutes after I sent the footage Todd's attorney provided, the detective called back. "I reviewed Todd's dashcam footage, and I believe it'll strengthen your case. Proving he altered it will be difficult, but his video conflicts with the date and time on the restaurant footage. I sent a warrant for Todd's arrest to the judge for signature."

"Wow, really? I—"

"Yeah. The first Violation of a Protective Order is a misdemeanor, which he was already convicted of. The second, which this one is, constitutes a felony, so there's a higher standard we need to meet. I'll call you back when I have more information."

"Thank you. I really appreciate all you've done."

"We'll be in touch," she said, then hung up.

My legs felt like lead weights, heavy with anticipation. I sat on the edge of my chair, waiting for news of Todd's arrest. I knew all too well the heightened danger in the window between warrant issuance and arrest.

My emotions shifted between relief and dread. On one hand, I was relieved justice would be served. On the other, I dreaded the lengthy court process ahead. The stalking case had taken two years to reach trial; I wasn't sure how long this one would take.

Several hours later, the detective called again. "The judge denied the warrant," she said.

"But why?" I asked, tears pricking the backs of my eyes.

"I'm sorry. The judge didn't give any explanation."

She had also reached out to Raymond. "He really wanted to help, but there's nothing he can do. Only in rare cases will the district attorney override a judge's decision. My investigation has concluded. Your case is now closed."

The flush rose in my face, and a tightness clenched in my chest. The rage was deep and powerful—it scared me. It didn't make sense that an eight-month investigation could be shut down in a matter of hours, but I lacked the strength to fight it.

CHAPTER SIXTY-SEVEN

Even though the judicial system had failed me, and Todd was now free, I couldn't imagine returning to a life of solitude. I didn't want to lose the progress I had made. I'd worked too hard to rebuild my life while he was in jail.

As I left Oskar's one day after meeting a friend, I saw Todd in his vehicle with the window rolled down and his phone held out. He appeared to be filming me. And there was nothing I could do about it—no crime had been committed.

Driving home, I realized I would never be able to return to the life that was once familiar and secure. Todd would never simply go away. My life would become a never-ending series of police reports, each one detailing how he skirted the line of criminal conduct. And even when he crossed the line, the punishment wouldn't fit the crime.

I sat at the kitchen table. To my right was the picturesque window overlooking the backyard—now tainted with memories of Todd deviously standing there in the dark. Looking down the hallway toward my bedroom, I reflected on the night I held vigil with my gun, cowering in fear after the breaker had been flipped, terrified I'd end up in a body bag. I peered into the kitchen, where I had brandished a knife when Todd refused to leave.

The truth was undeniable: every inch of my house was stained by Todd. And I knew I couldn't continue living my life as the target of a stalker.

I made the decision to sell. The house I had once brought out of foreclosure; the house that heard the pitter-patter of little feet—and now those of grown men. The day it went on the market, my heart shattered into a million shards of glass.

When I listed my house, I worried Todd would find a way to exploit it. If he came into the house posing as a buyer, he might figure out how to track me, even if it meant hiding something in an innocuous item that I wouldn't notice, and then move it with me.

The realtor eased my mind, explaining that all potential buyers would be required to submit a pre-qualification letter or proof of funds for a cash sale before viewing the house. She offered an app where I could log in and review each document submitted by potential buyers, then approve or deny a showing. But I didn't want an app on my phone—I was done with electronics.

The house was listed three years after Todd stole Winston. The first offer came in the next morning, followed by six more. With the house under contract, I made the difficult decision to quit my job. It had been my security blanket—funding my fight against Todd. My last day of work was also the day I closed on the sale of my house.

Packing up, I saved my shoe collection for last. I could wear a different pair each day for two months without repeating—flip flops didn't count. I owned only two pairs of sneakers, since exercise wasn't my thing. Even in jeans, I'd wear heels or flats.

I had several pairs of shoes in the same color. The black leather pumps with tassels were perfect for workdays, while the black heels with a single band around the ankle suited nights out. The sapphire velvet flats with a silk adornment across the pointed toes had been my go-to casual shoes for trips to the store.

I didn't have much money—often working extra jobs to support myself and the kids as a single mother. Most of my shoes were from secondhand shops in a ritzy part of town. Many looked brand new when I bought them. Others were carefully selected from clearance racks, some not even my size, but I was determined to fit into them regardless—a trade-off to own beautiful shoes at a price I could afford.

Gently, I lifted each pair from the shelf, reminiscing about the times I wore them before crime tainted my world. There were the sophisticated white and black two-toned Ralph Laurens I'd bought secondhand and wore to my college graduation at thirty-eight years old, with my children watching; the silver, strappy heels adorned with white rhinestones, a gift from Carleigh when I'd been her bridesmaid; and the leopard print flats I liked on a pub crawl with friends. I wrapped each shoe in tissue paper and carefully packed them into the box. Several boxes later, the entire collection was secured with rows of shipping tape.

I drove to a Dress for Success location and donated them all. I kept only the shoes I'd worn that day—Walmart shoes that had seen better days.

With everything moved out, I took one last walk through the house. In slow motion, I ran my hand along the empty, barren walls, feeling each nail hole where memories once hung—reminders of a life that once was.

A deafening silence filled the house—the complete absence of life, love, and laughter. I stared into the emptiness of the rooms where I'd tucked my children in at night. It was more than I could bear. For the last time, I locked up the house and backed out of the driveway. The moment I had to loosen the grip on the keys to hand them over was devastating. All the memories—friends, family, parties I had hosted—suddenly gone. As bittersweet as it felt, it had to be done.

Winston and I moved one town over, entering the nomadic life of apartment living, where not even Nathan or Lauren knew my exact whereabouts. Every corner of the unfamiliar space felt overwhelming and strange; yet, I felt liberated from the confines of a house that no longer kept me safe.

With no job to occupy me, I lived as a ghost. No matter how hard I tried to scrub away memories of Todd, they remained indelible. My only comfort came from the llama pajamas that Lauren had gifted me. After sleeping fully clothed for so many nights, I stayed in them for days.

I called a friend up north to vent about how the apartment felt like a morgue after a week. She listened sweetly. "My sister is terminally ill. I'm going to leave the country to care for her. You can stay in my house—free of charge. I have no idea how long I'll be gone, so it'll be nice to know my house isn't sitting empty."

"I would love that. Are you sure? Given everything I've been through, the mess I've been in, do you really want me to—"

"You'd be doing me a favor. Come as soon as you want and stay as long as you'd like."

The following week, I loaded up the car and hit the open highway, leaving my cell phone and every digital device I owned behind. Winston curled up on the backseat for our cross-country drive, and the collection of binders rested on the passenger floorboard—in case I ran into any trouble on the road. Though I was eager to escape Todd, I couldn't help but feel a wave of sadness leaving the state I'd called home for the last two decades. It felt like I was abandoning Caleb and Dylan, saying goodbye to a piece of my soul. Even with the convictions, I felt like I was the one who had lost everything.

Exhausted from the drive, my priority was a new cell phone. As the clerk unwrapped the package, I breathed a sigh of relief—at last, a device and number I could feel safe using. Once set up, I went through the familiar process of changing passwords using the list I'd compiled three years earlier, before Todd's initial arrest.

In an abundance of caution, I didn't tell anyone where I'd temporarily relocated—not even the boys. I rented a mailbox near my old home and another in a nearby town, ensuring my mail would be forwarded twice before reaching me. I needed to be untraceable.

I wasn't ready to delete my social media accounts. I wanted the day to come when I could post, publicly, that Todd was a convicted stalker—so everyone in our tight-knit community and the world could see. But I had to be patient while the felony theft charge was still pending.

The defense attorney again presented Todd's offer to repay the stolen money and plead guilty to a misdemeanor charge, but I remained firm—Todd should not get away with anything less. Especially given the leniency of the sentences for the convictions, and no punishment for the probation violations. I didn't want him to escape consequences he'd already avoided. He had taken everything from me. I didn't see why I should give him a break.

Matt declined the plea deal, and I received a subpoena requiring me to produce a comprehensive list of documents. This also meant transferring data to my new computer.

It was exhausting; I read, re-read, and scrutinized every document I was asked to produce. I spent hours comparing the stalking case documents with the new ones, ensuring I hadn't missed anything.

Once finished, I printed a full set of documents and arranged them into Binder No. 5 on the floor. I tabbed the pages, created a table of contents, and took it to a copy shop. One set totaled over four hundred pages, but I paid to have it all duplicated. I refused to rely on electronic copies, fearing Todd might access the metadata and see where I was.

After making five binders, I sent four to Nathan. He was the only one I trusted to deliver three copies—one for the prosecutor, one for the defense, and one for the judge—and one to Gina. I didn't put my address on the package, only the city and state, trusting Nathan to destroy the box afterward.

Having complied with the subpoena, I knew the real torture was just beginning. I analyzed the documents, trying to understand what link Todd's lawyer was trying to establish. Restless, I decided I needed some whiskey. That first sip was like a warm hug from an old friend. Though I knew this dependency wasn't healthy, it helped suppress the painful memories and my constant overthinking.

CHAPTER
SIXTY-EIGHT

Time passed, and I'd been living out of state for two months. I still had the apartment back home to muddy the waters if Todd was looking for me. With my mail being forwarded twice, I took comfort in these countermeasures. I felt better, lighter. Until I received a call from Dylan.

My palms started to perspire as he said Mark and his wife each received a social media message seeking information about where I had moved. Shortly after, another person contacted me, notifying me Todd had messaged two other people, inquiring about my whereabouts. I called the sheriff's department I had gone to so many times, and they reluctantly took a report over the phone.

Knowing the process—report being taken and then assigned to a detective to investigate—could take time, my thoughts turned to the unsolved case of the murdered woman. I rewatched the television episode I had seen with Lauren and scoured articles on the Internet for any new information that could put my mind at ease, confirming that Todd was not involved.

The more I investigated the publicly available information, however, the more I suspected Todd might be involved. The murdered woman had told people she was being stalked just three weeks before her death. She described a white truck following her. Todd's truck was white. She had security cameras at her house, which Todd said he installed. There were cigarette butts on her front porch. She and her husband did not smoke, but Todd did. And how was it that the smoker was not caught on camera? I could only think of my own experience—how Todd would be in my backyard, at my bedroom window, without ever getting caught on camera.

As I dug into the case, I learned that a camera overlooking the entrance to her driveway wasn't working the day she died. *Was this on purpose so she'd call Todd to repair it—a classic Todd move?* Family and friends were adamant that she would not have let anyone into the house she didn't know. But she knew Todd.

Her lifeless body had been discovered in her bedroom, with a fatal bullet wound to the head. Did she go in there thinking Todd was outside repairing the cameras?

The video recording system had been sent to the FBI, but they could not recover any data from it. *Did Todd use his technical knowledge of law enforcement methods to destroy it before leaving it behind, knowing it would be the first thing the police would look for?*

I thought I had experienced the extremes of depravity, but this revealed unexplored depths. Instead of calming my worries that Todd might have been involved, the pattern of events made it seem likely that he was. I had my own battle to fight with Todd, but I couldn't keep this to myself.

Within two days of filing the police report, the special crimes detective that handled the doggy daycare investigation called to discuss the social media messages Todd had sent. I was less concerned about this than I was about the connections I had made to the murdered woman, but I listened patiently.

"I was able to reach out to the recipients, and two provided me with screenshots, which is enough."

"Enough for what?"

"A warrant for Todd's arrest," she said, seemingly surprised by my question.

"Will the judge sign it?" I asked, unable to allow myself to believe it.

"He already has. Do you know where we can find him?"

Stunned, I told her I had no idea where Todd might be—or if he might have left the state to come find me.

"Stay vigilant," she warned, rattling off the usual statement I'd heard so many times before. I suspected this phrase was taught to all police academy cadets. It seemed like the police only cared about my safety after a warrant was issued and before Todd's arrest.

"If you have another minute, there's something else I'd like to discuss," I said sheepishly.

"Sure. How can I help?"

I spoke quickly, voicing my suspicions surrounding Todd and the unsolved murder case, unloading the burden I'd been carrying. I told her about all the ways I thought the evidence pointed to his involvement, the lines I'd drawn, and the eerie similarities between her case and mine.

"I'll pass this information to the detective handling the case. However, Todd's not a violent offender, so I don't think you have anything to worry about. He's just trying to scare you."

As I hung up the phone, I tried to steady myself. It filled me with dread that everyone around me—including the police and the prosecution team—tried to placate my fears, insisting Todd was not a violent person. And each time, my mind boomeranged to the statement I'd made to Aaron: "Nobody's a murderer until they kill their first victim."

I remembered seeing an email notice about the upcoming felony theft trial, so I opened my laptop and scrolled to it. Since he was released from jail, I had stopped looking at notices from the district attorney, relying on them to call me if they needed me, as Jacob had advised. My eyes widened, and my heart quickened when I saw the trial date. Todd had sent the social media messages to three people I knew about, the day before the theft trial was scheduled. This, along with the list Gina's paralegal prepared showing other incidents and court dates, is more proof that Todd was attempting to intimidate me. I pulled up the list, added this incident to it, and sent it to Sharon, hoping she would notice the correlations.

With things heating up, I worried about the weeks to come. Todd managed to evade the warrant for the second Violation of a Protective Order, and the police couldn't find him. I had already booked a plane ticket to attend my granddaughter's first birthday party, but I had mixed emotions about returning to the state where Todd lived, even though I still had the apartment there. Then, just days before I was scheduled to leave, I learned the party invitation had been posted on social media. I feared Todd would go to it, looking for me, and might use it as an opportunity to end my life. I worried that my granddaughter's birthday would always be associated with my death date.

My thoughts were interrupted when my phone buzzed with a text from Lauren. Using her "super sleuth" skills—developed from binge-watching endless hours of true crime television—she sent me a screenshot of Todd's company website. She noted that Todd's website listed a new address. *Could he have moved?*

Nathan knew the town so well that I forwarded the screenshot with the new address to him and asked if it was legitimate. His response came almost immediately—and it wasn't what I expected.

"Where did you get this?" he asked sharply. His voice sounded different than normal, and I could sense his anger through the phone.

"Lauren sent it to me," I answered quickly.

"This is my daughter's address!" Nathan shouted in disbelief.

My stomach dropped. His daughter was several years older than me and a single mother herself. Why would Todd post her address on his website? Unless, in my absence, he had decided to target Nathan or his daughter. Or both.

I was hit with a wave of guilt. I realized that my escape had unwittingly left someone I cared about to bear the brunt of Todd's vengeance. It was too risky to attend my granddaughter's first birthday, which tore at my soul, leaving me raw and bleeding with regret. The thrum of worry pulsed through me, a warning that he was out there, wild and hunting for revenge like a feral animal.

Thirty-eight days.

That's how long it took from the time the warrant was issued until Todd was arrested. And that's how many days I had to remain vigilant because the most dangerous period is after the warrant is issued and before the arrest. Even so, he was arraigned and posted bond within hours.

With his arrest came another attempt at a plea deal for the felony theft charge, which I refused. The prosecutor, Matt, seemed to be growing weary of my persistence, but was ready to move it to trial. However, the courthouse was still backlogged from the pandemic-induced shutdown.

Living in a temporary home meant living in limbo. I had no permanent residence, no job, and two cases pending against Todd in the judicial system. I felt like I was in a holding pattern, waiting for something to happen. The stress was taking its toll. I was anxious, irritable, and my sleep was restless.

I decided it was time to move on, to find a permanent home for Winston and me. Somewhere safe to re-establish roots. With Winston settled into a new boarding facility, I started a cross-country drive. Emotionally, I felt lost. In eleven days, I crossed through twelve states, eventually finding a beautiful place to call home along the way. I hired a local law firm, set up a limited liability company with my new identity, and purchased a house.

Reunited with Winston, I began collecting the few belongings I had at my friend's house. For the past seven months, fragments of my life sat in boxes—some in storage, some at the apartment, and a few at the temporary house. Moving into my new home just after Thanksgiving, I was finally reunited with all my belongings and began the arduous task of unpacking.

I carefully opened the first box and paused to look inside, questioning whether I had the strength to continue. As I unwrapped items one by one, memories flooded back. The first thing I saw was a figurine Caleb had given me years ago, a reminder of all the joyous moments in my former home. I carefully placed it back in the box and sealed it shut, unable to cope. I felt sorrow for what I had to give up because of Todd, which morphed into rage at him for pushing me out of the beautiful house I loved so dearly. The past and present collided inside me, plunging me into a devastating abyss of despair. With no job and only the equity from the house left in my bank account, the crushing depths of depression threatened to swallow me whole.

The days dragged on, and I lacked the motivation to get out of bed, except on the days I moved to the new sofa I purchased. Less than a month after moving into my new house, I was shuffling to the coffee pot when I saw Raymond calling. I greeted him with a quick, "Hello," and listened as he launched into an update.

"Although Todd was arrested for attempting to locate you, unfortunately, it's not a strong enough case to prosecute. He was clever in crafting his messages, which is the only evidence we have."

"I mean, he was clearly trying to—"

"I know, and I agree with you. But because of the way Todd phrased his message, it's unlikely we could win the case."

He then announced he was going to drop the charges, and part of me felt relieved. Now, I just had to wait for the felony theft trial Todd's *sixth* attorney had postponed. I settled into life in a new house, in a new city, in a new state I'd never even visited before my road trip.

He'll never find me here.

CHAPTER
SIXTY-NINE

After ringing in the New Year, I was in my kitchen when I received a call ending the exhausting four-year court battle. It was Aaron with an update about the felony theft charge. I was grateful that he dispensed with the pleasantries and got straight to the point.

"Matt is out on paternity leave, and because I'm familiar with your case, I'll be handling the felony theft case."

"That's great. Thanks for stepping in."

Aaron cleared his throat. "The district attorney has decided to accept Todd's offer to plead guilty to a misdemeanor charge of theft in exchange for reimbursing you the money he stole. As a result of this plea agreement, Todd will be sentenced to time served and won't receive any additional jail time. I know this isn't what you want to hear."

My stomach flipped.

My heart pounded.

I balled my hands into fists.

"How can this be happening? The law he broke makes this a felony. It's not about the money; it's about the *law*."

"I understand you're upset, I—"

"No, you don't understand. Why have I waited three years for trial?

Why have I rejected all plea deals, only to bow down to him now? Why did I spend weeks putting together the documentation to comply with the subpoena? I produced nearly four hundred pages!"

I could feel the fire of my anger radiating through the air and I remained impassive as I made it clear that I was not satisfied with them allowing Todd to plead guilty to a lesser charge. But it was a done deal. It didn't matter that I was the victim in the case. My opinion did not matter. There was nothing I could do.

"Look, funding for the prosecutor's office has been cut. The unfortunate consequence is we now lack the resources to take your case to trial."

"I can't believe this."

"To be honest, Kathryn, most first-time theft offenders are allowed to plead to a lesser charge. There's a huge precedent for the agreement reached with Todd."

My eyes burned with fury, but I kept my voice controlled. "But this isn't just a simple theft charge. It's part of a bigger picture of criminal behavior. The district attorney chose to handle these cases separately for strategic reasons. He decided to pursue separate charges for strategic motives, but it's all connected."

"I know, and I get your point. I'm sorry, but at least you can now move forward with your life."

My chest heaved with anguish; another injustice had been committed by the judicial system, and Todd was free to go on as if nothing had happened. With no felony record, he could get a job in another police department and even have the audacity to cast a vote against funding for the district attorney's office. I'd be lucky if he was denied a gun, since not all protective orders show up on a firearms background check. That was, of course, assuming he didn't just buy one off the street.

The plea deal was done, bringing closure from a legal perspective. I flew back to my former home to collect the restitution check. I couldn't risk providing my new address in case Todd hacked into their system. I picked it up from the courthouse and donated it to charity, but I couldn't leave without seeing my friends. I arranged breakfast with Nathan and, later that evening, dinner at Lauren's house. Although I had already said goodbye to them in my heart, I owed them a final, in-person farewell. I knew this would be the last time I'd see them. It was for their own good, as well as mine.

Before I left town, there was one more thing I had to do. I met the brave woman who reached out to me on social media about her own experience with Todd. I was deeply grateful for her courage in going to court for me and wanted her to know how much I appreciated it. As we talked, it was striking how similar our experiences with Todd had been. After what I'd been through, I didn't question why she didn't bring charges against him. I savored the moment, being with someone who understood.

Having been terrorized by Todd for years, I now knew one inevitable truth: he would do it again. He had perfected the game of manipulating the system. He'd continue searching for me, no matter what. I was painfully aware that even shifting focus to new prey wouldn't deter him from his mission.

Returning to my new home, I couldn't deny how drastically I'd changed on all levels: physically, I'd gained weight; emotionally, I was a wreck; mentally, I found it hard to concentrate; intellectually, I'd become a walking textbook on criminal law; psychologically, I was diagnosed with PTSD; and, physiologically, my body was still repairing itself from the stress and self-medication tools that carried me through my darkest days.

Dr. Saxton assured me that all of this was normal following a traumatic event. To address my current issues, he suggested we review the stalking experience in its entirety. "To take that step forward, I think you need to take a step back," he said.

The session was difficult and uncomfortable, but I trusted Dr. Saxton. He asked his questions, listened as I shared, then summarized what he'd gleaned during our time together.

"Kathryn, I see exactly why you find yourself in this heightened state of social paranoia. Your mind looks for these warning signs in new people because Todd was methodical in his actions. Random acts of flattery led to acts of kindness, enabling him to get close enough to learn your vulnerabilities. Armed with this insight, he exploited those vulnerabilities. As he started losing control, his acts led to your isolation before dissolving into the fear-inducing acts of coincidence. Chaos was his power. Yet, nothing was ever truly random. There was never a coincidence."

My mouth hung open, and my eyes widened as I slowly processed the information. A knot tightened in my stomach; my throat closed. After one thousand eight hundred ninety-six days of living life in this chaos, I finally understood.

Following that enlightening session with Dr. Saxton, I was able to stop hating myself for not recognizing the signs of Todd's insidious behavior earlier and for minimizing it when I did. I quit berating myself for not being able to handle Todd and the emotional damage he inflicted on me. My heart was no longer burdened with the typical feelings of a stalking victim—shame, blame, and guilt.

Even before that fateful day that Todd stole Winston, it was clear what drove him—his sordid need for possession. His words echoed in my head like a bad omen: *You are mine. And I don't share.*

A box with fraying edges sat in the corner of a room. It contained all my documentation on the cases. At the very top, lay The Black Binder.

With all court cases settled, and thanks to the help of Dr. Saxton, I was ready to put the box away and the experience fully behind me. Before I could seal the box shut, I logged into the court system's website one last time to print the case disposition for each conviction, as if to punctuate the end of an era.

The first court document I came across was the denial of Todd's appeal. I recalled his attorney saying they would appeal the judge's guilty verdict in the Violation of the Protective Order trial, but nothing more had been said about it. At least I now knew Todd's options to overturn the verdict had been exhausted.

I scrolled on and came across the witness list Todd had submitted for the stalking trial. Chuck, the bartender at Oskar's, who had once taken me out through the kitchen to avoid Todd; an ex-boyfriend I had years before I met Jason; John, who had so diligently reported his conversation with Todd to me but didn't want to get involved; and several other people, including men I had previously dated. Then there was Jason's subpoena, which I fully anticipated. It still disgusted me to see it.

Todd's witness list read like a sickening inventory. Some of these people had been friends. Others had covertly tried to help me, claiming they didn't want to get involved and cross Todd, yet there they were on a list to testify on his behalf. I felt like I had been played by people I trusted. I fought through the nausea as I printed the disposition and placed it in The Black Binder.

I came across another record in the stalking case that sent shockwaves through me. It was a *Motion to Suppress Confession* that Todd's original attorney had filed—I never knew about it. Apparently, Todd had been verbose when he was arrested for stalking, and his attorney's attempt to remove his confession from evidence was successful. As I read about Todd being under duress at the time of his arrest, I felt nothing. I was neither angry nor sad—just numb.

I printed the court documents in the theft case to tie up loose ends and found the plea agreement entered into the court record. I had not been present in court that day and only received the phone call from Aaron advising me of it. Now, I was reading new information. Not only was Todd allowed to plead to a lesser charge and pay restitution, but he was also ordered to serve six months in jail with credit for time served in the other cases. This credit meant his sentence was complete without it ever beginning. He never spent a day in jail for the stalking conviction. He never spent a day in jail for the theft conviction. Instead, the judicial system allowed Todd to keep applying his jail time for the violation of the protection order to the other convictions.

Reading further, I found out Todd was allowed to have the theft conviction expunged from his record. An IT professional who worked for the municipal police department stalked his prey, stole money to buy equipment for the same police department, and the judge authorized expungement?

I just couldn't make sense of it. I sealed the box with thick layers of packing tape, and pushed it into the farthest, darkest corner of my attic. Its only purpose now is to help the next unfortunate, unsuspecting victim. I hope it will never see daylight again, but it's there just in case.

I poured a splash of whiskey into a glass to celebrate. I loved whiskey. It had been my constant companion through the darkest days. But when I took a sip of it now, all I could taste was fear. With a sudden resolve, I emptied the bottle down the drain, watching the amber liquid disappear as I vowed never to drink whiskey again.

The taste of fear lingered on my tongue, and my thoughts turned to the murdered woman and her family. I never heard back from the police after my conversation with the detective. I have no evidence that Todd was involved with her death; only my suspicions and speculations based on my experience with him. To be fair, I don't know if Todd was ever questioned by the police and there have been no reports made public that he has ever been a suspect. Her killer is an enigmatic shadow that has eluded justice.

Another television episode aired about this unsolved murder case. Even though the coroner reported her death as a homicide, the police now said they believed it was likely a suicide, even though she was shot in the back of the head. I listened as her sister's voice shook with anger, adamant that she would have never killed herself.

A chill ran through me when my mind replayed Todd asking if I wanted to see death coming and I knew what I needed to do: delete all my social media accounts. A digital footprint could be a breadcrumb, compromising my safety. I had fantasized about the sweet satisfaction of calling out Todd online, giving him a taste of his own medicine, but when the moment came, I couldn't do it. I wasn't Todd, after all, and I wasn't going to allow myself to stoop to his level.

He mistook my kindness for weakness, but that's just me—it's who I am. I'd already lost so much through all this, and I wasn't about to allow him to taint another piece of my soul.

As I scrolled through a news feed one morning, headlines buzzed with the story of a woman murdered by a man who had stalked her eight years prior. When her protective order expired, she mistakenly thought he'd moved on since she hadn't had any further contact from him and hadn't renewed it. Five years after it expired, he murdered her. She let her guard down. Her mistake was fatal.

It affirmed the truth I was now living with: I must never become complacent. I will forever look over my shoulder, wondering when Todd might find me, and I won't see death coming.

As a child, I was told that monsters didn't exist. But now I know they do. They hide in the shadows and hunt. They evade detection and prosecution. They tease their prey. They wait for the perfect moment to strike. And my monster—he has a name.

Todd.

ABOUT THE AUTHOR

On the surface, I am like any other woman. I stay busy running errands, caring for my beloved dog, and cooking new recipes for dinner. Beneath the surface, I live a very different life than most—in hiding.

I was born and raised in the Deep South, where roots run cavernous. I've moved so many times that I've become efficient at it, which is funny considering I had lived in the same house for over seventeen years of my adult life—the house stained with memories of a stalker in my backyard.

Writing has always been a hobby I've enjoyed. After receiving a B.A. in journalism, I pursued a career in reporting. But assignments and deadlines suffocated me—there was no room for creativity. Instead, I launched a new career and attained an MBA. After years of climbing the corporate ladder, I had to leave it all behind to hide.

Alone in a new state, a new city, I wrote *Unfollow Me* three months after the last court case was settled to capture the details before time had a chance to erode the memories. I'd kept my family shielded from it as much as possible, but I knew one day they would want to know the full story. Dr. Saxton said it would be cathartic, but I found it painful to relive those moments.

Later that same year, I wrote *He Follows Me*—a fictional alternative ending to *Unfollow Me*. I needed to. For me.

A year since I had started writing passed when I began editing my first draft of *Unfollow Me*. Writing these books was emotionally draining. I suffered a stroke at the age of forty-nine. If a stalker wasn't going to stop me from telling my story, a stroke certainly wasn't.

To finally tell my story publicly, I had to weigh the risks. In the United

States, anyone can sue for anything. I find that sad, actually. I've seen firsthand how the judicial system treats people and how judges often want the parties to settle rather than rule on the facts of the case.

I have made a good life for myself, insulated by people who protect me and make me feel safe. Days before I sent this book to the printer, I had a reason to celebrate. It was 9:30 p.m., and I realized I had not taken my trash can to the curb for collection. It was full, and I didn't want to miss my weekly scheduled pick-up. I was home alone. I tied my shoes, opened the garage, and wheeled my trash can down the dark driveway. I walked back, closed the garage, and slipped off my shoes.

It was the first time I walked outside of my house at night, alone. These are the types of wins I celebrate now.

goodreads.com/kathryn_caraway
instagram.com/un.follow.me_kc
facebook.com/authorkathryncaraway
tiktok.com/@k_caraway
x.com/UnfollowMe_KC
threads.com/@un.follow.me_kc

HE FOLLOWS ME
HER NEXT MOVE IS HIS NEXT STEP

"While *Unfollow Me* reads like a memoir narrating one woman's desperate attempt to regain control over her spiraling life, *He Follows Me* is an action-packed thriller . . ." —*Chanticleer Book Reviews and Media*

Kathryn Caraway thought seeing him in jail was the end. She was wrong.

Kathryn survived a sadistic stalker—and she might not get that lucky twice. When Todd Bennett walks free, Kathryn is desperate for safety. She trades her identity for anonymity in the Victim Protection Program and finds herself in the hands of U.S. Marshal Wes Kade. He is controlled, detached, and dangerous in ways he doesn't explain.

But starting over is not the same as being safe.

Halfway around the world, Kathryn builds a new life: a job, an apartment, a best friend, even the tentative hope of romance. Yet some memories refuse to stay buried. Some follow.

Strange coincidences and subtle threats begin to unravel the fragile sense of security she's fought so hard to achieve. As the shadows close in, Kathryn realizes the line between vigilance and paranoia has blurred—and someone is watching more closely than she ever imagined.

With threats mounting, Kathryn discovers that in a world built on secrets, trust can be a dangerous weapon. Because the most terrifying question is not who's hunting her. It's *who is protecting her?*

RESOURCES

TO LEARN MORE ABOUT STALKING:

- **The Unfollow Me Project**—https://www.unfollowme.com

Stalking is a serious crime that can escalate quickly. It isn't just something that happens in movies—it's far more common than most people realize. More than 13 million people are stalked each year in the United States. The most common tactics include phone calls, uninvited appearances, text messages and emails, sending notes or gifts, and following or watching the victim[i].

TO LEARN MORE ABOUT VETERAN SUICIDE:

- **22 Too Many**—https://22toomany.org
- **VOW 22**—https://vow22.org
- **Travis Manion Foundation**—https://www.travismanion.org

We lose an average of 22 veterans a day to suicide. To my family, that number isn't just a statistic; it's a reminder of the pain so many families are living with.

Dear Reader,

My family lost someone we loved—a veteran. A hero in every sense of the word, he carried invisible wounds none of us fully understood until it was too late. If you are a veteran who's struggling, or if you know someone who is, please don't wait. Reach out.

Kathryn Caraway

NOTES

DEDICATION

i. McFarlane, Judith M., Jacquelyn C. Campbell, Susan Wilt, Carolyn J. Sachs, Yvonne Ulrich, and Xiao Xu. "Stalking and Intimate Partner Femicide." *Homicide Studies* 3, no. 4 (November 1999): 300–316.

AUTHOR'S NOTE

i. The Unfollow Me Project, "Home Page," The Unfollow Me Project, 2022, https://www.unfollowme.com/.
ii. Smith, Sharon G. and Basile, Kathleen C. and Kresnow, Marcie-jo "The National Intimate Partner and Sexual Violence Survey : 2016/2017 Report on Stalking — updated release" (2022)

RESOURCES

i. Smith, Sharon G. and Basile, Kathleen C. and Kresnow, Marcie-jo "The National Intimate Partner and Sexual Violence Survey : 2016/2017 Report on Stalking—updated release" (2022)

www.ingramcontent.com/pod-product-compliance
Lightning Source LLC
Chambersburg PA
CBHW020530030426
42337CB00013B/795